Praise for *Meeting the Enemy*

Kevin O'Brien has laid out a systematic case for blessed rage toward the fossil fuel industry. The intersectional forces of domination that have led to colonialism, racism, sexism, heterosexism, and ableism, and that reinforce anthropocentrism, are today exacerbated by fossil-fueled atmospheric defilement. Rather than placing the blame on our daily lives, even though we must recognize our complicity to varying degrees, O'Brien argues we ought to join forces against a strategic enemy, the fossil-fueled industrial complex, which exacerbates injustices on a global scale.

—Whitney Bauman, professor of religious studies,
Florida International University

Meeting the Enemy is an excellent book. Clear, well-written, and timely. Honest, yet hope-filled. A persuasive argument for resisting the structures at the root of our climate crisis. Take up and read.

—Steven Bouma-Prediger, professor of religion, Hope College,
and author of *Creation Care Discipleship: Why Earthkeeping Is an Essential Christian Practice*

In recent years, Christian environmental ethicists have begun the important work of interweaving questions of ecological concern with questions pertaining to the social, economic, and political realms. Kevin O'Brien has been at the forefront of this work. In *Meeting the Enemy*, O'Brien continues to expand his vision of the movement toward a world that more fully reflects God's love for all of creation. Engaging a diverse array of interlocutors while drawing upon Walter Wink's conception of the "powers that be," O'Brien gives us a way of conceptualizing and enacting the struggle against a fossil fuel industry that would devour the earth in its service to mammon. This book will be helpful to activists, scholars, and communities of faith alike.

—Daniel Castillo, associate professor of theology, Loyola University Maryland

Warning: this book will change the way you think about climate—and about everything else. In *Meeting the Enemy*, Kevin O'Brien is both readable and revolutionary, incisively exposing the deepest roots of the destructive powers behind climate change. Profound, yet practical, O'Brien describes a clear path from powers of evil to powers of renewal. Required reading for anyone who wants to create a greener, more just future!

—Laura M. Hartman, associate professor of environmental studies, Roanoke College

The title of O'Brien's book says a great deal about its content, which is innovative and accessible in its approach to this topic. While giving a clear and complex picture, *Meeting the Enemy* also helps the reader in how to respond. This book provides a comprehensive and creative way to teach about "atmospheric defilement," or global warming, empowering readers to understand and act; it will work in a wide variety of classrooms and subjects. I look forward to teaching it.

—Laurel Kearns, professor of ecology, society, and religion, Drew Theological School

With his usual clarity of vision, leading Christian environmental ethicist Kevin J. O'Brien mobilizes the rich biblical and theological tradition of nonviolent resistance against the destructive powers of the fossil fuel industries and the cultural myths that sustain them. The aim is not to demonize, but to narrate an altogether different story in support of the subversive, life-giving powers of faith-based intersectional alliances for an alternative energy economy. There is no other book yet that connects biblically informed moral argument against the fossil fuel industry with Christian practices of climate resistance in such a clear-eyed, yet hopeful manner.

—Hilda P. Koster, Sisters of St. Joseph of Toronto Associate Professor of Theology and director of the Elliott Allen Institute for Theology and Ecology, University of St. Michael's College in the University of Toronto

This is a marvelous and urgently needed book! Read it. Honest, courageous, faithful, theologically profound, politically savvy, and artfully written, it will direct our vital energies into redemptive, lifesaving, and hope-infused action toward a world in which all may flourish. O'Brien's brilliance shines light on pathways into a future where life together is grounded in cooperation, mercy, and renewable equitable energy, a future no longer dominated by fossil fuel industries and the myths that sustain them. This book is a healing gift!

—Cynthia Moe-Lobeda, professor of theological and social ethics, Pacific Lutheran Theological Seminary and the Graduate Theological Union, and author of *Resisting Structural Evil: Love as Ecological-Economic Vocation*

MEETING THE ENEMY

MEETING THE ENEMY

THE FOSSIL FUEL INDUSTRY AND THE POWER OF CHRISTIAN CLIMATE RESISTANCE

Kevin J. O'Brien

Fortress Press
Minneapolis

MEETING THE ENEMY
The Fossil Fuel Industry and the Power of Christian Climate Resistance

30 29 28 27 26 25 1 2 3 4 5 6 7 8 9

Library of Congress Cataloging-in-Publication Data

Names: O'Brien, Kevin J. (Kevin James), author.
Title: Meeting the enemy : the fossil fuel industry and the power of Christian climate resistance / Kevin J. O'Brien.
Description: Minneapolis, MN : Fortress Press, [2025] | Includes bibliographical references and index.
Identifiers: LCCN 2024020955 (print) | LCCN 2024020956 (ebook) | ISBN 9781506499338 (paperback) | ISBN 9781506499345 (ebook)
Subjects: LCSH: Climatic changes—Religious aspects—Christianity. | Fossil fuels—Environmental aspects.
Classification: LCC BT695.5 .O29 2025 (print) | LCC BT695.5 (ebook) | DDC 261.8/8—dc23/eng/20240708
LC record available at https://lccn.loc.gov/2024020955
LC ebook record available at https://lccn.loc.gov/2024020956

Cover image: Texas Oil Pump from Real Window Creative/Shutterstock
Cover design: Brad Norr

Print ISBN: 978-1-5064-9933-8
eBook ISBN: 978-1-5064-9934-5

CONTENTS

ACKNOWLEDGMENTS

Writing a book about enemies could be a sad, angry experience. It was not, and for that I thank the allies and friends who support me.

My family is a blessing. My wife Mary believes in me, challenges me, and teaches me to be a better human being. My parents are not only curious about my work and supportive in thousands of ways but are also inspiring models of how to insist that the world can and should be better. My brothers, sisters-in-law, nieces, and nephews teach me what it is to be part of something larger than myself and are a lot of fun in the process.

I am also blessed with good friends and intellectual interlocutors. One cherished colleague, Forrest Clingerman, unexpectedly died just as I finished this book. He had brainstormed about this project with me and offered thoughtful feedback on the first three chapters, which is just an example of how he helped me over twenty years of collaboration. I am honored to have known him and will keep learning from and teaching his work.

Kathryn Blanchard and Trevor Bechtel show me what ethicists can be and do. Rick Bohannon and Whitney Bauman challenge my ideas and refuse to let me take them or anything else too seriously. Adela Ramos and Jennifer Smith expand my engagement with intersectionality. Erik Hammerstrom, Michael Zbaraschuk, and Suzanne Crawford O'Brien help me begin to understand how I as a scholar of Christianity can learn humbly from other traditions. Laura Hartman read parts of this book and kept encouraging me to move from abstract analysis to impassioned exhortation. Christopher Carter, Sarah Fredericks, and Laura Yordy all inspired key ideas in this book during helpful conversations.

I also thank the friends who remind me of all that exists outside of books. The people with whom I game, walk, run, plunge, eat, drink, read, and talk keep me grounded in the real world and laughing at all that seems unreal.

I am grateful to Pacific Lutheran University, which granted me the yearlong sabbatical during which most of this book was written. The university's library and interlibrary loan services also make my scholarship possible. My colleagues in the religion department and the environmental studies program help me continue developing as a scholar and a professional. Most importantly, my students at PLU steadily show up willing to discuss the hardest questions we can find and think together about how our answers might matter.

An earlier version of chapter 1 was published in the *Journal of the Society of Christian Ethics* in 2021. Chapter 2 was first shared in conversation with a wise panel of discussants at Xavier University in 2023. Chapter 3 was originally a series of presentations at Hope Lutheran Church in Enumclaw, Washington. Portions of chapter 5 were first presented and discussed at Tulane University in 2019 and at the 2022 annual meeting of the Society of Christian Ethics. The ideas for chapter 6 were originally presented to Harbor Covenant Church in Gig Harbor, Washington, and Trinity Presbyterian in Tacoma, Washington. Thanks to all who responded to my work and continued conversations with me afterward.

I am grateful to Walter Wink, who taught me how to think as a Christian about enemies. I only met him once, very briefly. But I have been inspired by his life as well as his work, especially the way he engaged movements in his research and brought his personal and emotional life to his scholarship.

Inspired by Wink, I have tried to write a book that learns from the global movement for climate justice. To those in that movement—anyone who has ever written a letter to a legislator, picked up a sign, chanted a slogan, drafted legislation, chained themselves to a bulldozer, or anything else for the sake of climate justice—thank you.

Thank you to those who have brought snacks, support, or bail money to their protesting neighbors. Thank you to those who write bills and ordinances and lobby leaders inspired by this movement. Thank you to those who work on related causes and bring climate change into the work of racial, gender, economic, and disability justice. These coalitions of resistance made my thinking possible. Far more importantly, they help make our shared world just a bit more merciful, a bit more loving, a bit more sustainable.

Thanks to Laura Gifford at Fortress Press for supporting this book when she first heard about it, improving it in our conversations, and nurturing it through the production process. Her encouragement, advice, and professionalism have been a delight. Thanks also to Marissa Wold Uhrina, who ably managed the publication process, and to the rest of the staff who turned the pixels on my screen into a beautiful, shareable text.

Any good ideas and perspectives are gifts from these wonderful allies and friends. The mistakes, indelicacies, insensitivities, and failures are my responsibility. However, given the book's theme, I will note that I share that responsibility with the systems of domination that surround us all. They degrade our collective capacity to cooperate with, understand, and trust each other. Those systems are our enemies. My friends and allies give me hope that there is something more powerful than domination, that the systems degrading us will not win.

INTRODUCTION

Have We Met Our Enemy?

A FIRST-YEAR COLLEGE student in one of my classes reflected on how much she had learned in high school "about carbon footprints, pollution, and climate change, and how we can be sustainable as individuals to help the environment." She was grateful for the lessons, which motivated her to major in environmental studies. But she noted, "I think it also left me with a lot of anxiety about my own actions and measuring how 'good' of a person I am based on if I recycled that piece of plastic ten years ago."

Such anxiety about climate change, and guilt about our personal actions, is all too common. I hear about it from many students, colleagues, family members, and friends. I feel it myself when I put gas in my car or buy a plane ticket or turn on my stove.

This book is, in many ways, an argument that the best way to deal with anxieties about climate change is to channel them into resistance against enemies rather than guilt about our own actions. I will argue that privileged people should spend less time worrying about our personal choices and more time organizing against the destructive systems that limit our options. The most important work we can do is not to change our individual lifestyles but to resist the corporate and political structures at the root of the problem of climate change.

Historically, the environmental movement has been better at individual guilt than systemic change. For example, the iconic poster from the first Earth Day in 1970, drawn by cartoonist Walt Kelly, focused on convincing people to clean up litter. It featured Kelly's character Pogo, a friendly and philosophical possum. On the poster, Pogo is struck with guilt while looking at a trash-strewn corner of the swamp he calls home. With a bag in his hand to begin cleanup, he says, "We have met the enemy, and he is us."[1]

Never doubt that a single cartoon possum can make a difference. Pogo's phrase and image have been used thousands of times in speeches and campaigns about litter, pollution, vegetarianism, and climate change. The simple message has helped people accept our complicity in environmental problems. I hear echoes of it in my student's paper worrying that her worth is at stake in every environmental choice she makes.[2]

Today, most people concerned about climate justice do not urgently need to learn about their personal complicity. Those of us who are contributing to the problem should, of course, face our role in it, but it is far more important to identify the structures that shape our behavior. The deepest roots of climate change come from outside and around individuals.[3] We need to meet those enemies; we need to know that they are not us.

Naming anyone an "enemy" can be dangerous. The world already has so much us-versus-them rhetoric, and it is already too easy to mistreat and abuse opponents and those different from ourselves. But the enemy we'll meet in this book is not another person. We are not called to vilify other human beings but instead to name the systems and corporations that corrupt people's lives and limit people's capacity to address the problem. We should call these systems and structures—particularly the fossil fuel industry—our enemies.

Who "We" Are

Naming and understanding our enemy will take the first four chapters of this book. Before beginning that, though, it is important to be very clear about who "we" are, who particularly needs to meet this enemy.

Climate change and the systems that make it harder to stop are a danger to all life on earth. But I do not claim to speak for all life or even all of humanity when I refer to "we" and "us."[4] Instead, I have in mind a narrower group of people with four things in common:

1. We are privileged enough to have complicity in the injustices of climate change.
2. We are open to learning from Christian traditions about how to constructively have an enemy.
3. We are committed to resisting the degradation of earth's climate.
4. We know that a better and more just world is possible.

If you are part of this group, I hope this book will convince you to name fossil fuel corporations and other destructive systems as your enemy and to find creative ways to resist them. If you're not part of this group, I don't presume to tell you how to feel or what to do, though I hope you might learn something from what I've written.

1) We Have Complicity in Climate Injustice

The year I wrote most of this book, 2023, was the hottest year yet recorded on earth. As I write, the ten warmest years ever measured were between 2014 and 2023.[5] The primary cause is industrialized technology that releases greenhouse gases, which in turn trap heat in the atmosphere.

While these scientific facts about climate change have been clear for over four decades, the rate of fossil fuel emissions still increases. Industrial activity put about fifty-nine billion metric tons of carbon dioxide, methane, and nitrous oxide into the atmosphere in 2019. The heat trapped by these emissions leads to broad and unpredictable changes in weather patterns, including more frequent droughts, more extreme flooding, stronger hurricanes, and rising sea levels across the planet.

According to the Intergovernmental Panel on Climate Change (IPCC), the impacts of climate change are also unfairly distributed.

Most fossil fuel emissions come from wealthy corporations, governments, and people in the industrialized world. However, the worst impacts are felt by marginalized peoples, particularly those in Africa, Asia, Central and South America, small islands, and the Arctic. Poor and Indigenous communities in these vulnerable places were fifteen times more likely than wealthier people to die from floods, droughts, or storms between 2010 and 2020.[6] In other words, climate change intersects with global poverty, racism, colonialism, and many other injustices; its impacts are most severe on those who are already marginalized.

Responding to these worrying trends, scientific experts have recommended reductions in fossil fuel usage since the 1980s. Activists have proposed political and economic tools that would encourage or require such reductions. But very little has been done. Ever more fossil fuels are extracted, sold, and burned.

Since the 1990s, vulnerable nations have called for resources from richer countries to help them adapt to a changing world and relocate vulnerable populations. The United Nations has established a "Loss and Damage" fund for this purpose. But as of 2024, the fund has received only modest contributions and vague commitments.

In recent years, increasing attention has been paid to engineering solutions that could remove climate-changing gases from the atmosphere or block sunlight. But at the moment, no such viable technology exists.

In summary, the climate is changing primarily because of how privileged industrialized societies are structured, the worst impacts are being felt by less-privileged peoples in other parts of the world, and not enough is being done in response.

My actions are part of this problem. My life is supported by the burning of fossil fuels, and it is difficult to imagine an alternative. To research and write this book, I used electricity from a grid that depends on coal and natural gas. I drive in a gas-powered car to reach the classrooms where I teach about these issues. I love people who live across the country, and it is only feasible to see them by traveling in planes that burn jet fuel. Life, for me, includes having complicity in the changing climate.

But the same factors that make my actions complicit also protect me from many of the worst impacts of climate change. The systems designed to keep the oil, gas, and coal supporting my lifestyle flowing are also protecting me from the worst impacts of emissions. In the Pacific Northwest of the United States, where I live, a strong infrastructure is helping me adapt, and there are government agencies planning to offer people like me assistance as wildfires and extreme heat and droughts become more common. Though I am endangered by increasing extreme weather, wildfires, and droughts, I am safer than most. I am privileged.

One of my privileges comes from being a citizen of the United States. My country—amid repeated tests and stumbles—remains rich, powerful, and willing to spend resources protecting people like me who are educated, white, male, heterosexual, cisgender, and middle class. And yet my country, the largest historical contributor of greenhouse gases to the planet, continues to stand in the way of meaningful global action to reduce climate change. The arguments of this book are therefore primarily focused on how the United States and other powerful, industrialized nations can reform in a world of climate change.

You may be less privileged than me, but it is likely that at least some of your actions are still complicit in climate change. You have at least enough education and time to read these words, which suggests you probably have some privilege that leads to the emissions of greenhouse gases. I do not say this to add to anxiety or guilt but to empower you. Those of us who have privilege can use it to make things better. After acknowledging that our actions contribute to the problem, we can recognize our power to make meaningful changes in the world.

While the burdens of climate change are unfairly distributed, the benefits of resisting it can help everyone. We who are privileged must resist what Heather McGhee calls "zero-sum stories," which insist that our comfort and health depend on the suffering of others. Societies work better when they nurture solidarity, seeking benefits for a wider rather than a smaller community. We will be better off in a world that offers everyone more safety and security.[7]

The first chapter of this book will argue that climate change is caused by the same structures of injustice that created other privileges; it is an intersectional problem. I will suggest that we learn to think of the problem as "atmospheric defilement" by connecting the burning of fossil fuels to the defilement of bodies in the slave trade, the theft of resources in imperial expansion, the capture of lands in settler colonialism, the exploitation of workers in extractive capitalism, and the exclusivity and limitations of ableism and heteronormativity. I'll also argue that we are best equipped to talk about climate change when we listen humbly to and learn from marginalized peoples.

Chapter 2 will then argue that the injustices of atmospheric defilement are rooted in particular ways of thinking that justify and excuse oppression and injustice. Identifying three myths of domination—human exceptionalism, radical individualism, and infinitely expansive wealth—this chapter will argue that these habits of thought have taught people in industrial societies to ignore or downplay the problem of climate change. The solutions that have so far been proposed and tried are too small and ineffectual because they assume separation and competition rather than seeking unity and collaboration.

Overcoming broad cultural patterns and deeply rooted injustice will not be simple. Individualism, human exceptionalism, global capitalism, racism, colonialism, sexism, ableism, and heteronormativity are deeply entrenched in industrialized societies; there will be no easy way to end them. But when those of us who are privileged understand these issues as part of climate change, we find the power to act meaningfully. We can advocate for political and economic structures better than those we've inherited. We can make the world fairer, more sustainable, and more just than it is now. We can name fossil fuel corporations as our enemy.

2) We Are Open to Learning from Christian Traditions

I used to be uncomfortable with the idea of having enemies and even more uncomfortable publicly naming them. In an earlier book, I argued that the climate movement "ultimately needs empathy even more than it needs enemies."[8]

I was wrong to contrast empathy with enemies. Since I wrote those words, the Black Lives Matter movement and youth-led climate protests have taught me that sometimes genuine empathy for those who suffer requires naming the enemies hurting them. One cannot claim to be in solidarity with the victims of police violence without taking a stand against the systems that disproportionately harass, abuse, and kill people of color. One cannot genuinely advocate for future generations without naming the structures defiling the atmosphere and clouding their future. I am convinced, now, that if we want to build coalitions that make the world better, we need to name the enemies who are making it worse.

As we do so, we must remember that having enemies is dangerous. It is all too easy to lose ourselves to negativity and bitterness, to focus more on destroying what we dislike than building up what we love. It is all too easy to become defined by our enemies and to warp ourselves into a mirror image of what we oppose. We risk being corrupted by bitterness and cynicism; we can be tempted to believe we only succeed when our enemies suffer. It is important, therefore, to learn from wise people and traditions about how to have enemies in a constructive and healthy way.

My own guidance comes from Christianity, and so this book is particularly addressed to those who are open to learning from Christian traditions. It's important to note this does not only include Christians; *we* and *us* in this book refer to anyone who is open to the idea that Christianity might have something to teach. I am a Christian, but you will see in this book that I have learned a lot from atheists and Muslims and Buddhists and Jews and Hindus. These people and their traditions help me think about how the world works, how to be a good person, and how to stand up for climate justice. And I've learned the most when they spoke honestly from their own traditions and beliefs. So this book tries to speak honestly from my tradition and beliefs in hopes that you can learn from them and reflect on your own traditions and beliefs.

Christianity, as I understand it, is a call to believe and live as though the world and everything and everyone in it were made to live together in loving, just community. All of creation is meant for connection. This, I believe, is the core message of Jesus's teachings and the most faithful expressions of Christian traditions. Of course, many Christians and Christian institutions have failed and continue failing to live up to this ideal of loving justice. I certainly do. But that ideal remains the heart of what Christianity can be.

I used to think that because Christians were supposed to love everyone, we were not supposed to have enemies. I should have known better. Jesus taught otherwise, and he was not subtle. In Matthew's Gospel, he commands, "Love your enemies and pray for those who persecute you" (5:44).[9] Notice that the fact of enemies is straightforwardly assumed here. Jesus was speaking to a group of people colonized and oppressed by the Roman Empire. They had enemies, Jesus knew it, and he did not try to talk them out of it. Rather, he taught them how to treat those enemies. If we want to learn from these instructions in the twenty-first century, then we must first understand that we, too, have enemies.

This point is made well by pastor and activist Melissa Florer-Bixler, whose book *How to Have an Enemy* grows out of her work in movements for peace and racial justice. She writes, "To have enemies as a source of liberation—for ourselves and for those who do harm—is to recognize structures of power and their relationship to identity. . . . Christians not only have enemies but have them well. We have enemies in particular and curious ways, ways that do not make sense within the structures of violent power-keeping around us."[10]

Christianity, Florer-Bixler insists, can teach people how to have enemies well. This means resisting evil without being warped and corrupted to compromise our own beliefs and ideals. It means standing up for justice even when we must do so against the norms and ideals of the wider culture. It means maintaining an attitude of love even when we are hated.

The biblical stories of Jesus are about a man who was hated by his enemies. He argued against the injustices of the Roman Empire, and that empire killed him. He warned those who followed that they would be hated too: "If the world hates you, be aware that it hated me before it hated you . . . Because you do not belong to the world, but I have chosen you out of the world—therefore the world hates you" (John 15:18–19). Those who hate us are our enemies, and Jesus teaches us how to oppose them without hating them back.

Chapter 3 will explore a theology that helps Christians treat destructive systems as enemies. Drawing on the work of New Testament scholar Walter Wink, I will argue that when Jesus refers to "the world" in the passage just quoted, he means not all of creation but a corrupted system of domination. Jesus was not warning followers that they would be opposed by the Planet Earth but by a network of structures that push people into violence and irresponsible consumption. That network, which Wink learns from the Bible to call "the fallen Powers" and the "Domination System," put Jesus to death. The same network is changing the climate and distributing the burden of that change unjustly.

This book is about one specific group of fallen Powers: the fossil fuel industry. I take my lead here from the climate movement, which is increasingly naming that industry as its enemy. For example, Methodist climate activist Bill McKibben argued in 2012 that the fossil fuel industry is "Public Enemy Number One to the survival of our planetary civilization." He emphasizes the point with a reference to our friend Pogo: "The more carefully you do the math the more thoroughly you realize that this is, at bottom, a moral issue; we have met the enemy and they is Shell."[11] In chapter 4, I will bring McKibben and other activists into conversation with the theology of the Powers, arguing that the fossil fuel industry contributes enormously to climate change, exacerbates unjust and imperialist power structures, and institutionalizes dangerous myths of domination.

3) We Are Committed to Resisting Degradation

It might seem unwise to cite Jesus's commandments to love and pray for our enemies because some people interpret this to mean Christians should only sit quietly and reflect on the problem without doing anything to fix it. They assume we name our enemies only to wish them well. After all, shortly before Jesus advises us to pray for those who persecute us, he also says, "Do not resist an evildoer" (Matthew 5:39). This all feels very passive, as though our only response to systemic destruction and violence should be thoughts and prayers.

This book is written for people who believe, instead, that we should actively oppose evil. Put in Christian terms, the God who made the world and declared it good expects human beings to use our power to resist destruction and division. But we need not use violence and domination to do so. Jesus offers a range of creative and constructive methods with which to resist the domination system. Christians are called to use these methods, and to create new ones, against the systems causing our neighbors to suffer. Christians are called to turn love and prayer into action for systemic change.

As chapter 5 will emphasize, Jesus's instruction to "not resist" was a caution against violence, not against all protest. So we will explore three strategies for resistance and the ways they are already being demonstrated by activist for climate justice. Protests on the streets, political organizing in the halls of legislation, and creative opposition to the fossil fuel industry all demonstrate that people can constructively resist the Powers and that we do best when we form coalitions with others who seek to do the same.

When we name fossil fuel corporations as our enemy, we will find many allies. With those allies, we will gain resources to challenge, change, and overcome the systems defiling the atmosphere. This will help us build collectives powerful enough to make meaningful, systemic change. Chapter 6 will draw on the biblical story of manna in the wilderness to argue that Christians can build democratic structures that gather and share the abundant energies of the sun and wind, share them fairly, and support a slower and more participatory culture. While fossil fuel companies are based on assumptions of scarcity and habits of hoarding, climate citizens should instead seek a transition to a new, more cooperative world.

The work of resistance is hard. We must take seriously the anxiety and guilt my student and so many others have expressed about climate change. Even as we work against the fossil fuel industry, those of us who use its products must recognize that we have complicity. Like those we oppose, we are flawed and imperfect. Like those we oppose, we live in a fallen world.

The School of Life, a secular organization that draws wisdom from across human cultures, offers a helpful interpretation of the Christian idea of human fallenness. While the idea of a "fall" from grace is often dismissed as harsh or cruel, it should instead be understood as "generous." The truth of fallenness is that our limits are not the simple result of our own choices. The School of Life explains, "We suffer, feel lost and isolated, are racked with worry, miss our own talents, refuse love, lack empathy, sulk, obsess, and hate: These are not merely personal flaws, but constitute the essence of the human animal." In contrast to self-help that promises "solutions" to human failings, Christianity teaches that it is part of human nature to make mistakes and that we should accept this rather than futilely scrambling to change it.[12]

Christians and climate activists share a reputation for being sanctimonious, for scolding others, for relentlessly seeking purity, for being no fun at parties. These reputations are sometimes, unfortunately, deserved. But the doctrine of the fall offers a defense against it, insisting there is no purely "right" place from which anyone speaks; no one has all the answers. As we resist our enemies, as we work for a better world, we must accept and remember our limitations, and use them to grow better at understanding others'.[13]

Chapter 7 will build on this wisdom to reflect on the inner work of climate resistance, focusing first on how to process and build on the guilt and anger that many of us feel about climate change. That chapter will also argue that such feelings can help us build up the loving mercy and joy that are required to live well, and have enemies well, in a fallen world.

The resistance this book advocates is ultimately rooted in mercy; it names and opposes enemies while seeking to avoid domination. These strategies focus on supporting and nurturing the habits and institutions that help human beings live well together. Ultimately, resisting the Powers of the fossil fuel industry is less about taking them down and more about building up better institutions. The most effective resistance comes from nurturing a politics and an economy that bring people closer to both one another and the entirety of creation.

4) We Believe We Can Build a Better World

Climate change is real; it is unjust; it is terrible. And it is not going away. Carbon dioxide emitted into the atmosphere remains there for hundreds or thousands of years. This means we are still dealing with warming caused at the start of the Industrial Revolution and that fossil fuels burned today will change the climate for many generations to come. Perhaps it will someday be possible to efficiently remove CO_2 from the air or block the sun's heat and rebalance weather systems. But even then, human life will have been fundamentally altered by climate change.

Like the pernicious injustices of racism and colonialism and patriarchy from which it emerged, climate change will be part of human life for generations to come. People driven from their homes by wildfires today will feel some measure of fear and insecurity for years. Families forced to abandon their farms to drought will live with that loss for decades. Nations endangered by rising seas will have reason to resent the wealthy people and institutions who allowed it to happen for centuries.

This is the bad news: There is no action you or I could take that would end the problem of climate change. We cannot wipe the slate of global inequities clean. The earth's atmosphere is irreparably changing, making life harder for many of God's creatures and increasing the injustice and violence of contemporary human existence. We must accept that we cannot solve this problem. We cannot make the world right.

But this is the good news: we can make it better. Those of us with privilege have power to resist the enemies causing the problem. We can build systems that help us and everyone else live more in harmony with other people and the earth. We can prepare ourselves, our communities, our nations, and our world to be as loving and just as possible as the climate changes.

That preparation will redeem the Powers. We use our power to heal and re-create the institutions our world needs to help people care for one another, connect to strangers, and serve those in need. We work toward the hope of a loving and just world by giving our energy to the most just and loving systems we can find.

Films about climate change are frequently apocalyptic, imagining a future without civilization as we know it. The dry deserts of *Mad Max*, the frozen tundra of *Snowpiercer*, the meteor-ravaged landscape of *Don't Look Up* all share a sense that our world will completely collapse. The most important thing about those stories is that they are cautionary rather than predictive. Humanity is not doomed. Our civilizations are not inevitably about to end. We do not need to live in a world where every individual must fend for themselves. Instead, we are called to work very hard to preserve the structures that prevent violent wastelands, protect those in need, and share the excesses of those who prosper. Even in a changing world, we can sustain and build healthy communities. We can insist on governments and community organizations that are just and resilient enough to be sustainable.

The corporate and political systems that structure industrialized life are corrupt, and it is tempting to give up on them entirely. But this is not the answer. Not all systems are bad. Not all that is corrupted is irredeemable. If we want to live in diverse communities, we need to support the institutions that make cooperation and collaboration possible. We need to help make them democratic, trustworthy, and inclusive.

As the climate changes, we're going to need the best institutions we can get. This book is about naming the enemies that defile our climate and resisting them by building toward something better. As we will see, one of the defining characteristics of the fossil fuel industry is a repeated insistence that the forces warming the earth cannot change, that humanity is stuck with atmospheric defilement. We must call this out as a lie. A better world, a better future, is possible.

Nevertheless, *Meeting the Enemy* will not satisfy readers who are looking for the solution to climate change; instead, it assumes at the outset that there is no solution. Part of accepting our limitations, accepting the fallenness of human life, includes recognizing that we will not repair the entire world. This helps us treat ourselves with grace when we make mistakes, when we feel overwhelmed by problems, or when we are tempted to wallow in guilt about our complicity. It helps us be empathetic toward people who disagree with us, recognizing that they are limited too. It helps us serenely accept what we cannot change while courageously focusing on what we can. It can help us be merciful to our enemies.

There is much to do. We can resist the Powers of climate change, we can work toward a more just world with a healthier climate, and we can repent when we make mistakes. We can start the process of healing in our human and more-than-human communities; we can build and support better and more just systems. We cannot fix it all; we cannot make a perfect world. But we have reason to hope and work for a better future.

The Enemy Is Not Us

Over a semester, I tried to offer new perspectives to the student who felt anxious and guilty about climate change. I tried to help her and the rest of the class put their personal actions in perspective, comparing them with the broad and powerful systems that are closer to the root of the problem. We thought together about how to learn from and consider participating in acts of resistance and restoration. We studied time-tested resources from Christianity and other faith traditions that help people process the overwhelm that comes from living in a fallen world. I hope it helped.

Similarly, I hope this book will help you if you have privilege, care about climate change, are open to learning from Christian traditions, are committed to resisting injustice, and believe that a better world is possible.

Those of us who feel guilty about climate change can progress from that feeling into a more systemic analysis and critique of the powers that make us complicit in the problem. To do this, we need to understand the depths of the challenges we face, name the enemies most at fault, strategize ways to defeat them without using their methods of domination, and work toward a more just and sustainable future.

Beginning in 1970, Pogo and Earth Day helped people across the industrialized world understand we all have complicity in the degradation of the environment. This is an important lesson. But it is time to move past it, to turn our attention away from our own small failings and toward the monstrous divisions and fractures created by the fossil fuel industry. It is time to meet our enemy. That enemy is strong, but once we face it clearly, we will see that our communities and traditions are even stronger.

Part I

THE PROBLEM

FOR SIX WEEKS in 2022, the Bolt Creek fire burned sixty miles northeast of my house in Washington State. Our forests were dried out from a long summer that stretched into an oddly rainless October, so this was one of many long-burning fires in the region.

It made life worse. Ash hung in the air for weeks, and most days included a strange orange haze in the eastern sky. By mid-October, we had the worst air quality measured anywhere in the world and were advised to avoid exercising or even lingering outside. I felt anxious. I worried about the impact of these fires on my health, on the health of my family, and especially on dear friends with breathing difficulties. I worried about the long-term health of the forests and trees iconic to this place.

Sadly, seasons like this are becoming more common across the Pacific Northwest and the world. The next summer was better here but far worse across Canada. Global trends also show increasing risks of wildfires in Greece, Indonesia, Australia, and many other places. By the time you read this, it is almost certain that more terrible fires will have burned across the world. Warming air and changing weather patterns make long-standing forests more vulnerable to burning, and the continued development of cities near these forests endanger human health and communities.

Even during our wildfire experience, I didn't talk much about climate change with friends and family. We focused on practical topics like building air filters out of box fans and how to stay sane while getting some exercise indoors. We speculated about when rains might start and offer relief. We made brief, knowing references to the foreboding sense that the sky's strange color was a sign of troubling times, but we avoided any explicit reference to the warming globe.

This is, unfortunately, a common trend. Most of us worry about climate change far more than we talk about it. In a survey the same year as the Bolt Creek fire, the Yale Program on Climate Change Communication found that 64 percent of people in the United States are either very or moderately worried about global warming, but only 32 percent even discuss the issue with family and friends occasionally.[1] Only half of the people who are worried about the issue talk about it.

I understand why we avoid conversations about climate change. The world is full of other challenges and entertaining diversions. During the Bolt Creek fire, I sought distraction. I wanted to deal with the inconveniences and anxieties of the defiled atmosphere privately and quickly, and then I wanted to stop talking or thinking about it.

But those of us with privilege who want to do something about the problem of climate change can resist the temptation to turn away or stay silent. We can learn to communicate about what is happening to our atmosphere. We can help others join the conversation. Such honest communication is essential before we can take meaningful action.

The difficulty in talking about climate change is in part reflected in the name. The scientific community originally called the phenomenon the *greenhouse effect*, naming the chemical reaction that causes the atmosphere to trap more heat. This evolved to focus on results rather than causes, so *global warming* became the common term. But the issue is about much more than just rising temperatures, and so the discourse evolved to focus on the more comprehensive *climate change*. Yet most advocates and communications experts agree this term is too bland and tame to capture the myriad challenges facing contemporary global communities.[2]

Climate change is also hard to talk about because it is so complicated. To grasp the issue requires some understanding of chemistry, biology, meteorology, history, economics, sociology, theology, and many other ways of looking at the world. As geographer Mike Hulme writes, climate change is "multifarious," too complicated for any one explanation: "There is no single comprehensive account of climate change that can do full justice to the physical manifestations, political discourses, and imaginative power of the phenomenon." So, rather than seeking a singularly accurate accounting of the issue, Hulme calls for "different and richer accounts of what climate change is and what climate change *means*."[3] Inspired by this call, I will not try to capture all the complexity of the problem in this book but instead offer one perspective that I hope can facilitate more and deeper conversations.

Chapter 1 argues that the problem should be understood as atmospheric defilement, a term I adapt from theologian Delores Williams. Atmospheric defilement includes increasing global temperatures but also the intersectional injustices wrapped up with the causes and impacts of the extraction and burning of fossil fuels. When we understand the problem this way, we are called to a broad conversation about what is happening to our planet and every community on it. We are called to listen to as many voices as possible to understand the problem. The chapter works toward such a conversation by learning from people of color about how atmospheric defilement intersects with racism, from Indigenous and postcolonial people about its roots in imperialism and colonialism, from working people about how it damages human as well as ecological communities, from those who have been dismissed as "queer" or "wrong" about how the world could be different.

Chapter 2 then begins to develop a particularly Christian understanding of these intersectional injustices by identifying three destructive habits of thought, myths that normalize and excuse atmospheric defilement. Human exceptionalism, radical individualism, and infinite expansionism are myths of domination that Christian communities have too often embraced and taught. Naming this fact makes it more possible to see where we have gone wrong.

It may seem counterintuitive to suggest that atmospheric defilement will be easier to talk about when we connect it to other things that are also hard to talk about. Bringing racism, colonialism, sexism, and ableism into dialogue with climate change requires nuance. Raising questions about human uniqueness, individualism, and capitalism can make conversations more tense. But these myths and injustices are part of the problem; talking about them will help us to honestly account for what is going on. They also help us develop a language rich enough to begin responding meaningfully.

I hope the next time my community experiences the fear and reality of climate change as directly as we did during the Bolt Creek fire, I will be better equipped. I hope I will talk to leaders in my city and region about how the firefighters risking their lives and the people evacuated from their homes deserve a stronger social safety net. I hope I will talk with my neighbors and friends about how unhoused people and farmworkers, who have no choice but to stay outside breathing polluted air, deserve better institutions that are built to truly care for them in dangerous times. I hope I will amplify the voices of local Indigenous groups who incorporated small, controlled burns into their lives with these forests for centuries before settlers came to this place. I hope I will have learned more about the trees that burn, the animals that called those trees home, and the multiple ripple effects from this disaster on so many other ecosystems. I hope I will have reached out to more Christian communities to consider together how our tradition has contributed to the problems we face and how we can do better.

1

CLIMATE CHANGE AS ATMOSPHERIC DEFILEMENT

IN 1976, EMMA Degraffenreid and a group of colleagues sued an auto assembly plant in St. Louis for discrimination, arguing that their opportunities there had been limited because they were Black women. A district court ruled against them, suggesting they could not legally be discriminated against that way. If they had proven discrimination based solely on gender or solely on race, they would have had a case. But, according to the court, Black women were not a protected class.

Legal theorist Kimberlé Crenshaw responded by arguing that the law was missing something vitally important: the experience of Black women is shaped not just by race and gender but also intersection. So, discrimination cannot be understood with the "single-axis analysis" of the court system. From this insight, Crenshaw began to interrogate "intersectionality," tracing multiple dimensions of discrimination and oppression and insisting that all people are shaped by multiple identities. She writes, "Because the intersectional experience is greater than the sum of racism and sexism, any analysis that does not take intersectionality into account cannot sufficiently address the particular manner in which Black women are subordinated."[1]

Since this early articulation, Crenshaw and many others have developed intersectionality as a key concept in law, ethics, and cultural analysis. Racism intersects with sexism; neither can be understood well if the other is ignored. Furthermore, myriad other identities intersect with race and gender: ability, age, class, nationality, religion, sexual identity, and sexuality, among others. No identity exists in isolation, so no prejudice or oppression ever exists in isolation. If a society discriminates against immigrants, this will affect wealthy immigrants differently from those experiencing poverty. If disabled people are treated dismissively in the workplace, this will pose different challenges to disabled people who are cisgender than to those who are trans. All people exist at the intersection of multiple identities. So all injustices intersect. Intersectionality, a concept that traces part of its history to an auto assembly plant, has important implications for climate change and for those of us who want to resist the industry most responsible for it.

Climate "Coalitions Waiting to Be Formed"

In a talk at a TED conference, Kimberlé Crenshaw said, "If we can't see a problem, we can't fix a problem."[2] Those of us who want to see the problem of climate change need to understand it intersectionally, learning to talk about the atmosphere in conjunction with the complexities of human identity and social injustices. Poor and Indigenous communities are more threatened by rising seas and raging fires than others. Women and children are more likely to be driven from their homes by droughts and typhoons. Disabled and elderly people face more challenges than others when heat waves strike. People of color whose lands have been colonized tend to have fewer resources with which to adapt to a changing world.[3]

Note that the concept of intersectionality applies to everyone and invites everyone to learn from other people. This is an important corrective to public discourse, which too often presents intersectional thinking as divisive, forcing people into identity categories with exclusive walls around them. That approach continues the "single-axis analysis" that Crenshaw criticized; it assumes that people are shaped by just a single identity. Intersectionality asserts the opposite: people are most empowered when they understand the multiple identities that shape them and the many connections this provides to others.

Identity categories, Crenshaw writes, "are in fact coalitions, or at least potential coalitions waiting to be formed."[4] When people gather with others who share their racial identity, they find diverse classes and genders represented. When people gather with others who share their ethnicity, they meet others with diverse sexualities and religious affiliations. Every human being belongs to multiple, overlapping identity groups. So intersectionality provides opportunities for anyone and everyone to communicate and work together.

Intersectional perspectives are particularly important for those of us who experience climate change with some privilege. We have too often been taught that our privileged experiences are universal. In discourses on climate change, this is frequently expressed with assumptions that "we" human beings all have the same experiences: "we are all in this together," or "we all share this planet," or "we have met the enemy, and he is us." There is, of course, truth to such claims. Everyone in the industrialized world has complicity in the problem, it is changing the entire planet, and every human being has reasons to be concerned. But beyond these generalities, it is hard to say much about the experience of climate change that is truly universal.

An intersectional perspective insists that humanity is made up of many diverse communities, many different "we"s. This makes conversation more possible. It reveals important truths that can only be seen from particular perspectives. Some communities are more threatened than others, and some communities have done an especially poor job sharing our pieces of the planet with other people and other creatures. Some of us have more complicity than others.[5]

Intersectionality makes learning possible because it makes coalitions possible. Even those of us who are privileged in every identity—whiteness, maleness, heterosexuality, upper class, able-bodied adulthood, for example—are included in identity-based coalitions; we share our identities with people who are marginalized in other ways. Men are privileged in patriarchal societies but can connect through that identity with gay, trans, and disabled men who are marginalized. Christians are privileged in most of the Western world but through that identity can meet fellow Christians who are female, poor, and migrants. Identity groups make it possible to connect and to learn from connections.

Climate Change at Six Intersections

This chapter learns from six people who have drawn insights from their marginalization to explain systems that oppress them and alter the climate. They can teach us about racism, imperialism, colonialism, capitalism, ableism, and heterosexism.[6] Their insights coalesce into an empowering, intersectional understanding of climate change.

"The Sin of Defilement": Intersections with Racism

In 2014, a Staten Island police officer killed Eric Garner, a Black man, by pinning him to the ground in an illegal chokehold. As he died, Garner pleaded, "I can't breathe." The medical examiner's report deemed Garner's death a homicide, caused by the choking. But it also listed asthma as a contributing factor. This is a disproportionately common disease among African Americans in New York City, who tend to live and work amid high levels of air pollution. Garner's tragic death therefore occurred at an intersection of injustices: police violence, racism, and pollution.[7]

In trying to understand this intersectional violence and what it might teach us about climate change, we have much to learn from the Christian theologian Delores Williams. Over twenty years before Garner's death, Williams wrote a sadly prophetic essay titled "Sin, Nature, and Black Women's Bodies," arguing that the best way to understand the contemporary degradation of the nonhuman world is to identify roots in the ways the bodies of Black people have been treated in North America since the slave system.

Slavery, Williams writes, was based in part on "the sin of defilement," the "wanton desecration" of Black people's bodies.[8] The slave system abused and degraded human beings at the whims of those who believed themselves to be owners. This sin was most acute in the treatment of Black women, who were not only forced to work for and serve white people but also routinely raped and tortured by men who used sex and violence to assert power. That is defilement.

This sin did not end with emancipation. Even after slavery, Black women were expected to play surrogate roles, caring for children and physically laboring with minimal compensation for the profit and comfort of white people.[9]

Williams identifies the same sin of defilement in environmental degradation. Focusing on the strip mining in her native Kentucky, she argues that the technologies stripping vegetation from mountains to extract coal are justified by the same thinking that justified slavery. Those who believe themselves to "own" mountains believe they have a "God-given right" to destroy them and justify doing so to provide "greater profits, comfort, and leisure for more Americans."[10] The earth is defiled, just as Black women's bodies are defiled. Williams writes, "Put simply, the assault upon the natural environment today is but an extension of the assault upon black women's bodies in the nineteenth century."[11]

It is important to note that this is not just an analogy between slavery and environmental degradation. Instead, Williams argues that the same sin of defilement is expressed in both. The intersection is historical and real; the same social structures that justify white supremacy justify the defilement of the earth. This also means that those of us who have been socialized not to notice the oppression of Black women are ill-equipped to understand the realities of environmental degradation. Only by learning to broadly recognize oppressive systems can we develop a realistic understanding of climate change. Only by standing against the defilement of women's bodies and bodies of color can we effectively resist the defilement of the atmosphere.[12]

Williams offers an important way to name and see the problem of climate change as atmospheric defilement. Global warming, like the polluted air that degraded Eric Garner's lungs, is rooted in patriarchy and white supremacy. Unjust systems constructed a world where powerful people believe they can wantonly desecrate both the bodies of others and the ecosystems on which all bodies depend. This leads not only to strip mining but also to the careless burning of coal, oil, and methane.

When we understand climate change as atmospheric defilement, we understand that it intersects with Eric Garner's death. The sin of defilement is sadly still evident when the lives and bodies of Black people are treated as if they do not matter. The same sin that led to Garner's strangulation also led to the degradation of his lungs. That same sin continues to defile the entire atmospheric system.

"A Viscerally Human Conflict": Intersections with Imperialism

Racism intersects with the related injustice of imperialism, a system that assumes European and European-descended people have the right to control lands and ecosystems across the world. That control has been used to justify the extraction of fossil fuels, and so is an essential part of why and how the climate is changing.

Consider, for example, the nation of Burma in Southeast Asia. A Burmese town called Yenangyuang, "Stinking Water Creek," used to be one of the few places on earth where petroleum naturally bubbled to the surface. For centuries, people there harvested it to burn for light and other household purposes. One scholar suggests that before the invention of the combustion engine, the Burmese were the largest petroleum users in the world.[13] But when the British Empire became interested in oil, they stole Yenangyuang. Their army invaded and claimed ownership over the entire country of Burma in the nineteenth century and ran it as a colony for almost seventy years. Ownership of all the nation's oil was transferred to a company that is now part of the BP corporation.

In 1948, the people of Burma achieved independence and formally changed the country's name to Myanmar. However, they continue to struggle with the legacy of imperialism, which includes poverty, military rule, and rising seas. Between 1998 and 2017, Myanmar had a higher death toll from extreme weather events than any other nation in the world.[14] In 2015, a flood in the Bay of Bengal killed thousands and forced over 1.5 million people to leave their homes. Recovering from such a severe disaster is particularly challenging because one-third of the nation lives below the international poverty line.[15]

Essayist and novelist Amitav Ghosh argues that the contemporary climatic threats to Myanmar cannot be understood separately from the history of empire. British colonization took wealth out of the nation; the industrialized extraction and burning of oil added greenhouse gases to the atmosphere. Thus, the same imperialism that defiled the atmosphere also degraded the Burmese people's capacity to adapt to it.[16]

This history is just one of many examples of colonialism. Ghosh writes, "The fact is that we live in a world that has been profoundly shaped by empire and its disparities." The logic of colonialism taught white people that they are entitled to the oil under faraway lands, which in turn justified treating the peoples in those lands as hostile and ignoring their suffering when a changing climate threatens them: "The distribution of power in the world therefore lies at the core of the climate crisis."[17]

Like Delores Williams, Ghosh calls for an understanding of atmospheric defilement that takes its history seriously. While many have tried to label climate change a "new" problem in the twenty-first century, he finds roots in centuries of violence against colonized peoples and lands: "Behind the increasing derangement of the air, the landscape, and the bodies of those who inhabited it there lay a viscerally human conflict."[18]

Imperialism is not just a political and economic phenomenon; it is also a set of cultural assumptions. It assumes there is a single standard of "civilization," that those who are "most" civilized have the right and responsibility to force others to conform to their standards. Climate change is a result, an expression, and a continuation of this assumption. It is also an indictment. Western empires were built on a belief that "civilized" people from Europe could control other peoples and the earth.[19] It did not work. The result has been, instead, defiled lands, peoples, and atmosphere.

For those of us who descend from colonizers, these can be hard truths. It is easy for people who are white, European, and prosperous to feel personally attacked when the realities of imperialism are laid out. But Amitav Ghosh argues that one of the habits of thinking we need to unlearn is the colonial individualism that insists we are the center of every story. The world does not need more people who feel individually guilty. Instead, it needs people who can help imagine a new global future. The work Ghosh calls for is not to feel bad but instead "to find a way out of the individualizing imagery in which we are trapped."[20]

Ghosh hopes that people can transition away from the mistakes of empire, preventing and healing the defilement of the atmosphere by developing alternatives to replace greed and individualism. He writes, "I would like to believe that out of this struggle will be born a generation that will be able to look upon the world with clearer eyes than those that preceded it; that they will be able to transcend the isolation in which humanity was entrapped in the time of its derangement . . . and that this vision, at once new and ancient, will find expressions in a transformed and renewed art and literature."[21]

Understanding atmospheric defilement as a product of imperialism as well as racism helps us to look honestly at the world and to make decisions about what we want it to be in the future. If we can imagine new ways forward, then we can disrupt the worst patterns of the past.

"Colonial Déjà Vu": Intersections with Settler Colonialism

One of the most powerful examples of such imagination occurred in 2016, when the Water Protectors of the Standing Rock Sioux opposed construction of the Dakota Access Pipeline on their traditional lands. For almost a year, this movement drew international attention, teaching the world that the pipeline violates Sioux sovereignty and endangers water supplies for communities across North Dakota. While the protesters were eventually forced out by police and the pipeline was built, the face of the climate movement changed. The intersection of atmospheric defilement with Indigenous rights became indisputable; new coalitions formed that continue to resist and demand change.

Potawatomi scholar Kyle Powys Whyte insightfully explores the links between contemporary global warming and the "invasion that began centuries ago" in North America. He insists that climate change is not new for the Indigenous peoples of this continent, who already experienced "deforestation, pollution, modification of hydrological cycles, and the amplification of soil-use and terraforming" when European settlers invaded and changed the land.[22]

From an Indigenous perspective, Whyte argues, atmospheric defilement can be understood as "colonial déjà vu." It is one more expression of the invading settler culture that takes away "Indigenous peoples' adaptive capacity and self-determination by repeatedly containing them in different ways, destroying the ecological conditions that are tightly coupled with Indigenous cultural and political systems."[23]

While media coverage of the Standing Rock protests frequently noted that the pipeline poses risks to tribal health and water, they less often noted that it was being built on land ceded to the Sioux in the 1858 treaty of Fort Laramie. In an act of colonialism, the US Congress redrew the border in 1889 after gold was discovered in the Dakotas. Congress did not consult with the Sioux, acting as though the Indigenous people had no rights so that white people could make money.

In the 1960s, the treaty rights of the Sioux were denied once again when the Army Corps of Engineers created Lake Oahe, flooding 200,000 acres of reservation land that displaced over 1,000 Native families. Again, the government did not ask. So in 2016, when Dakota Access LLC proposed building a pipeline across this land and under Lake Oahe without meaningfully consulting the Sioux, they were continuing a long tradition of invasion and defilement without consultation.[24]

The theme of this story, Whyte argues, is "a lack of indigenous consent." From the creation of reservations to the siting of dams to the construction of the pipeline, the invasion of Native lands has led directly to environmental degradation and climate change: "U.S. settler colonialism continues to work to erase Indigenous peoples culturally, economically, and politically. It is hard to distinguish U.S. protection of gold miners from similar protections of [Dakota Access Pipeline] workers and investors."[25]

This understanding of the problem is sobering, forcing those of us descended from settlers to admit that the lands we inhabit were, in most cases, unjustly stolen. But it also offers a way to begin imagining alternatives, to work for a better future. If climate change is rooted in the invasion of Indigenous lands and the destruction of Indigenous cultures, then healing involves returning land and power to Indigenous people, who have managed climate changes for centuries.[26] As Whyte puts it, "Climate justice is a matter of breaking the cyclical history of colonial strategies that interfere with [Indigenous] rights."[27]

The water protectors at Standing Rock offered an example of resistance. They asserted their right to determine their own future and that of their ancestral lands. In doing so, they attracted a diverse coalition of support. At its peak, the Sacred Stone Camp housed representatives of three hundred distinct tribes from across the world, each supporting the sovereignty of the Sioux. They were joined by a wide range of activists from other identities who were motivated by commitments to racial justice, climate, and many other issues. There was no single reason that activists came to Standing Rock; instead, many communities, identities, and belief systems intersected there. They formed an intersectional coalition of resistance and demonstrated what climate justice can look like.

"Hiding Away the Human Wreckage": Intersections with Extractive Capitalism

One thousand miles northwest of Standing Rock are the oil sands of northern Alberta. There, corporations extract three million barrels each day using a process of pumping that separates oil and leaves behind piles of toxic, muddy waste. This extraction takes place on the traditional lands of the Dene and Creek peoples without their consent.[28]

In the graphic novel *Ducks: Two Years in the Oil Sands*, artist Kate Beaton tells the story of her time as a worker in Alberta. She worked for the fossil fuel industry between 2005 and 2008, beginning when she was twenty-one. She had grown up on the island of Cape Breton and completed college with majors in history and anthropology. She felt the loan she'd taken for that degree as "a foot on my neck,"[29] and the only job she found that would allow her to quickly repay it was in northern Alberta. The booming oil industry was paying premium wages.

One theme of Beaton's book is that almost everyone she worked with also migrated to Alberta, temporarily, for the money. When she asks a coworker if he was a fisherman before, he replies, "I'm still a fisherman. I'm just here." Another, asked if he likes it in the camps, says it "doesn't matter" because his job in the oil sands is the only way to pay his bills.[30] The workers of the oil sands were there to support families and pay debts. The difficult, dangerous work of extracting fossil fuels is often done by people who feel they have no other economic choice.

This marks out an important connection between climate change—caused in significant part by the production and burning of oil like that in the tar sands—and extractive capitalism. Oil is pulled from the ground by employees who justify it because they need the money paid to them by corporations, who justify the work because they need to make money for their investors. Economic need drives people and systems to do things that exacerbate climate change. Marxist historian and activist Andreas Malm argues that most people in the industrialized world live under what he calls "the fossil economy," a system "of self-sustaining growth predicated on the growing consumption of fossil fuels, and therefore generating a sustained growth in emissions of carbon dioxide."[31] The economy justifies climate change and human complicity in it, and the economy requires that extraction and burning continue at any cost.[32]

Market exchanges do not cause climate change, but the unquestioned adherence to market logic and the imperatives of market growth that characterize contemporary capitalism do. Markets and economic exchange are long-standing ways to organize people and have accomplished a great deal. But, in the twenty-first century, extractive capitalism has become not just an economic option but a hegemonic system that increasingly degrades all other aspects of culture.

Kate Beaton's *Ducks* offers a powerful reflection on what it is like to be a worker in an extractive capitalist economy. The corporations that employed her are a powerful, faceless presence throughout the book. The most consistent impression of these corporations is that they care about nothing except the profit to be made from extracted oil. For example, the book takes its name in part from an event in 2008 when hundreds of ducks died in a pond of sludge, coated with suffocating toxin that made flight impossible. Beaton, who had worked at the camp where this happened, is troubled and saddened. But she and her coworkers continue about their business of extracting oil and producing tailings.[33] No one is allowed to stop and consider whether the death of these ducks should call their work into question. What matters is not whether the workers care about ducks or what the ducks reveal about the poison workers are pulling from the ground. What matters is that the corporations require the work to continue.

Beaton suggests that her employers barely cared more about the lives of workers than the lives of ducks. Regular safety briefings ignore the perilous roads between the camps, the rampant drug use among workers, and the persistent coughs and rashes developed from working in oil fields. She writes, "The industry prized itself on having millions of hours without lost time incidents while hiding away the human wreckage."[34]

One product of this uncaring quest for profit is gendered violence. Throughout the book, Beaton recounts the casual sexism and microaggressions she encountered, with men staring at her, objectifying her, and making incessant sexualized comments. During her time in the camps, Beaton was raped twice, horrible events she depicts in spare drawings and dark pages in the middle of the book.

Beaton's critique focuses more on the system than on specific perpetrators. The first time she complained to a supervisor about men objectifying and harassing her, his response was dismissive: "listen, you knew this was a man's world when you came, it's not always nice."[35] This discouraged her from complaining again. It tragically motivated her to make no reports when she was raped.

Beaton insists that extractive capitalism makes this type of abuse likely. An economic system that prioritizes profit over all else removes people from the support systems that hold them accountable: "Gendered violence does happen when men outnumber women by as much as fifty to one, as they can in the camps or work sites. Of course it does. Of course, this happens when men are in isolation for long stretches of time, away from their families and relationships and communities, and completely resocialized in a camp and work environment like that of the oil sands."[36]

Nothing can excuse harassment or rape. But it is important to recognize that such violence is made more likely by an economy that degrades community for the sake of profit. The fossil fuel industry as Kate Beaton experienced it cares about its bottom line so much that it allows ducks to die, it allows its workers to risk their lives, and it allows men to assault women. All that matters to the system is the continued flow of atmosphere-defiling oil.

"We Must Speak the Truth": Intersections with Ableism

While Kate Beaton worked in oil fields to pay for college, Greta Thunberg became famous for refusing to go to high school. Going on strike at the age of fifteen, she bravely sat outside the Swedish parliament building and demanded meaningful political action on climate change before she would return to class.

Thunberg became the most prominent face of the climate movement. With that platform, she has insisted on an intersectional understanding of the problem. She regularly calls attention to the injustices experienced by poor and Indigenous peoples, and she demands equitable and differentiated responses to climate change. She also offers a powerful image of a coalition forming to resist atmospheric defilement. She pictures feminism "standing outside one door stamping its feet," while "humanism, anti-racism, the animal-rights movement, those who fight for refugees, or against mental illness" each stand at their own doors. "The climate movement has a key that fits all the doors" and can bring all movements together.[37]

While Thunberg acknowledges her privilege as a white, relatively wealthy citizen of Sweden, she also emphasizes that she speaks from marginalized identities. Most famously, she identified herself in her strike and her subsequent public appearances as a young person. She accused previous generations of a failure to act on climate change that makes people her age deeply afraid of the future. Thunberg and the Fridays for Future movement that she inspired insisted young people have been marginalized from conversations and decisions about climate change. They emphasized that young people had no agency in causing the problem but are most affected by future threats of atmospheric defilement. While "future generations" had been discussed for many years, Thunberg and her peers insisted the future cannot be treated as an abstraction. The next generation is present, and they demand a seat at the decision-making table.[38]

Thunberg also speaks from another marginalized identity as a person with Asperger's syndrome, on the autism spectrum. Indeed, she presents the identification of her neurodiversity as the turning point that made her protest possible. Before she understood that her brain worked differently from many others, she was overwhelmed by loneliness and sadness. But with the support of her family and the guidance of professionals, she learned to understand what made her different and now routinely insists that it is an advantage: "Asperger is not a disease, it's a gift."[39]

The gift of neurodiversity leads Thunberg to reject marketing and spin when defenders of the fossil fuel industry distract from simple truths. She insists that if oil, methane, and coal emissions are degrading the prospects for life on earth, then they must be stopped. Those of us with so-called "normal" brains, she writes, live in a world where "whoever is best at packaging and selling their message wins. And since the truth is uncomfortable, unpopular and unprofitable, the truth doesn't stand much of a chance." But Thunberg refuses to accept anything she knows to be untrue. She can see that "the emperors are naked. Every single one. It turns out our whole society is just one big nudist party."[40]

So, Thunberg argues that the ways of thinking and communicating that have ignored or minimized climate change must be rejected. Embracing her neurodiversity emboldened Thunberg to speak up and demand action. It gave her the strength to speak honestly and forcefully to the General Assembly of the United Nations, US Congress, wealthy industrialists at Davos, and many other audiences.

Greta Thunberg helped inspire thousands of others to go on strike, to speak up, and to take leadership in the movement for climate justice. She attributes her groundbreaking activism in part to her neurodiversity, to her brain's ability to see things those of us believed to be "normal" have missed and ignored. We all have much to learn from her, and from other young and neurodiverse people, about how to respond to the complexities of atmospheric defilement. Thunberg's most basic message is a simple but challenging call for honesty: "We must speak the truth and tell it like it is."[41]

"Searching for a Messier Story": Intersections with Heterosexism

Thunberg teaches us that dominant ideas about what is "normal" have been deeply destructive to human societies as well as to the climate.

Another important messenger for this perspective is the writer and disability activist Eli Clare, who adds additional critiques of ableism while also insightfully exploring the intersections of that issue with norms about gender and sexuality.

Much of Clare's childhood was spent in doctor's offices. Medical professionals tried to help him speak without slurring, walk without bobbing, and stand without trembling. When he was twelve, he was diagnosed with cerebral palsy, and doctors sought to stop his tremors by instructing him to strap heavy weights to his arms every day. He felt uncomfortably burdened and shamed by the weights, which emphasized how different he was from other students. Eventually, he rejected the braces and their attempt to cure him. Instead, he accepted his tremors as part of his identity. He learned to use an electric typewriter, which allowed him to write while trembling, accommodating to his body rather than expecting his body to accommodate to the school's idea of "normal."[42] What he needed, he writes, was not a cure for his condition but an adaptation that helped him thrive with it.

Clare and many contemporary disability activists work from a social model of disability, which focuses on the political and cultural contexts in which people live rather than the conditions of their individual bodies and minds. The more dominant medical model aspires to a world where medical professionals cure disabled people. The social model, by contrast, insists that disabled people themselves can define what they want and that this will often mean they do not need to change at all. Instead, the society they live in needs to learn to accommodate them as they are.[43]

As Clare puts it, disability is "a matter of social justice . . . residing not in paralysis but in stairs without an accompanying ramp, not in blindness but in the lack of braille and audio books, not in dyslexia but in teaching methods unwilling to flex."[44] Clare has cerebral palsy, but that impairment only becomes disabling when sidewalks are hard to navigate, when conversation partners refuse to listen to slurred speech, when people make prejudiced assumptions. The solution to his challenges is not to cure him but to adapt society so that it welcomes him and everyone else.

If a treatment were found to repair the brain cells damaged at his birth, Clare writes, he would not take it: "I'm not broken. . . . I have no idea who I'd be without my tremoring and tense muscles, slurring tongue."[45] Insisting he is liberated by accepting the way he was born and rejecting any notion that some part of him does not fit, he embraces his "body-mind" exactly as it is.

Clare also insightfully connects his critique of ableism to the gender norms into which he was born and which he has had to resist for his entire life. When he was born and throughout his childhood, the world considered him female based on his body. But as he got older, he rejected stereotypes of femininity and began to understand himself better. His father and medical professionals continued to insist he should fit cleanly into existing gender categories. Just as they wanted to "cure" his disability by making him more like "normal" people, they asked him to fit neatly into the gender he had been assigned. But Clare refused. He now identifies as genderqueer and uses masculine pronouns. Eventually, he had chest reconstruction surgery so that his body better matched his self-understanding.

Clare reflects thoughtfully on the tension between, on one hand, his use of a medical procedure to align his gender identity and, on the other, his suspicion of medical "cures" for disability. This is not hypocrisy because in both cases he insists he is the primary authority about his own body-mind. Ableism and heterosexism both expected him to conform to the "normal" society around him; in both cases, he instead learned to trust his own self-understanding. Eli Clare is best equipped to know who Eli Clare is, his gender identity, and how his abilities can be accommodated by the wider world.

But the question nevertheless remains: why did he find liberation in accepting cerebral palsy but seek intervention to better live out his gender identity? Clare embraces the seeming contradiction, without closure, as a sign of the complexity of social justice: "I'm searching for a messier story."[46]

Clare also suggests a messier story of climate change. He notes that many environmentalists seek a "cure" for defiled ecosystems, hoping to restore some ideal past. This is the same kind of simplistic thinking that insists disabilities should be "cured" or that gay and trans people should be "converted" to cisgender heterosexuality. Such hope does violence to who disabled and queer people really are; it prevents those around them from acknowledging and accepting them. People born with disabilities have no "nondisabled" state to return to; believing that some imagined technology can return them to "normalcy" treats their body-minds as "fantasies and projections."[47] Similarly, the landscapes that industrialized human beings have managed and exploited for centuries have been permanently changed: "The damage may be irreversible; some ecosystems, irreplaceable," and "there is no return to the past."[48] There is no way to rebuild a world without anthropogenic global warming, no "cure" for atmospheric defilement.

Systems of power and domination seek clean stories. They offer a simple standard of good and evil, a straightforward measure of progress. They suggest that problems should be conclusively solved so that everyone can move on. As a disabled and queer person whose basic identity has frequently been labeled a "problem," Clare rejects such thinking. He embraces, instead, a messy story in which people learn to trust themselves and accept their limitations, adapting to reality rather than hopelessly trying to change it to match simplistic ideals.

Whatever future is ahead for our species, it involves a climate fundamentally changed by human activity. Eli Clare offers tools to accept this truth and then focus on how people can lovingly support one another in that climate. This does not mean ignoring the roots of climate change in villainous negligence and sin; it does not mean excusing the forces hiding and exacerbating the problem. It certainly does not mean we allow emissions to continue unchecked. But it does mean we accept that there will be no simple resolution to atmospheric defilement. The messy story ahead involves enabling as many beings as possible to thrive in a changed and changing climate, to adapt as inclusively and justly as possible.

Expanding Conversations

Many voices are still missing from this intersectional analysis of climate change. For example, climate change intersects with the power dynamics of caste, colorism, and citizenship, although these are not the focus of the thinkers and activists I've explored here. And, of course, the identities that have been discussed are not fully represented: Delores Williams does not speak for all Black women; Eli Clare does not speak for all disabled or queer people.

So this conversation is incomplete. Intersectional conversations always are. And anyone who participates in an intersectional conversation runs the risk of missing or misunderstanding something. But an incomplete conversation is better than no conversation at all. Worse than misunderstanding someone is not trying to understand them at all. Worse than forming an imperfect coalition is forming no coalition at all.

Hopefully, the six people introduced here will help those of us who care about climate change to think and talk more, more deeply, and more effectively about the issue and its intersection with so many other injustices. Hopefully, we will carry their lessons forward as we decide how to resist the forces that continue to fuel this problem.

Resistance requires that we understand where climate change has come from. Delores Williams helps us understand that climate change results from the same "sin of defilement" that creates and justifies racism and patriarchy. The globe is warming because of the defilement of the atmosphere; this is a cruel, destructive crime.

Amitav Ghosh makes further connections between atmospheric defilement and the "viscerally human conflict" of imperialism. While some who deny the depth of the problem attribute it to natural forces and unintended consequences, Ghosh insists that the deliberate choices of colonizers created the conditions for climate change. This creates an opportunity: different choices can make a different future.

Resistance requires that we understand why climate change continues. Kyle Powys Whyte emphasizes that colonialism is not only about the extraction of resources but also the continued erasure of Indigenous people when settlers claim their lands and spaces. By characterizing climate change as "colonial déjà vu," Whyte emphasizes that contemporary challenges grow out of the cultural destruction and lack of consent that have defined the treatment of Indigenous North Americans for centuries. Breaking this cycle is an essential part of responding to global warming.

Kate Beaton encourages us to recognize that the systems most responsible for changing the climate are explicitly motivated by extractive capitalism and its insistence on profit above all else. She demonstrates that this system hides "away the human wreckage" it causes. Those of us who want to resist climate change should explore changes and alternatives to capitalism that will prioritize healthy communities over corporate bottom lines.

Resistance requires that we speak honestly. Greta Thunberg offers a deceptively simple-sounding remedy for these many complexities: "We must speak the truth." Anyone who has sought to talk publicly about atmospheric defilement—or witnessed Thunberg vilified for her efforts—knows this will not be easy. But her experiences as a young person on the autism spectrum demonstrate the power of honesty. We can all join her in speaking directly and truthfully about the challenges we face.

Finally, Eli Clare offers a way to embrace the inevitable complexity of climate change at the intersections. It may lead to a "messier story" than some of us would have wanted, but that messiness is the only path to genuine change that avoids the worst pitfalls of the past. To learn from those whose queer and disabled identities are outside of "normal" is to learn how we can hope for a new way of life that does not defile the atmosphere.

These perspectives put climate change into historical and cultural contexts. They make it clear that anyone who cares about global warming needs to care about justice and vice versa. They demonstrate that we all have much to learn from those who speak from the margins. The intersections between these perspectives suggest we can all benefit from a broad conversation as we learn to resist climate change.

2

MYTHS OF DOMINATION

I ONCE WORKED out of a communal graduate student office in an environmental studies department. When I met the climate scientists with whom I shared the space, our first conversation was tense. An atheist deeply devoted to the scientific method, he was nervous when he found out I was a Christian studying faith-based responses to environmental issues. He feared that I, like so many Christians who talked about the issue in the media in the early 2000s, would deny anthropogenic global warming entirely. Attempting to reassure him, I said, "No, of course I believe in climate change."

That didn't help. He insisted I was using the wrong category to think about the issue. The truth of climate change, he said, is based on evidence and data; the "beliefs" of any individual are irrelevant. What is happening in the atmosphere, he argued, has nothing to do with anyone's faith or opinions. He was right in important ways, and our conversations throughout that year taught me a lot about climate change and the importance of respecting the scientific method, the care with which scientists make claims, and the distinction between tested observations and ideas.

But I also spent the year trying to convince him that questions of faith and belief do matter when we talk about climate change. The chemical reactions of CO_2 in the atmosphere and the average global temperature may not be directly determined by what I or anyone else thinks, but many important things are. Whether we accept scientific evidence about the problem, who we trust to respond, and whether we are willing to make any changes in the ways we live, vote, and act are all wrapped up in our beliefs. How we make sense of the reality of climate change, how important we decide it is, and what we think should be done about it are influenced by faith.

My office mate was worried about Christians because Christian beliefs have caused great harm to public discussions of climate change and many other issues. Some Christians have justified the exclusion of racism, the arrogance of empire, the greed of colonization, the extraction of capitalism, the ignorance of ableism, and the narrowness of heterosexism. Some Christian institutions have used theology to excuse these injustices for centuries and profited in the process.

But Christianity has also given some believers the courage to assert that people of all genders, ages, and abilities should be fully included in decisions that affect them, the hope to insist that inclusive communities could be stronger, the humility to seek reparations for stolen land and lives, and the strength to fight for justice and sustainability. Some Christian institutions have transformed the cultures around them to be more inclusive and loving.

My office mate taught me to take seriously the limits of Christian beliefs; I tried to teach him to take seriously their potential. To borrow a word from Eli Clare, the relationship between Christianity and atmospheric defilement is messy. Just as climate change is too complicated to be explained in any one way, Christianity is too complicated to have just one relationship to intersectional injustices. There are over two billion Christians in the world, who learn from traditions that have developed for over two thousand years. In the face of such diversity, Christianity cannot be all good or all bad; it cannot be entirely on the side of justice or against it. Anyone who claims to explain or evaluate Christianity simplistically is dealing with something much smaller than reality.

The solution to this complexity is to take the diversity of Christian beliefs seriously and to recognize their power, for good and evil. This chapter will focus on some Christian beliefs that have been part of the problem, studying three myths that contribute to atmospheric defilement. This is, of course, not the whole story, and we will see in the next chapter that Christianity also has better myths that can contribute to redemption. First, though, we attend to the divisive myths of domination—exceptionalism, individualism, and expansionism—that put people in competition with one another and with the nonhuman world.

How Myths Matter

I do not mean the word *myth* dismissively or pejoratively. While people sometimes associate myths with lies or irrationality, I do not understand them that way. Instead, I see myths as foundational to human life. We depend on them to make sense of the world around us, to organize its complexity, to orient ourselves amid a reality that no one person can ever fully, rationally understand. Human culture, nature's diversity, and challenges like climate change are bigger than we can ever understand with only facts. We depend on myths to orient us and help us communicate about complexity.

It is tempting to assume that myths are things of the past, that people once needed big stories to make sense of the world, but don't anymore. This isn't true; people still need myths. It is tempting to think that rational science gives us all the answers we seek. This isn't true either; people have questions of meaning and purpose and ultimate reality that don't have scientific answers.

Myths are broad stories that attempt to capture big realities about human existence and ultimate reality. While not necessarily factual, myths seek to tell truths bigger than data. They prioritize broad meaning over specific accuracy. They do not make a claim to literal truth but to something timelessly insightful about human existence. Myths offer lessons about ultimate reality, about what it is to be human, and about the key principles that can guide human lives.[1]

The first chapter of the Jewish and Christian Bibles, for example, offers a myth about the creation of the world. If we take it literally, it is simply false. The separation of light from darkness, the formation of seas and land, the evolution of plant and animal life did not happen in six days. This is not a story about how the earth as we know it physically came to be; it does not lay out scientific facts. That was not what the people who originally told this story nor those who put it into Scripture were trying to do. Instead, they were trying to tell a mythic story that presents life on earth as carefully, lovingly structured. That mythic truth does not need to compete with scientific stories about the origins of life and the universe; it can instead be a complement that encourages readers to approach the world with respect and reverence. When I want to know how long the human species has existed on earth, I turn to the best scientific evidence I can find. But when I want to know whether I should trust in a basic sense and order to the universe, I need a more mythic story. The Book of Genesis offers one such myth.

Myth is a tool people use to make sense of the world and their place in it. Like most tools, myths can be used constructively or destructively. Some interpreters of the Genesis story emphasize that it presents our species in the context of large and complex systems of other creatures and ecological systems. In this interpretation, the important lesson is one of humility, emphasizing that human beings are one part of a broader whole that God created to be unified. But, as we will see below, other interpreters have drawn the opposite conclusion, using this myth to justify the uniqueness and singular importance of the human species. Both interpretations are reasonable because the myth does not offer an incontestable lesson. Instead, mythic stories invite reflection. They require interpretation and can always be understood in multiple ways.

Those of us who want to respond to the intersectional injustices of atmospheric defilement need to carefully analyze religious myths and thoughtfully discern which ones are constructive and which are not. Author Karen Armstrong offers a helpful formula for this. In the book *Sacred Nature*, she argues that such discernment is particularly important as we face the uncertainties of our time: "We need good myths that help us identify with our fellow human beings, and not just with those who belong to our ethnic, national, or ideological tribe. We need good myths that help us to realise the importance of compassion, which challenges and transcends our solipsistic and tribal egocentricity. And, crucially, we need good myths that help us to venerate the earth as sacred once again, because unless there is a spiritual revolution that challenges the destructiveness of our technological genius, we will not save our planet."[2]

Myths, Armstrong suggests, are constructive when they connect people, build compassion, and teach respect for the world beyond our species. They are destructive when they fail to do so. Even destructive myths seem like common sense until we recognize and reflect on them. So we turn now to that recognition and reflection, identifying the pernicious myths of domination that have helped to justify and permit atmospheric defilement.

Human Exceptionalism

The first myth of domination emerges from the second interpretation of Genesis just mentioned. In the biblical text, after creating most of the earth and its systems, God turns to humanity, saying,

> *"Let us make humans in our image, according to our likeness, and let them have dominion over the fish of the sea and over the birds of the air and over the cattle and over all the wild animals of the earth and over every creeping thing that creeps upon the earth" (1:26).*

The most common interpretation of this passage extrapolates from it to argue that the human species is more important than any other. While the text does not say that human beings are the *only* species made in God's image, most interpreters have assumed this to be the case. While the text does not say that "dominion" includes the right for human beings to do whatever they want with the creatures of this planet, most interpreters have drawn that implication. While the text does not say that humans should have control over the oceans and the land and the sky as well as the creatures that call those places home, most interpreters have made that leap.

This is the myth of human exceptionalism, which teaches that our species has the right to control and utilize the rest of creation, that human beings are more important than any other creature and so do not need to concern ourselves with the rest of the world, except when it is useful to us.

Outside of Christianity, other justifications of human exceptionalism are based on different stories. Many philosophers assume that human reason and sentience are unique to our species, making us uniquely important. Many narratives of biological development have been interpreted to say that humanity is the pinnacle of evolution, and so our species matters more than others. Many moral systems suggest that it is "natural" for beings to value their own species most highly, justifying an exclusive focus on human well-being. These stories are different from Genesis, but they justify the same myth of human exceptionalism. All assume that the nonhuman world should be understood as a set of resources meant as a backdrop, a fuel, or an antagonist for human life.

In this myth, "humanity" is a singular character, the unquestioned protagonist in the history of Planet Earth. The land exists as a setting for human action; other species exist as—at best—supporting characters. The primary and most interesting driver of change and action is humanity. Our increasing control over the rest of the planet is a narrative of progress to be celebrated and extended.

Human exceptionalism either ignores the fact that human life depends on healthy ecosystems in symbiosis with a diverse array of species or baselessly assumes we can technologically replace any resource from the nonhuman world that we use up.

This myth has been used to justify and sustain atmospheric defilement. People who believe in human exceptionalism tend to assume their distinctions from other species are more important than connections.[3] They do not feel personally concerned when they learn that the earth is now in its sixth period of mass extinction, that polar bears are threatened by melting ice, that coral reefs are bleaching in warming oceans, that rainforests are being burned. People who believe in human exceptionalism pay less attention to the limits of the natural world than to the expansiveness of their own desires.[4] So they participate in defiling the atmosphere and expect not to have to live with the results.

For example, the theologian and pro-fossil fuel activist Calvin Beisner interprets Genesis 1:26 as appointing human beings the "covenant head" of the planet, with the vocation from God to "subdue and rule the earth." That justifies the premise at the foundation of his thinking that "the most valuable resource in Creation of course remains the human person." On this basis, Beisner argues that Christians do not need to take climate change seriously; Christians are instead called to support and encourage the extraction and usage of fossil fuels.[5] He believes human beings, made in the "likeness" of God and given "dominion" over the rest of creation, are entitled to whatever resources serve our desires.

Sadly, this myth of exceptionalism is so widespread that it has become common sense across the industrialized world. Most legal systems offer no rights to nonhuman creatures, treat animals and land as property that human owners can dispose of as they please, and regulate harm to the natural world or nonhuman creatures only when it directly affects people.

Potawatomi botanist Robin Wall Kimmerer argues this destructive exceptionalism is built into the dominant language of the industrialized world, which teaches us to refer to most nonhuman nature with the pronoun *it.* She writes, "In English, you are either a human or a thing. Our grammar boxes us in by the choice of reducing a nonhuman being to an *it.* . . . The arrogance of English is that the only way to be animate, to be worthy of respect and moral concern, is to be a human."[6] She also notes that her scientific training emphasized this same approach, teaching her to preserve her objective distance from what she was studying by never personifying or anthropomorphizing the natural world.[7]

When I first read this indictment, I resisted it. I thought about how I would never refer to either of my cats as *it*, how I lovingly use *he*, *she*, and countless adoring nicknames. I also thought about the scientists I know who research birds and small mammals, motivated in part by deep respect and wonder. But the more I sat with Kimmerer's critique, the more I recognized its truth. My scientific colleagues may respect the animals they study, but their field and their universities assume they have every right to capture and kill those creatures. I love my cats as individuals, but they have no legal rights and only get the respect and care my family decides to extend to them.

While you and I may not agree with the myth of human exceptionalism, we live in systems that assume its truth. Most nonhuman animals in the world are not treated like my cats. Chickens are piled into restrictive cages; cows and pigs are confined to small pens and have their children taken away at birth. Wild habitats can be burned or paved over with no consideration to animals or plants unless a narrow set of laws is applied to protect the ones humans have decided to care about. Such defilement is only possible because most animals, and most ecosystems, have been "reduced to an it." Our species remains the main character in virtually every story we tell.

Like all myths of domination, human exceptionalism has intersectional impacts. When only humans matter, the boundaries of who counts as human can exclude people or justify their abuse. If the rest of creation is less important than humanity, then those who want control can shrink the circle of who counts as human. Men who want to justify the mistreatment of women decide that women are closer to nature.[8] White people who want to justify the enslavement, mistreatment, and segregation of other cultures claim that people of color are less "civilized" or "rational" and therefore less exceptional.[9] Colonists who seek to profit from distant parts of the world decide that they deserve "dominion" over not only the land but also the human beings and human cultures they find there.[10] Ableists and heterosexists who seek a uniform way of being in the world argue that those who think, ambulate, or love differently from them are somehow less human.[11]

In other words, when that which is not human can be dismissed, the boundaries around what is human become dangerous. Christian ethicist Christopher Carter puts it well: "The core message embedded within colonial Western Christian theological anthropology is that in order to be Christian, one must become 'human,' and in order to become human, one must become white, and in order to become white, one must accept the hierarchy that protects the image of the heterosexual white male as the image of God on earth, the pinnacle of Creation."[12] For Carter, this calls Christians to reject human exceptionalism. Instead, he seeks a myth that emphasizes the interdependence of all life—including humanity—within God's creation. This myth should stress cooperation, encouraging the liberation rather than domination of other creatures.

We will consider such a myth in the next chapter, but first we must sit with the challenges to it. An egalitarian view of other creatures is countercultural. The societies, languages, and systems in which most of us live have been developed out of a story of human uniqueness, a belief that our species has the right to define what counts as human and to control everything that does not. This divisive, hierarchical story continues to justify the intersectional injustices of atmospheric defilement.

Radical Individualism

Another myth of domination shrinks attention even more narrowly than exceptionalism, treating independent individuals as the fullest expression of what it is to be human. In this story, the structures that bring human beings together—nations, institutions, neighborhoods—are optional constructions; what is real is the self, the human individual. The social and ecological networks that connect life are pushed into the background: the embodied and singular person is pulled to the foreground. In the most extreme versions of this story, true success can only come if people leave behind the trappings of the communities that raised them, forging entirely new paths to the future, alone.

This individualism is not as prominent in the traditions of Christianity as human exceptionalism, but many Christians nevertheless find justifications in Scripture. For example, consider these lines from the letter to the Ephesians:

> *You were dead through the trespasses and sins in which you once lived, following the course of this world, following the ruler of the power of the air, the spirit that is now at work among those who are disobedient. All of us once lived among them in the passions of our flesh, following the desires of flesh and senses, and we were by nature children of wrath, like everyone else. But God, who is rich in mercy, out of the great love with which he loved us even when we were dead through our trespasses, made us alive together with Christ. (2:1–5)*

Many interpreters read this text as starkly contrasting the deadly evils of "this world" against the individual who is revived alone. The redeemed person is "together" only with Jesus, apart from the rest of the world. On one hand, "the passions of the flesh" and the way of "everyone else" are corrupting and degrading. On the other hand, the individual "you" is liberated and revived by a private relationship with God. The masses—the broad human community, the structures in which most of us live—are deadly. Freedom comes from turning away, embracing Jesus in one's own heart, and beginning an individual journey to a new way of life.

This myth is particularly prominent in the Protestant Christianity that dominates religious discourse in the United States. Historian

Alex Zakaras argues that what he calls the "Myth of American Individualism" became particularly prominent during the Second Great Awakening in the early nineteenth century, when popular preachers were stressing private faith while criticizing religious establishments, elites, and institutions. They taught that "individuals should cast aside received truths, heed their own intuitions, follow their own prophetic visions, and that the individual might read Scripture for himself and receive instruction directly from it."[13]

Such suspicion of institutions is not just a religious phenomenon; it has also profoundly shaped politics in the United States and beyond.[14] This is perhaps most famously demonstrated by the campaign line that earned Ronald Reagan accolades in the 1980s: "The most terrifying words in the English language are: I'm from the government, and I'm here to help." This talking point efficiently communicates a deep suspicion of governmental institutions and a confidence that the best solutions to people's problems can always be found by individuals rather than institutions.

An even more revealing version of the myth is found in UK Prime Minister Margaret Thatcher's answer to an interview question in 1987. Explaining that she believed anyone who expected the government to solve their problems was making a mistake, she said, "They are casting their problems on society and who is society? There is no such thing! There are individual men and women and there are families and no government can do anything except through people, and people must look to themselves first."[15]

This is the myth of individualism: human life is most real, truest, and most important at the level of individuals; collectives like governments are, at best, secondary and ineffectual. This myth asserts that what matters is the freedom of individuals to do as they wish; what keeps people at peace is when they leave one another alone.

Radical individualism makes social reform and collective work for justice unlikely. For example, W. E. B. Du Bois's classic analysis of why former slaves were never given the resources they deserved after the Civil War is that all efforts at reparations and payments were stopped by arguments that freed slaves needed to earn their own way. This tortured logic depended on what Du Bois calls "the American Assumption" that success can only emerge from individuals, never from social structures. For the government to award land to freed slaves was, he reports, widely seen as paternalistic and unnecessary because "any American could be rich if he wanted to" based on individual hard work and motivation.[16] The stark and horrible fact that generations of people had been enslaved—had been prevented from benefiting from their individual hard work and motivation—was not powerful enough to overcome the myth of individualism.

In the contemporary United States, the assumption that individuals can and should ultimately be responsible for their own health and success makes it hard for children, those who are elderly, and disabled people to advocate for the kinds of social supports and changes that allow them to thrive as full members of an interdependent community.

Celebrations of individualism tend to ignore the structures that make individual successes possible. "Self-made" businesspeople have often worked hard and brought brilliant new ideas to the market, but they have also generally benefited from schools, infrastructure, and legal systems that collective institutions maintain. Evangelicals who read the Bible "for themselves" depend on translations and interpretations and cultural contexts that were formed by generations of communities. The myth of individualism ignores a patently obvious truth: individuals depend on institutions.

This myth has also discouraged meaningful action on climate change. As journalist Kate Aronoff argues, those who embrace radical individualism cannot meaningfully respond to a problem as complicated and multifaceted as atmospheric defilement: "Faced with the greatest existential threat the world has ever faced, [individualistic politicians] suggest that there is no such thing as an organized, society-wide response, and no meaningful role for the government to play.

There are only individuals, each of us is equally to blame, and each of us must do our small part in isolation, becoming more conscious consumers and sacrificing for greater good."[17]

Sadly, evidence of Aronoff's thesis is not hard to find. In 1988, a year after Thatcher theorized that "there is no such thing" as society, the United Nations formed the Intergovernmental Panel on Climate Change, which has ever since issued regular warnings about the reality of climate change and increasingly called for meaningful political action to mitigate the problem. But political systems have failed to act meaningfully, allowing corporate structures to deny the problem while blaming it on individual rather than collective actions.

The myth of individualism cannot explain a problem as big as atmospheric defilement. No one person could dig billions of tons of coal from the ground. No one person could raise and eat millions of cattle every year. No one person could alter the atmosphere as fundamentally as corporations and nations have. If there is "no such thing as society," then it is hard to fully grasp a problem that is caused by collective action.[18] We need to abandon the myth of individualism before we can even begin to comprehend the problem.

We must also move past the myth to begin working toward solutions. If the government is understood only as a problem and never the source of possible solutions, then the only reasonable responses to a challenge like global warming are private.[19] Thus, decades of public discourse about climate change have been aligned with the environmentalism of Pogo, encouraging individualistic, voluntary changes. The dominating myth of individualism conceals both the nature of the problem and the possible remedies.

Infinite Expansionism

A third myth of domination assumes that the scope of individuals and the human species can and should continually expand, that growth is always possible and always good.

Many Christians who believe in this myth find justification in the Parable of the Talents from Matthew's Gospel. Jesus tells a story of a man who entrusts three slaves with great wealth. Two double their investments, and the master calls them "good and trustworthy," rewarding them with more responsibility on his return. But the third buries the treasure and can only produce the amount of money he was originally given. The master's response is blistering:

> *You wicked and lazy slave! You knew, did you, that I reap where I did not sow and gather where I did not scatter? Then you ought to have invested my money with the bankers, and on my return I would have received what was my own with interest. So take the talent from him, and give it to the one with the ten talents. For to all those who have, more will be given, and they will have an abundance, but from those who have nothing, even what they have will be taken away. As for this worthless slave, throw him into the outer darkness, where there will be weeping and gnashing of teeth. (Matt 25:26–29)*

Like all biblical texts, this can be interpreted in multiple ways. I understand it as a cautionary tale; I read the master as a villain in the story and believe Jesus expects followers to reject his behavior.

But many Christians see it differently, understanding the master as a model, whose behavior Jesus puts forward with praise. The master rewards those who get richer and throws the one who does not "into the outer darkness." If we are to emulate the master in this story, then those of us with money should use it to make more money. This myth suggests that privileged people should "reap" and "gather" ever more.

That interpretation supports the extractive capitalism discussed in the previous chapter, which has become the dominant economic system of the industrialized world. The myth of infinite expansionism teaches that acquisitiveness is fundamental to human nature, growth in economic activity is inherently positive, and the expansion of markets and consumption is necessary for thriving.[20] My word choice is awkward: *expansionism* is a strange, unnatural term. This is on purpose because the belief it stands for is strange and unnatural too. Expansionism, the idea that something in the created world could and should grow indefinitely, makes no sense.

And yet this myth is prominent. In contemporary economic discourse, individuals, corporations, and nations are often considered "healthy" only if their wealth is growing. Throughout the industrialized world, success is primarily measured based on growth. Our economic system assumes unchecked growth, depends on it, and is willing to sacrifice for it. This is possible because of the widespread acceptance of the myth of expansionism.[21]

Ecofeminist theologian Sallie McFague criticizes the mainstream of Christianity for aligning itself to expansionist capitalism, arguing that this myth does not come from biblical texts like the Parable of the Talents but instead from the propaganda of corporations. Most churches and believers, she fears, have accepted "almost without question, an economic theory that supports insatiable greed on the part of individuals, regardless of its consequences to other people or to the planet."[22]

McFague also articulates the dangers of this myth. In a limited world, material growth requires the consumption or reduction of something. If our energy sources come from the earth, consuming them means they are not available to other life forms or other people. If our wealth comes from other people's bank accounts, then its growth requires their impoverishment. The myth of infinite expansionism creates competition, degrades the planet, and pushes people to continue enriching themselves no matter the cost. As we will see in chapter 4, the quest for expansive wealth among fossil fuel companies has meant not only that they extract ever-more resources from the earth but also that they discourage the growth of alternative, cleaner energy sources. The myth of expansion, like the myths of exceptionalism and individualism, encourages domination.

The ideal of ever-expanding wealth is at the roots of atmospheric defilement. The corporations Kate Beaton worked for in the tar sands of Northern Alberta excused the mistreatment of their workers and ducks based on the profit they were making. The conquest of colonial empires was justified, in part, by the unquestioned assumption that Europeans deserved to get rich at the expense of other cultures. The violent capture of Native lands in North America was motivated, in part, by the ideal of "manifest destiny" that assumed settlers should control and profit from the entire continent. The defiling of Black bodies in slavery was allowed, in part, by the unquestioned assumption that white people who owned land deserved access to inexpensive labor at any cost. The technologies of the Industrial Revolution were adopted, in part, because they made it possible to use more energy more quickly. In each case, degradation is justified by unquestioned embrace of expanding wealth.

The myth of expansion has also made political action in response to the changing climate more difficult. For example, as the scientific establishment was solidifying the evidence of global warming in 1988, George H. W. Bush campaigned for president with a promise to take on the problem, predicting that he would match "the greenhouse effect" with the "White House effect." He began his administration with serious attention to the issue and proposed substantial funding to research solutions. But by the end of his term, his primary advice on the subject was not coming from scientific experts but from economists who opposed meaningful action. He was convinced by advisers who worried that most solutions would have steep economic costs, and so his administration resisted all binding agreements at the 1992 Rio Summit. He repeatedly insisted that no action on environmental or climate issues could be allowed to deter economic growth.[23]

Almost thirty years later, when Greta Thunberg demanded that leaders "immediately and completely divest from fossil fuels" at the 2020 World Economic Forum in Davos, US Treasury Secretary Steve Mnuchin dismissed her comments by saying, "After she goes and studies economics in college she can go back and explain that to us." Only economists, he assumed, are equipped to understand climate change. Mnuchin also insisted at the same meeting that the only viable solutions to climate change were those produced by expanding technological capacity in the private sector.[24]

Naomi Klein argues that this "logic of indiscriminate economic growth," exemplified by President Bush and Secretary Mnuchin, prevents people from even considering the possibility that responding to climate change is worth an economic cost. The myth "fetishizes GDP growth above all else, regardless of the human or ecological consequences" and so has led to a public debate that assumes any climate action that costs real money is untenable.[25] If expanding wealth is more important than all other goals, Klein argues, there can be no reasonable solution to climate change. We need a better myth.

Moving beyond Bad Myths

It is tempting to argue against these myths of domination with simple facts. Unlimited material expansion is impossible in a finite world. No individual can be totally independent, ever. Our species developed out of and continues to depend utterly on the rest of earth's living diversity. The myths of domination are not, in any literal sense, true.

But myths do not need to be true to be powerful. The validity of a myth comes from the view of the world it creates. The three myths discussed in this chapter have been validated by the industrialized cultures that embraced them; those cultures have spent centuries building systems that make the myths seem sensible. It is possible to live in the United States and rarely think about nonhuman animals as anything other than a resource, to be told throughout one's public education that individuals are more real than institutions, and to see only the positive aspects of economic growth. Our culture makes these myths feel true. And so the domination they justify continues.

The solution to bad myths is not fact-checking. It is better myths. We need myths that emphasize connections among people, institutions, and the natural world. We need myths that respect limits instead of exclusively celebrating growth and expansion. We need myths that help us admit the depth of injustice in atmospheric defilement and inspire us to resistance.

Part II

THE FOSSIL FUEL POWERS

WE HAVE NAMED the problem. Atmospheric defilement is intertwined with white supremacy, colonialism, empire, economic inequality, ableism, and heterosexism. Climate change is a product and a producer of injustice, degrading human communities and ecosystems. This domination is justified by myths that have come to define the industrialized world: exceptionalism, individualism, and expansionism.

But we still do not know what to do about it. There are no simple answers. When we see someone choking, we know to give them the Heimlich maneuver. When a house is on fire, we know to call the fire department. But the intersecting challenges of atmospheric defilement are much more complicated; the best response is less clear.

If I had a straightforward answer to what you should do about the intersecting injustices of atmospheric defilement, I would tell you. This would be a shorter book. But I don't know. And I suspect you don't either.

Ecofeminist philosopher and cultural critic Donna Haraway offers a helpful distinction between "emergencies" and "urgencies." Emergencies are serious, immediate problems with clear solutions. The blazing house, the obstructed airway. We know what to do about an emergency. An urgency, by contrast, is a serious, immediate problem that is too intricate to have obvious answers. Unlike the immediate action of emergencies, urgencies "have other temporalities, and these times are ours." Offering her trademark elliptical wisdom, Haraway insists, "These are the times we must think; these are the times of urgencies that need stories."[1]

Amitav Ghosh was driven to write about climate change by his work as a storyteller, and he agrees with Haraway that stories are essential for any reasonable response to the problem: "Storytelling needs to be at the core of a global politics of vitality," he writes, because stories teach people the empathy required to survive amid the urgency of atmospheric defilement.[2] Climate reporter Kendra Pierre-Louis also emphasizes that "the stories many of us are telling about ourselves are hurting us," and so "we should start telling ourselves a different story."[3]

This section will develop a story with which to face the urgency of atmospheric defilement. First, it will offer a myth that is more constructive than the ones previously criticized. Chapter 3 develops a climate ethics based on the work of biblical theologian Walter Wink, suggesting that myths of domination can be opposed with the myth of the Powers. This myth is based on the story of creation and fall: God created the Powers that structure human life to serve loving connection, but they have fallen and mistakenly serve domination. However, they can be redeemed. This is a story of spiritual forces that animate both the natural world and human institutions, a story that offers a vision of deep connection among people, institutions, and all of creation.

Chapter 4 moves from the mythic to the factual. It narrates, in broad strokes, how the fossil fuel industry has contributed to, worsened, and slowed solutions to atmospheric defilement. This is not an attempt to reduce the complexity of the problem or to argue that one industry is responsible for all the world's injustices. Naming this enemy does not offer a complete account, but it does offer a way to move forward.

Together, these chapters will argue that fossil fuel companies should be understood as fallen theological Powers. Like all other institutions, these companies are meant to connect and coordinate human beings into social and ecological harmonious communities. They have failed in that task. They have, instead, fallen under the sway of a system that dominates and destroys. And so they must be resisted until they are redeemed or replaced.

The environmentalist story of Pogo told us that we are the enemy and promised easy solutions. It suggested that if we just pick up our litter, recycle our waste, and buy slightly more efficient appliances and cars, we will solve the problem. This is no longer a helpful approach. In the myth of the Powers, we find a better story, one that names the fossil fuel industry as our enemy, explains our enemy's fallenness, and then helps us find communities that will empower us to act.[4]

3

POWERS THAT BE

MANY PEOPLE IN the industrialized world want to leave Christian traditions and their myths in the past. They associate Christianity with the myths of domination, with intersectional injustices, with climate denial. Rejecting these mistakes, they also hope to live without myths, or to find myths in other religious traditions, or to develop new mythic truths.[1]

I wish those people well, but I take another approach. I assume the traditions we inherit, along with their flaws, can still offer wisdom and comfort. I believe the religious stories with which I and so many other Christians were raised, which billions of people have treated as sacred for millennia, include guidance relevant to atmospheric defilement and intersectional injustice. As a Christian, I believe the best myths of my tradition can help people to transcend and resist structures of domination. Sacred texts offer resources with which to imagine a better world and name the forces standing in the way of that world. Christianity includes myths that resist all the "-isms" discussed in previous chapters.

This chapter is about one such myth, the myth of the Powers, which can support and inform meaningful resistance against the fossil fuel industry and other forces of atmospheric defilement.

The myth of the Powers as I understand it is based on a set of assumptions, stories, and ideas that New Testament scholar Walter Wink (1935–2012) found in his extensive study of the Bible and other ancient literature. Wink spent most of his professional career as a professor of biblical interpretation at Auburn Theological Seminary in New York City. In that role, he became an international leader at applying Christian ideas to the work of progressive activism. He assumed that the Bible should be interpreted as a resource for social change and that those who study Christianity's sacred texts should use what they learn to shape contemporary Christian communities into advocates for justice.

The texts of the Bible were written long ago, in cultural contexts vastly different from ours, but they nevertheless offer wisdom on vital questions about how human beings work, what shapes our behaviors, and how we can change. Those who have eyes to see and ears to hear can learn a great deal from the Bible about intersectional injustice and the best ways to resist it.

An Introduction to the Myth of the Powers

The myth of the Powers asserts that the systems structuring human life—governments, corporations, churches, universities, nature—are not only the sum of their parts but also coherent entities in their own right. These Powers have personalities and inner spiritual lives. So, for example, the cities and towns in which we live are not just physical plots of land managed by administrators and elected leaders. They are also Powers, with identities that persist even as personnel come and go and landscapes change. People gesture toward that idea when they say "that's New York for you," or "keep Austin weird," or "you can't fight City Hall," or "this is a friendly town."[2]

When a new mayor or pastor or president seeks to make dramatic change but finds the inertia of an institution's politics, culture, and attitudes hard to shift, they experience a Power. When someone travels to a new country and senses a different vibe, they experience a Power. When people feel deep loyalty to a brand, they have become attached to a Power. When a rivalry between two teams, universities, or companies takes on a multigenerational life of its own, there is a clash between two Powers.

The word *Power*, in this usage, is taken especially from the biblical Letters to the Romans and the Ephesians. In Romans, Paul asserts that "neither death, nor life, nor angels, nor rulers, nor things present, nor things to come, nor powers, nor height, nor depth, nor anything else in creation, will be able to separate us from the love of God" (8:38–9). In Ephesians, Paul writes that the struggle of Jesus's followers is "against the rulers, against the authorities, against the cosmic powers of this present darkness" (6:12). In both cases, readers are asked to prove their faithfulness by setting themselves against corrupted institutions, or "powers." A contemporary shorthand for such institutions is "the Powers that be."

As the biblical quotes suggest, the Powers are connected to, and sometimes synonymous with, angels and authorities and rulers. Other texts and translations relate the Powers to principalities and demons. What is consistent is that a Power is the personality of a collective, and all collectives have a Power. According to this myth institutions, structures, and systems have their own identities. They, like the beings they organize, are creatures.

Walter Wink began researching biblical language about the powers to "demythologize" it. He hoped to find the seed of verifiable truth in the language of "angels" and "demons," separating out psychological and sociological insights from superstitious metaphors. But as he studied, he began to see something in the myth of spiritual Powers that he could not reduce to a purely rational explanation. He began to suspect that the biblical texts had an insight that contemporary, scientifically informed culture is lacking.[3]

The more Wink read, the more he found that even biblical texts that do not explicitly mention powers and angels assume everything in creation has a spiritual identity. In the ancient world, he suggests, the existence of the Powers was common sense and conventional wisdom. Just as most writing about the solar system today doesn't need to explicitly say that the earth circles the sun, the authors of biblical texts assumed that everyone reading would already know about the collective spiritual forces at work in the world. Scientists today have better evidence than the ancient world did about the relationship between our planet and its star. But, Wink argues, people in the ancient world had insights we lack into the spiritual realities of nature and human institutions.

Wink offers this summary of the myth of the Powers: "Every business, corporation, school, denomination, bureaucracy, sports team—indeed, social reality in all its forms—is a combination of both visible and invisible, outer and inner, physical and spiritual. Right at the heart of the most materialistic institutions in society we find spirit. IBM and General Motors each have a unique spirituality, as does a league for the spread of atheism. . . . There is nothing, from DNA to the United Nations, that does not have God at its core. Everything has a spiritual aspect. Everything is answerable to God."[4]

To many, this might sound like naïve superstition. DNA has a scientific explanation. The United Nations is a political entity created through negotiation and compromise. General Motors is a corporation built by human beings. But the myth of the Powers does not contradict these facts. Instead, it suggests such facts are not the whole story. DNA, the United Nations, and GM are also part of God's creation; therefore, they are spiritual beings. Speaking of the "Power" inherent in each system is a way to remind ourselves that all things can and should be part of the love and justice God wants for the world.

These can be difficult arguments to make among educated people in the industrialized world. Wink writes, "If you want to bring all talk to a halt in shocked embarrassment, every eye riveted on you, try mentioning angels, or demons, or the devil." He speaks from experience, noting he has found these ideas the "unmentionables of our culture," dismissed as simplistic, old-fashioned beliefs at which intelligent people should scoff.[5] But such rejection is a category mistake. Whether the Powers are factual, whether our institutions are "really" animated by winged beings invisibly floating around us, is neither the most interesting nor the most important question about them.

The Powers are mythic. The stories and images of the Bible train readers to understand the ways human behavior is shaped by and shapes forces bigger than individuals and to see that these forces are spiritual as well as material. The myth of the Powers should be tested not based on scientific evidence but based on whether it helps those who accept it understand something important about reality.

The Created Powers

The myth of the Powers helps us better understand and appreciate the systems that structure our lives. Consider the fascinating account of creation in the letter to the Colossians: "For in [Christ] all things in heaven and on earth were created, things visible and invisible, whether thrones or dominions or rulers or powers—all things have been created through him and for him" (1:16).

The direct argument of this sentence is that the God revealed by Jesus is the ultimate creator of everything that exists. The energetic force behind reality is the same force that also calls people to love their neighbors, blesses peacemakers, and hungers for justice. This is a central idea in Christian faith, and it remains revolutionary.

Notice, also, the interesting variety of beings included in this list of what makes up creation: "all things" includes "things visible and invisible." This text, like many others in the Christian Bible, assumes that God's creation includes not only the material world we can sense around us but also a less concrete set of forces that spiritually connect the material world to its creator. Those connections shape, direct, and change human experience. This is fundamental to the myth of the Powers: There are important things in the world that cannot be directly sensed or measured. Reality is bigger than what we immediately see and know.

The Powers are part of God's world, they are meant to exist, and they are meant to be good. This includes "thrones," "dominions," "rulers," and "powers," each a metaphor for the institutions that govern and shape human life. Churches and nations have not only the material realities that can be seen and touched; they also have soul, personality, and identity. Governments and corporations are part of God's good world. Like human beings, the Powers are part of creation. Like human beings, every Power was made by God and is part of God's ideal plan for a world of loving and just harmony.

However, the Powers do not always live up to their created purpose. Indeed, as the texts from Ephesians and Romans quoted in the previous section suggest, the Powers are too often contributors to "this present darkness," agents of "death." Most of the Bible's direct references to these forces emphasize their fallenness, that they have turned away from the connections for which they were created. When fallen, they act as obstacles, blocking the justice and love at the heart of Jesus's teaching.

Human institutions are not the only Powers. God made "all things," including animals and plants, places and landscapes, and the earth itself. These elements of nature, too, have spiritual connections to God. Coral reefs are part of the world God made and loves. The wind is animated by spiritual energy as well as by physics.

The myth of the Powers reminds us there are more things in heaven and earth than any one person can fully understand, experience, or control. It insists that human beings are one part of the wide and diverse world. It insists that people who want to make the world better must first engage with its multifaceted complexity.

Most of us in the industrialized world have been taught to believe that reality is fully explainable through material measurements and that people can and should control the world around them. Our dominant culture teaches us that we are completely in charge of our own fates, that individual choices are all that matter. They teach that a problem like climate change can be solved purely by human action. But humans are not fully in control and should not seek to master the world. There are spiritual realities beyond us. God's creation is bigger than just our species. Unless and until we understand this, we cannot make effective change; we cannot achieve the love and justice to which all of creation is called.

Wink summarizes the implications of the myth this way: "Humans *can* change things, but not if they are so naïve as to think that they are only changing human things."[6] I propose this as a motto for any Christian response to atmospheric defilement. To meaningfully respond to climate change, we must recognize that the problem involves the entire earth and its ecosystems. To meaningfully respond to all the injustices that go along with that problem, we need to recognize that human beings exist in the context of social structures and institutions far beyond any one individual. We can never just change the people and things we can see. God's creation is bigger and more complicated than that.

The Spiritual Life of Nature

Many biblical texts refer to the spiritual aspects of the natural world. Consider Psalm 96:11–13:

> *Let the heavens be glad, and let the earth rejoice;*
> *let the sea roar, and all that fills it;*
> *let the field exult, and everything in it.*
> *Then shall all the trees of the forest sing for joy*
> *before the Lord; for he is coming,*
> *for he is coming to judge the earth.*

In this text, the "heavens" and the "sea" and the "trees" all relate to God and hope for God's arrival. The world beyond human beings communicates with its creator. The story told in these verses does not mention human beings, offering a compelling alternative to the myth of human exceptionalism.

Industrialized cultures have treated the nonhuman world as if it were merely a set of objects to be manipulated at our whims. The myth of exceptionalism has taught people to believe that only our species could have meaningful thoughts, desires, intentions, and purpose. By contrast, the biblical myth of the Powers suggests that all of creation has a foundational connection to love. Nature is made up of Powers, of spiritual entities. Each one has a direct relationship with God.

The same point is made in the book of Revelation, which uses the language of the Powers to personify the natural world. The book refers to four angels at the corners of the world who control the wind (7:1), an "angel of the waters" (16:5), and an angel "standing in the sun" (19:17). These Powers capture the spiritual aspect of creation, the connection between nature and God.[7]

Of course, as discussed in the previous chapter, the book of Genesis tells us that God has given human beings "dominion" over the rest of creation. But if we use texts from Revelation and the ninety-sixth Psalm to interpret that, we will be more likely to notice that most of that chapter from Genesis is about God's attention to and appreciation of the nonhuman world. The skies and seas and all animals are also part of the story. Like Psalm 96, Genesis insists that every part of creation is directly connected to God. Like Revelation, Genesis insists that natural forces are ultimately accountable to God rather than human beings. In this interpretation, what matters most about human beings is not what makes us different from the rest of creation but what makes us part of it.

Human exceptionalism makes no sense in a world where fields exult and forests sing for joy, where natural forces know and are part of God's plan. All of life on earth, the ecosystems that support that life, the planet itself, and the thin envelope of atmosphere around it were created by the God who is love.

Those of us participating in industrialized cultures that pollute the atmosphere and change the chemistry of oceans, fields, and trees have something to learn from Psalm 96. Those of us sweltering as more of the sun's heat reaches earth and fearing that the winds will blow the ash of burning forests into our lungs should consider the angels mentioned in Revelation. When we degrade other creatures and ecosystems, we degrade God's creation.[8]

Understood through the myth of the Powers, climate change is a spiritual phenomenon, an attack on the angels of nature. The sun and the wind and the trees have spiritual interiority; they are hurt by the defilement of the atmosphere. Climate change harms not only the human families driven from their homes but also the caribou whose habitat is shrinking. It harms the ice shelves that fall into the ocean and melt away. We cannot know what this harm feels like. What can a human know about what caribou or ice feels? But that limitation in our knowledge should inspire humility rather than carelessness. The God who is love cares about them and imbues them with a spirit. And yet we are hurting them.

If we can learn from the myth of the Powers that the heavens can be glad and that trees can sing for joy, we will be better equipped to admit the damage industrialized life is causing to them. Our complicit actions contribute to the defilement of the atmosphere, and we must face the enormity of that. But we also have the capacity to stop making the problem worse and to repair some of the damage we have caused. We can help restore forests and begin healing the atmosphere. However, to do that effectively, we must first wrestle with the complexity of the social systems that shape our actions.

The Powers of Society

The myth of radical individualism is not compatible with the predominant worldview of the Bible. Biblical texts repeatedly refer to collective groups as if they have a coherent identity, emphasizing the importance of social systems as well as individuals. Consider this text from the book of Isaiah, addressed to the nation of Israel:

> *I am the Lord, I have called you in righteousness,*
> *I have taken you by the hand and kept you;*
> *I have given you as a covenant to the people,*
> *a light to the nations,*

to open eyes that are blind,
to bring out prisoners from the dungeon,
from the prison those who sit in darkness. (42:6–7)

God addresses the nation as a singular entity. Israel is charged with being a light to other nations, with sharing a radical truth that will bring freedom to the world. These are not tasks that any one person could take on; they are not even achievable within one generation. The prophetic text offers a vocation for an entire community, a unified group that is assumed to have coherent and enduring identity. Nations and institutions are creations, made to be part of God's plan, to achieve a shared purpose.

According to the myth of the Powers, every institution—not just Israel—has a coherent identity and calling in the world. Every Power has a mission, a vocation. How might we engage politics if we fully accepted that every nation is part of God's plan, with an inner spiritual reality that matches its outward material reality? What might it mean to treat every country, corporation, and collective as a creation meant to build connection and love? Could we understand the Intergovernmental Panel on Climate Change as a Power with a spiritual calling to coordinate, make sense of, and share scientific data? Could we celebrate the Extinction Rebellion movement as a Power with a spiritual calling to remind industrialized peoples of our failure to truly face the peril of climate change? Could we hold the United States of America accountable to its calling to advocate for justice and freedom in a degraded world?

It is hard to imagine such rhetoric taking off in politics and governance. But it—or something else that replaces the myth of radical individualism—is necessary if we are to respond to the enormous, collective problems of atmospheric defilement. Resisting atmospheric defilement requires collective action. Individual scientists, activists, and citizens can do important work, but that work will only match the scale of the problem if it is organized and connected by institutions.

The myth of radical individualism celebrates loneliness. Every person is asked to define their own attitudes and understanding of the world. Every person is expected to solve their own problems. The myth of the Powers, instead, teaches us that we are meant to be together, with each other, with institutions, and with the rest of the world.

The last chapter quoted lines from Ephesians that have been read as individualistic, encouraging readers to remove themselves from the "death" of "this world." But while a rejection of "this world" sounds to modern ears like an individualistic call to make one's own way, it reads very differently when we attend to its historical context. *World* is a translation of the Greek word *kosmos. Kosmos*, Walter Wink explains, referred in Jesus's time not to the entirety of creation nor of human society but to "*the human sociological realm that exists in estrangement from God.*"[9]

In context, the "world" that Jesus's followers are called to resist is, specifically, the part of human systems that goes against God's call for love and connection. The *kosmos* that leads to death is not all of creation; instead, it refers specifically to the aspects of society that degrade and dominate. Rejecting that *kosmos* requires the connection and community that Powers make possible.

Over and over, the Bible emphasizes social connections. It assumes that nations and churches and other collectives matter, that they have coherent identities, and that they shape human action in the world. In the Gospel of Luke, Jesus instructs his disciples that "repentance and forgiveness of sins is to be proclaimed in his name to all nations" (Luke 24:47). In his letter to the Romans, Paul insists that governing authorities "have been instituted by God" (13:1). In the book of Revelation, an angel proclaims "an eternal gospel" to "those who live on the earth—to every nation and tribe and language and people" (14:6). The consensus across these texts seems to be that God created not just human individuals but also the collectives into which humans are organized.[10] In other words, the Bible offers a lot of evidence against Margaret Thatcher's assertion. There is such a thing as society.

Again, the myth of the Powers names something that is true in human experience. Any fan of team sports knows that groups with a sense of common identity can empower, excite, and energize. To be human is to be part of social institutions, and to live a good life requires healthy and constructive institutions that structure relationships. Powers can bring people together, nurture connection, and help people understand that we are part of something bigger than our individual selves. The myth reminds us that God's plan is for a world of loving, harmonious connection.

The Fallen Powers

When institutions build such connections, they fulfill their purpose. When they fail to do so, when they create divisions and separation, they participate in fallenness. The Bible repeatedly insists that most Powers have fallen under the sway of the *kosmos*, that nations and institutions are mistakenly training people for domination rather than loving justice.

For example, the book of Genesis includes stories not only of individual sin—Adam and Eve betraying God's first commandment and their son killing his brother—but also of institutional failings, as when an early society used its power to build an idolatrous "tower with its top in the heavens" in the city of Babel (11:4).[11] Institutions fail. These fallen Powers serve domination and destruction rather than loving connection.

This does not contradict the idea that the Powers are part of God's good creation. As we have seen, Romans (13:1) insists that the authorities were created by God; Colossians (1:16) says the same about the Powers. The Powers are good, but they have fallen; they have come up short of the love for which they were created.

Walter Wink's primary examples of fallen Powers are nations. He insists they can and should be good. National identity should bind people together with common identities; coordinate the sharing of resources; set laws to limit and adjudicate conflict; and protect citizens from the harms of violence, war, and natural disasters. Nationalism should inspire people to respect and collaborate with their fellow citizens and to make sacrifices for the common good. But nations fall short. They fail to protect their citizens or do so only at the expense of others. They neglect to make or enforce just laws. They refuse to rein in the whims of those who are rich and powerful. Nationalism too often becomes exclusive rather than inclusive, teaching people to fear and hate those outside their borders and then to fear and hate compatriots with different ideas. The nations are fallen Powers.

Writing near the end of the Cold War, Wink emphasized the danger of such fallen Powers in control of nuclear weapons: "we are now watching in a kind of mesmerized horror as the two superpowers escalate the probability of destroying the planet—*in order to defend their nations.*"[12] When a Power justifies weapons of mass destruction, Wink insists, it has replaced God's good purposes with its own survival. Decades after Wink first wrote about this threat, it remains disturbingly relevant.

Other systems and structures have fallen, as well, by prioritizing domination over the common good. Too often, universities that should devote themselves to liberating students' minds instead hoard fortunes in endowments devoted to preserving the status quo. Too often, neighborhood associations that should focus on hospitality instead seek to prevent change and protect property values. Too often, churches that should focus on spreading love and justice instead devote themselves to consolidating power and security. Too often, fossil fuel corporations degrade the world and its peoples. These are fallen Powers, and God calls people of faith to resist them.

Biblical texts prepare readers for such resistance. Consider the instructions offered in the letter to the Ephesians: "Put on the whole armor of God, so that you may be able to stand against the wiles of the devil. For our struggle is not against enemies of blood and flesh, but against the rulers, against the authorities, against the cosmic powers of this present darkness, against the spiritual forces of evil in the heavenly places" (6:11–2). Here, followers of Jesus are called to struggle against both "authorities" and "Powers" and are promised the "armor of God" that will help them resist the devil's influence.

The structural injustices of our world are, in part, spiritual challenges. To stand against the "wiles of the devil" requires discipline and wisdom, as well as political and material strategy. It requires recognizing that our real enemies are systems that warp human life rather than the individuals subject to those systems.

One of the most powerful myths animating the fallen Powers of our time is that of infinite expansionism. This myth has been wildly successful at convincing people that most human relationships should be defined by the profit motive.[13] The industrialized world increasingly affirms the assumption that making money is a valid and reasonable goal around which to build a life.[14] As we saw in the previous chapter, this idea can be justified by the Parable of the Talents, which many Christians interpret as teaching them to imitate the "good and trustworthy" servants who increased their wealth and expected to be given more.[15]

The myth of the Powers helps us not to take this parable so literally. Immediately after that story, Jesus predicts a time when the nations will be judged based on whether they gave the food and drink to those who hungered and thirsted, housed strangers, clothed the naked, healed those who were sick, and visited prisoners. Those who fail to do so are sent "into the eternal fire prepared for the devil and his angels" (Matthew 25:41). No story about Jesus suggests that he cared about money, and he certainly never instructed anyone to hoard it. The stories of Jesus are about a man who focused on love and community. He asks his followers to increase their compassion, not their wealth. In that context, the Parable of the Talents makes more sense as a critique rather than a celebration of the cruel master who punishes his servant.

The Powers that embrace the myth of expansionism are fallen. The God of love offers the faithful "armor" to prepare us to stand against such "wiles of the devil."

The Domination System

But what is "the devil"?

One place to begin answering is in the Gospel of Luke's narration of Jesus's temptation in the wilderness. Before beginning his public ministry, Jesus spends forty days in the desert, where he eats nothing and is "tempted by the devil." One temptation is particularly instructive: "Then the devil led him up and showed him in an instant all the kingdoms of the world. and the devil said to him, 'To you I will give their glory and all this authority; for it has been given over to me, and I give it to anyone I please. If you, then, will worship me, it will all be yours'" (Luke 4:5–7).

Jesus refuses this and the devil's other offers. But notice that the devil here claims authority over "all the kingdoms of the world." These are Powers, and the devil believes himself to control them.

Based on this text, Walter Wink understands the devil as the spiritual force tempting institutions away from their created purpose. This is the spirit that corrupts, a personification of fallenness, a metaphor for the root of all temptations to greed and anger and hatred. So Wink defines the devil as "the world-encompassing spirit of the Domination System."[16]

Wink first learned to recognize the devil as a system not from the Bible but from anti-apartheid activists with whom he worked in the 1980s: "Blacks struggling against apartheid in South Africa were fully aware that they were fighting not merely white people but the apartheid system. When police were at the door, people inside would warn, 'The System is here.' When they would see propaganda on television, they would quip, 'The System is lying again.'"[17] This "System," Wink argues, is a corollary to the *kosmos* of the New Testament, the social structure that works for domination and against the connectedness of creation.

In South Africa, "the System" primarily referred to the apartheid government and its predilection for dishonesty, exclusion, and violence. In the New Testament, "*kosmos*" primarily refers to the Roman Empire and its systems of oppression, hierarchy, and domination. The "Domination System" is a general term with the same meaning: it refers to any structure that inspires division rather than connection, any institution that serves the myths of human exceptionalism, radical individualism, and infinite expansionism. The fallen Powers are in the thrall of the Domination System, and so they tempt us to believe that we should separate ourselves from other people and other creatures. They tempt us to believe that the suffering of strangers is not our problem. They try to convince us that the defilement of the atmosphere is inevitable.

Understanding climate change and injustice as the work of the Domination System helps explain why it is so often hard to do the right thing. It explains why politicians with good intentions so often feel pushed to serve short-term interests and blocked from making significant changes for the long-term good of their constituents. Professionals who go into business with high-minded ideals often find that every structural incentive pushes them to prioritize profit over all other concerns.[18] Activists who dedicate themselves to genuine social change often find themselves burned out and exhausted. This is the Domination System, the structure that makes it easier to do bad than good, punishing those who stick to their principles and rewarding those who do not. This is the *kosmos* that hated Jesus because he revealed its fallenness.

At the same time, naming an external Domination System that is personified by "the devil" does not let people off the hook for our bad choices. It is not enough, for example, to say that racism is created by a system bigger than us and then give up trying to be anti-racist. It is not enough to exploit workers or vote for self-interest over common good and say that the devil made us do it. It is not enough to say that my city's bus system isn't reliable enough so that I must buy and drive a car. We are responsible for our actions. When we recognize the Domination System, when we see that our institutions are corrupted by forces beyond any one human being, we are empowered to begin strategizing our resistance.

Exposing the Lies of the System

Such resistance involves, first and foremost, telling the truth.

John's Gospel says of the devil, "There is no truth in him. When he lies, he speaks according to his own nature, for he is a liar and the father of lies" (8:44). The book of Revelation describes the Power of the Roman Empire as a dragon who is also called "the Devil and Satan, the deceiver of the whole world" (12:9). The Domination System depends on lies.

Anyone who pays attention to politics and culture knows how destructive lies can be. As media companies are tempted to serve corporate profit rather than public interests, they degrade truth and feed division. As fake texts, audio recordings, and videos become increasingly common, they degrade the very idea of a shared reality. Most relevant to this book, as networks of corporations and institutes devote themselves to casting doubt on scientific consensus about the reality and injustices of climate change, they degrade the truth about atmospheric defilement.

We are not the first people to live under systems that lie to us. Pharaoh lied to keep the Israelites enslaved in Egypt. Jesus's accusers lied to have him crucified. The apartheid system lied to continue the oppression of nonwhite South Africans. The Domination System always lies because lies increase division and destruction. It insists that human beings cannot live peacefully with one another or with the nonhuman world. It teaches that conflict is inevitable. It assumes that relationships among genders, ethnicities, races, classes, nations, and species are inherently competitive. The Domination System trains us to believe that resources are scarce, to be hoarded and fought over. It teaches that flourishing is comparative so that my life can only be good if it is better than someone else's. It tempts people and institutions to live as though all these things are true and so to deny the connectedness and collaboration at the heart of God's plan for creation.

The System lies. So an essential strategy of resistance is, as Greta Thunberg taught us in chapter 2, to insist on truth. Wink writes, "Truth is medicine" because "domination cannot exist without the Big Lie that persuades the many to offer their lives for the protection of the privileges of the few."[19]

This means insisting that the violence of racism persists today, resisting the lies of those who want to continue reaping the benefits of white supremacy. It means admitting that the attempted genocide of Indigenous peoples continues, resisting the lies of those who want to erase history. It means insisting that extractive capitalism as practiced in industrialized societies is destructive and dangerous, resisting the lies of those who assume there is no alternative to our economic systems. It means insisting that democracy cannot thrive when some voices are silenced and marginalized, resisting the lies of those who want to suppress others. It means insisting that differences among human beings are opportunities to grow and learn, resisting the lies of homophobes, transphobes, and ableists who insist that society requires uniformity. It means insisting that there are ways to reverse and redress the injustices of climate change, resisting the lies of deniers.

Resistance also means insisting on the broad truth that human beings cannot thrive alone, that we need one another, we need other species, and we need ecosystems. One way to tell this truth is through the myth of the Powers, a vision of reality that insists God made the world for connection. God intended human beings and human institutions to thrive in harmony with nature and other creatures. This truth is medicine against the Domination System.

An Empowering Myth

The myth of the Powers suggests that we can better understand reality if we learn from the biblical language of "angels" and "authorities," spiritual beings created by God to animate the forces of earth. It suggests that the corruption of such forces can be helpfully understood as the work of the "devil," the Domination System that has corrupted the world and contributes to the ongoing, wickedly complex injustices that face human beings in the twenty-first century.

I am not particularly interested in discerning whether there are "really" angels and authorities with personalities that exist somewhere, nor whether the devil is a "real" being. Are the Powers metaphors or something more? I'm not sure, and I don't think I need an answer to resist the injustices of atmospheric defilement.[20] The myth of the Powers does not depend on the factual reality of angels or devils. It depends, instead, on faith that nature and human institutions are creations of a loving God and so animated by spiritual as well as material forces. When we believe that, we are better equipped to take on the challenges in front of us.

To repeat what I take to be the most powerful conclusion Walter Wink draws from the myth of the Powers, "Humans *can* change things, but not if they are so naïve as to think that they are only changing human things."[21]

The myth of the Powers empowers. We can change things. We can care about, learn from, and coexist with the nonhuman world on which all life depends. We can redeem the fallen institutions, structures, corporations, and nations that shape our lives. We can make material change by making spiritual change. We can resist the injustices of atmospheric defilement. We can take on the "armor of God" and resist temptations to dominate. When we understand the Powers as part of the world we live in, part of the world we seek to change, we are better equipped to work toward a healthier climate and healthier societies.

4

THE FALLEN FOSSIL FUEL INDUSTRY

COSTA RICAN DIPLOMAT Christiana Figueres ran the United Nations Framework Convention on Climate Change from 2010 to 2016. The culmination of her work there was the Paris Agreement, which remains the most ambitious international climate agreement as I write almost a decade later. While negotiating that agreement Figueres assumed, like most world leaders, that it was important to keep the fossil fuel industry at the table. She ensured that they contributed to and bought in on the proposed plans and goals. The UN processes she coordinated included extensive input, presentations, and advice from private corporations and state-owned companies.

In 2023, Figueres wrote about how her mind had changed. She reported that she had become skeptical that the industry could ever be part of the solution. Even after decades of clear evidence that oil, methane, and coal are fundamentally destructive to the atmosphere and human health, fossil fuel companies refuse to make significant changes. After years of record-breaking profits, they continue to invest trillions of dollars to explore and extract more fossil fuels. Despite repeated promises to move toward renewable energy and carbon capture, they spend very little in these areas and often quietly cancel the projects they do start in these areas a few years after announcing them. Figueres insisted that the global community "has reached the point where decarbonization will happen with the fossil fuel industry or without them."[1]

Demonstrating the grace of a diplomat, Figueres begins with gratitude: "Let's be thankful to the oil and gas industry that powered at least half of the world and gave creature comforts to half of the world in the past century." However, she continues, "My dear oil and gas industry, you are now facing your expiration date. Because we no longer need you. We now have much better technology that can actually power the whole world."[2]

Others in the climate movement have decried the industry even more forcefully for years, and many express less gratitude for those companies' past actions. But Figueres's conversion to this point of view demonstrates that the idea is spreading. The fossil fuel industry is and should be treated as an enemy of climate justice.

The logic is not complicated. A small number of private and state-owned companies across the world have dedicated themselves to digging up coal, oil, and methane to sell it to the rest of us. Those companies have aggressively marketed their products and helped build infrastructure that makes them seem essential. They actively discourage the development of alternatives. They have also refused to take responsibility for the damage fossil fuels cause to the global atmosphere, only recently and inconsistently admitting the damage is even real.

The theology explored in the previous chapter offers another way to make the point: the fossil fuel industry is animated by fallen Powers that exacerbate the injustices of atmospheric defilement through their spread of dominating myths.

Fallen Powers

Atmospheric defilement is destroying the northwest Alaskan village of Kivalina. Currently less than two square miles in size, the village is steadily shrinking as sea levels rise and erode the land from under its people's feet. A self-governing community of Native Alaskan Inupiat, the residents of Kivalina have long understood what is happening to their home. They decided in 1992 to migrate the entire population to safer ground. But they have still not moved, in part because they cannot afford—and no one else will pay—what it costs to move an entire village.[3]

In 2008, Kivalina filed a lawsuit against twenty-four oil, coal, and power companies. Their lawsuit asserted that these companies "are responsible for more of the problem than anyone else in the nation" and so requested $400 million to fund relocation. The lawsuit was thrown out of court, with the judge declining to make "a political judgment" that fossil fuel companies are responsible for climate change.[4] In the United States, most prominent court cases about climate change have since sued governments rather than corporations. But despite the legal failure, the moral logic of the Kivalinans' argument has never been refuted: fossil fuel companies are more responsible than anyone else for climate change.

In 2011, a group of students at Swarthmore College used the same premise to justify a different tactic. They had initially come together to fight mountaintop removal mining, but soon realized their college's endowment was invested in companies that benefited from these mines and other fossil fuels. They began a campaign to divest, and the idea quickly spread to other universities and organizations.[5] Within a year, the international organization 350.org was advocating divestment from all fossil fuels. One of that organization's founders, Bill McKibben, wrote an influential essay called "Global Warming's Terrifying New Math," which made the case for divestment by insisting that "the planet does have an enemy . . . the fossil fuel industry" because "wrecking the planet is their business model."[6]

The divestment movement is still growing. In 2022, a global database estimated that over 1,500 institutions, worth a collective $40.5 trillion, had divested from fossil fuel industries.[7] They take inspiration from the 1980s divestment campaign against South African businesses, which contributed pressure to end the apartheid system. In making this connection, the movement demonstrates an important link between atmospheric defilement and racist oppression. They also suggest that fossil fuel companies, like repressive governments, are enemies to be exposed and opposed.

The efforts in Kivalina and at Swarthmore share an insight that the fossil fuel industry is destructive and dangerous, that people who understand the threat of climate change and want to meaningfully respond need to set themselves against the companies that extract and sell coal, methane, and oil.

Activists are increasingly explicit about this approach. In 2019, the Indigenous Environmental Network released a statement insisting that the best way to address atmospheric defilement is "to keep fossil fuels in the ground" and that "we can no longer leave any option for the fossil fuel industry to determine the economic and energy future of this country."[8] A year later, Greta Thunberg and colleagues issued an open letter to demand "that all companies, banks, institutions and governments immediately halt all investments in fossil fuel exploration and extraction, immediately end all fossil fuel subsidies and immediately and completely divest from fossil fuels."[9] The implication is that politicians, banks, and other institutions can still be part of the solution, but fossil fuel companies cannot.

This approach is also supported by evidence from journalists who study the industry. Jeff Goodell's book *Big Coal* argues that the global coal industry depends on ignoring "the costs of air pollution, miners' safety, devastated mountains, and global warming."[10] Steve Coll's history of ExxonMobil in the 1990s and 2000s suggests its critique with its title: *Private Empire*.[11] In her book *Overheated*, Kate Aronoff argues that fossil fuel companies "can only play a destructive role in the climate policymaking process."[12]

The destructiveness of this industry is further chronicled by scholars. Historians Naomi Oreskes and Erik Conway presented foundational evidence in their 2010 book *Merchants of Doubt*, demonstrating that fossil fuel companies adopted the same tactics as the tobacco industry to disguise and deny the harms of the products they sell.[13] Climate scientist Michael Mann calls "the fossil fuel companies, right-wing plutocrats, and oil-funded governments . . . forces of denial and delay" that deceive the public to keep "the oil flowing and fossil fuels burning."[14] Geographer Andreas Malm articulates the expansive influence of the "fossil economy" on all aspects of contemporary industrialized life in his book *Fossil Capital*.[15] Sociologist Holly Jean Buck analyzes the practical steps required to phase out coal, oil, and methane in *Ending Fossil Fuels.*[16]

There is no single definition of the "fossil fuel industry" across all these critiques. For purposes of this book, this category includes the one hundred fossil fuel producers that the Climate Accountability Institute labels "the Carbon Majors." According to the institute's research, over half of the greenhouse gases (GHGs) emitted since the Industrial Revolution can be traced to one hundred companies: forty-one of them publicly owned, sixteen privately owned, and forty-three owned by nation-states.[17]

While it is true that the atmosphere has been defiled by the collective action of billions of people over hundreds of years, it is empowering to learn that over half of that defilement can be directly traced to just one hundred companies. These companies make up the fossil fuel industry, the Powers that I argue are the enemy.

One could come up with a longer list of companies responsible for climate change. Smaller companies have also been destructive and divisive. Some, like the Koch conglomerate in the United States, have an outsized influence on discourse.[18] But the "Carbon Majors" are a good place to start, and so those constitute the fossil fuel industry at the center of this book. As we will see, these companies are responsible not only for considerable emissions but also for extensive lobbying and propaganda to ensure that extraction and emissions continued even after the damage of atmospheric defilement was well known.

As a citizen of the United States, I am particularly interested in the publicly traded companies based in my country, including Chevron (responsible for 3 percent of the world's GHGs), ExxonMobil (3 percent), Peabody Coal Group (1 percent), and ConocoPhillips (1 percent). I am also interested in BP (2 percent), which supplied the gas station I used for years in Atlanta, and Shell (2 percent), which supplies gas to the station nearest my house now, where I reluctantly continue to buy their product.[19]

Other state-owned fossil fuel companies are, of course, important and villainous in their own ways. For example, the profits of Saudi

Aramco (4 percent) and Russia's Gazprom (2 percent) support authoritarian regimes, stifling democracy while defiling the atmosphere. These are also our enemies, and they must be resisted. But those of us who live in democratic nations have less direct, more complicated connections to such state-owned companies. We will be best equipped to resist authoritarian fossil fuel regimes after we learn to meaningfully resist the private companies with which we interact more directly. So this book focuses on resisting privately owned and publicly traded fossil fuel corporations, with the hope that this will someday also inform resistance against the state-owned fossil fuel industry.

To understand Chevron and Exxon and Peabody as fallen Powers is to take the focus away from individuals. Each corporation has a CEO, who represents it publicly, and thousands of other employees who do all the rest of the work. My focus is not on those people or the choices they make. As a Christian, I am called to see them as my neighbors and work to love them. When I have met and talked with people who work for the fossil fuel industry, I have not found it hard to wish them well. They care about their families, they want to do good, and they are largely trying their best. I suspect the same is true of most of their colleagues. But I worry that they are working within deeply corrupted systems. The Powers that employ them serve domination, warping the attention and action of us all.

Fossil fuel companies are corrupted institutions that serve atmospheric defilement rather than the good of creation. Perhaps, in some unlikely future, even ConocoPhillips could participate constructively in a healed world. But before considering that glimmer of hope, we must explore how far these Powers have fallen.

Lies and Dissembling

As noted in the previous chapter, the Domination System and its fallen Powers depend on lies and deception. The fossil fuel industry offers many examples as it regularly spreads lies and half-truths to justify and defend itself.

Consider a Canadian advertisement meant to make viewers feel irrevocably dependent on petroleum and methane. It begins with a white man stirring something on the stove while an adorable terrier looks on. As he walks away, the flame under the pan quietly goes out. He doesn't notice, blithely turning away from his cooking to watch a game. But then his glasses and his television disappear. Ominous music begins to play while his carpets fly away, clothes fall off, and the dog's plastic bone vanishes. As the house begins to fall apart, he steps outside to see his car disassembled. At the end, he is standing in the lawn in his underwear, and a voiceover—by an uncredited Anthony Hopkins or someone who sounds impressively like him—asks, "Have you ever considered how much your world depends on petroleum-based products?"[20]

The message is clear: the lives of middle-class, suburban people depend on fossil fuels, which provide not only the gas for our stoves but also the raw materials and power to make the plastics that surround us.

The ad was produced by Oil Sands Action, whose Facebook site explains that it is "fighting back by sharing the science, facts, and positivity about Canadian oil & gas." Who exactly they are fighting against goes unsaid. Instead, most photos feature smiling people in t-shirts that say "I ❤ 🍁Oil & Gas," giving the impression of a widespread grassroots movement. Also unsaid in their public materials is where the organization gets its funding. Independent journalists have tracked considerable donations from the Canadian oil and gas industry to Oil Sands Action.[21]

The premise of the advertisement—that life as we know it could not continue without fossil fuels—is not true in any helpful sense. While TVs and cars and dog toys are currently made with plastics from the oil industry, it is possible to build substitutes with different materials. Many people across the world live today without plastics and methane; most people for most of human history lived without either. The advertisement is a work of propaganda on behalf of the fossil fuel industry. It is an example of the dishonesty and fearmongering of the fossil fuel industry.

The "Inevitability" of Fossil Fuels

The implication of that advertisement, and much of the public messaging from fossil fuel companies, is that without fossil fuel products, life as we know it is impossible. This is a version and an extension of the myth of infinite expansionism discussed in chapter 2. Drawing on that myth, fossil fuel companies insist that the status quo of industrialized nations—and their increasing profits from it—can and should continue indefinitely.

For example, Rex Tillerson, then CEO of ExxonMobil, gave a 2009 speech advocating more access to oil drilling sites in the United States and offshore. He admitted that climate change was "an important global issue," but insisted that for the next twenty years, global demand for oil and gas would nevertheless inevitably continue to rise.[22] He did not mention that his own company was actively advertising and lobbying to ensure such an increase in demand. During his tenure as leader, Exxon spent hundreds of millions of dollars to expand fossil fuel markets, to convince political leaders to provide subsidies and permits, and to support the expansion of oil-dependent infrastructure.[23] Perhaps most frustratingly, even after Tillerson admitted that climate change was an important issue, he and his company continued to sow doubt about the problem, insisting that scientists did not know enough to act. A year after the speech declaring oil and gas consumption inevitable, Tillerson testified to Congress that scientific understandings of the issue were simply not complete enough to make sense of: "There is not a model available today that is competent. . . . So we say keep studying it."[24]

Note that Tillerson presents one prediction as "inevitable"—more and more people will continue to buy fossil fuels—while suggesting that another prediction is unreliable—no model is "competent" to make sense of the impacts of climate change. The economic prognostication that benefits Exxon's bottom line is beyond doubt; the climatic measurements that threaten it are too murky to justify any action.

Both leave people powerless, as if there is no possibility of reducing fossil fuel consumption and no way to make sense of climate change.

This is the Domination System at work, offering a simple, disempowering lie and declaring it common sense. The myth of the Powers insists the opposite: humans can change things when we wrestle with their complexity and interconnections.

Tillerson sought to protect the profits of his corporation, regardless of the cost to others. But the point is not to vilify him. The enemy is not one man; it is the system that produced and shaped him. His public statements continued a tradition at ExxonMobil, one that existed before he took over and continued after he left. The problem is not any single person; it is the institution. ExxonMobil, like the other fossil fuel corporations, is corrupted and fallen. It serves extractivist interests even as the evidence of their destruction has become undeniable. It is part of the Domination System.

Fossil fuel companies also respond dishonestly to the increasingly popularity of alternative energy sources. One analysis of energy industry messaging found a pattern of strategically mentioning renewable energy in conjunction with methane, creating the sense that so-called natural gas is more like solar and wind power than oil and coal.[25] This implication is simply not true. Methane is a fossil fuel; burning it adds enormous amounts of GHG to the atmosphere. The hydraulic fracturing often used to extract it disrupts ecosystems, and the distribution of the gas involves significant leaks, meaning that a great deal of methane defiles the atmosphere without even producing energy for human use.

The myth of infinite expansionism suggests that corporations can and should exist forever, that their profits should always increase. Fossil fuel companies are caught in and serve this myth. Analyzing the Dutch energy company Shell, Kate Aronoff insists it has "a constitutive block that keeps it from being an ally in the climate fight: an inability to envision a future without Shell. The company's overriding mission is to ensure an indefinite life for itself and its profits."[26] The same is true of ExxonMobil and Peabody Energy and all the other fossil fuel companies. All have demonstrated a willingness to sacrifice a healthy planet for the sake of their own profits.

Arguments against Regulation

Aronoff notes that fossil fuel companies also protect their profits by organizing powerful campaigns against any attempts to regulate them. These companies have contributed to an international discourse that insists "the private sector—and its visionary founders, in particular—are better at coming up with world-changing ideas than the public sector, which is allegedly bloated and allergic to outside-the box thinking."[27]

For example, proposals for carbon taxes and limits on emissions in the United States have consistently faced powerful opposition from the fossil fuel industry and the advocacy groups it funds. These groups point out the limitations of any proposed regulations while working to keep populations skeptical of any government attempts to reign in emissions. In 2009, the same year Rex Tillerson spoke about the inevitable growth in demand for fossil fuels, Congress considered a bill to cap carbon emissions by issuing permits that companies could trade. Over the 18 months the bill was being discussed, oil and gas companies and utilities spent over $500 million on lobbying.[28] The proposal failed, and no significant national climate legislation was even attempted for another decade.

In 2014, when the Environmental Protection Agency was writing its Clean Power Plan to put limits on the emissions of coal-fired power plants, a lobbyist began publishing a series of advertisements comparing the agency to terrorists and anarchists, attacking the very idea of regulating emissions. The arguments were persuasive to many legislators, who demanded that the Environmental Protection Agency reduce its restrictions. Two years later, the Natural Resources Defense Council was able to confirm that the lobbyist was hired by Peabody Energy, which sells over a hundred million tons of coal to power plants each year.[29] The truth came out, but the damage had already been done. The Clean Power Plan was less restrictive than it would have been without organized, secretive opposition.

Some of the fossil fuel industry's arguments are subtler, suggesting that meaningful change is the responsibility of individual consumers rather than the government. For example, in 2004, BP released a "carbon footprint calculator" and invited consumers to figure out the impact of their transportation, food, and housing choices on the climate. The ad campaign included an assertion that "It's time to go on a low-carbon diet" as part of a $200-million advertising campaign that rebranded the company from "British Petroleum" to "beyond petroleum."[30]

The burden of moving "beyond" oil was placed on consumers: BP admitted that climate change was a problem caused by fossil fuel emissions and then encouraged every individual to determine how they could make small lifestyle changes to reduce it. BP did not stop extracting oil from under the earth's surface nor stop promising investors that it would make billions of dollars in profit every year by selling it. Indeed, they kept investing in more ways to extract and sell their product. John Kenny, an advertising executive who helped to design parts of the campaign, wrote with regret in 2006 that it was "just advertising," that "they didn't go beyond petroleum. They are petroleum."[31]

In 2010, the world got a terrible reminder of this fact when an explosion on BP's drilling platform *Deepwater Horizon* led to the largest marine oil spill in history. Eleven people and uncounted animals died as oil leaked into the open ocean for almost a full month. The company that had rebranded to celebrate moving "beyond petroleum" spilled over 200 million gallons of the substance.[32] And yet, as I write, BP is still promoting its carbon footprint calculator, encouraging consumers to do our part as individuals.

The implication that climate change is caused by personal choices—that the enemy is us—is always, at best, a partial truth. When it comes from the fossil fuel companies that spend millions of dollars to convince us to buy their products and influence lawmakers, it is a dangerous lie. The idea that individuals should make small changes distracts from the fact that the fossil fuel industry has set us all on a fundamentally destructive course.

Individualism also distracts people from the fact that it is the job of governments to stop such destruction. Fossil fuel companies continue the worldview Margaret Thatcher and Ronald Reagan exemplified, that "there is no such thing" as society and that government regulations can only make things worse. These companies spend millions of dollars to convince us that governments cannot helpfully address the problem of climate change. They do not do this because it is true; they do it because it allows them to continue to get rich by defiling the atmosphere.

Climate Denial

The fossil fuel industry, as we have seen, regularly asserts that demand for their product is inevitable and that individuals are most responsible for that fact. These assertions are particularly ironic given that fossil fuel companies spent decades funding campaigns of doubt and denial. They paid to spread the idea that the climate isn't really changing or that its changes aren't caused by industrialized activity.

The most famous investigation into campaigns of denialism is summarized as "#ExxonKnew." This phrase became common in 2015, based on reporting from Inside Climate News, which revealed that scientists within the Exxon corporation were measuring the changes caused by fossil fuel usage and modeling climatic changes starting in the 1970s. The corporation's leadership knew about the problem and the damage it would cause. But Exxon did not rethink their business model. Instead, it stopped paying researchers to study the phenomenon by the late 1980s and began to release statements and advertisements questioning climate science. Having faced reality, the company turned away and worked to spread lies to the rest of us.[33]

Exxon did not do this alone. Denying the reality or seriousness of climate change was a widespread strategy in the fossil fuel industry at least through the 2010s. Much of this work was coordinated by trade groups that support the interest of the whole industry. Historian Benjamin Franta found evidence that the American Petroleum Institute was spreading "disinformation" about global warming as early as 1980.[34] James Hoggan recounts the way a group of coal producers pooled $500 million in 1991 to fund the Information Council for the Environment. Its goal was "to reposition global warming as a theory (not fact)" while also offering "alternative facts to support the suggestion that global warming will be good."[35] Other companies and executives have helped to set up think tanks and grants and university endowments offering clear incentives to academics willing to question climate realities.[36]

In 1997, journalist Ross Gelbspan summed up the situation efficiently: "The reason most Americans don't know what is happening to the climate is that the oil and coal industries have spent millions of dollars to persuade them that global warming isn't happening."[37] Such outright denial is thankfully less common as I write in 2024. But fossil fuel companies continue to sow doubt about proposed solutions, and none of them has admitted that their past public statements were lies. None of them has accounted for funding campaigns of denial; none has demonstrated a willingness to fundamentally change corporate cultures. Extraction, burning, and defilement continue.

The denial of climate change depends on a kind of human exceptionalism, a belief that the clear evidence of chemical, atmospheric, and physical science can be ignored if it conflicts with human desire. Denialists find a small piece of evidence in human experience—an uncharacteristically cold day, for example—and insist that it is more important than the collective weight of years of research by thousands of experts. This is effective only because people in the industrialized world have been trained to believe that humans are so uniquely special that we can ignore the rest of the world.

Walter Wink writes that propaganda is "the manufacture of idolatry," that "if you can cause people to worship the Beast, you have created a public immune to truth."[38] This is what the fallen Powers of the fossil fuel industry did. They used the myths of human exceptionalism, radical individualism, and infinite expansion to justify the defilement of the atmosphere. And they continue to do so. They are our enemies.

Injustices at the Intersections

Writing about fossil fuel companies, it turns out, tempts me toward cynicism. As I have been researching the lies and manipulations of the industry, I have found it harder and harder to be surprised. The depth and seriousness of atmospheric defilement have been concealed, minimized, and then declared inevitable by some of the most powerful and wealthiest institutions in the world. And yet I sometimes find myself thinking, *Well, of course that's what they did.* I am tempted to stop believing that fossil fuel companies could ever have been better.

This is dangerous. Once I see their corruption as predictable, I am more likely stop believing an alternative was or is possible. The myth of the Powers is therefore an important reminder to me—and anyone else cynically tempted to believe this level of deceit and destruction was inevitable—that it did not have to be this way. Fossil fuel companies could have been more open in the 1970s and 1980s to learn from the data of their own scientists and so many other experts. They could have helped the world understand and respond to climate change before it got as severe as it is today. They could have diversified their portfolios to transition their expertise and workforces into other forms of energy generation. They could have recognized that their employees, executives, and customers are all better off when governments are healthy, democratic, and trusted. They could have used their profits to chart a new and cleaner future.

But they didn't.

The fossil fuel industry could still partner with democratic governments to deal responsibly with the problem. But they don't. They could still invest the massive wealth they've extracted from the earth and from their customers into the desperately needed energy transition. But, it seems, they won't.

Fossil fuel companies are a part of creation, and so they have always had the potential to be good. But they denied this potential. They are fallen. That fall is revealed not only in their participation in the myths of domination but also in their relationship to the many injustices that intersect with climate change.

In chapter 1, we saw that Delores Williams connected the extraction of coal to the abuse of Black women, naming both the "sin of defilement." She is not alone in this insight that fossil fuel production has a common root with racism. Many have argued that slavery—a moral horror on which entire economies were based for far too long—is the best historical analogy for what the climate justice movement is fighting against today.[39] Journalist Chris Hayes, for example, suggests that contemporary calls to leave unextracted coal, gas, and oil in the ground are morally and economically comparable with the historical argument of abolitionists. In both cases, a righteous movement calls on people who believe themselves to be rich to recognize that their wealth is based on cruelty and destruction. The movement then calls on governments to take that wealth away.[40]

In the United States, fossil fuel companies' profits were based largely on the extraction of settler colonialism. Rights to coal seams and oil deposits depended on the violation of Indigenous rights and the willingness of Congress and law enforcement to ignore treaties.[41] In the late nineteenth century, oil was discovered on Osage lands, and the Osage themselves initially grew rich from it. But in the 1920s, Congress put white lawyers and businessmen in charge of managing it, quickly using enormous fees and illegal transfers to take away land rights. Even more troublingly, the guardians appointed by Congress used sexual exploitation and murder to transfer property rights away from the Osage.[42]

Extractive capitalism is at the root of every justification for the fossil fuel industry. Advocates insist that the wealth and jobs created by mining oil, methane, and coal justify the harms caused. Perhaps this was once defensible, but economic research on the "resource curse" increasingly shows that the money generated by fossil fuels goes into the hands of a few owners and leaves regions and nations as a whole poorer.[43] As suggested in Kate Beaton's *Ducks*, many people who work in fossil fuel jobs would be safer and happier if their economic needs could be met in other ways that better supported healthy communities.

Extractive capitalism also connects fossil fuel companies to the injustices of imperialism. Geographer Farhana Sultana, writing on behalf of the Global South, insists, "We are still colonized, this time through climate change, capitalist development industry, and globalization, colliding into centuries of varied and overlapping oppressions."[44] Fossil fuel companies continue to assume the right to extract wealth from the lands of poor people and communities of color and to downplay the dangers posed to those communities by drilling, mining, and changing the climate.[45]

Sexism, ageism, and ableism are also part of the history of fossil fuels. For example, political scientist Cara Daggett argues that oil and other fossil fuels have become a part of identity formation for a certain kind of men. Her analysis of this "petro-masculinity" reveals there are cultural as well as economic reasons people are susceptible to the manipulations and excuses of oil, gas, and coal companies.[46]

In sum, the fallen Powers of the fossil fuel industry are complicit in atmospheric defilement. They not only sell products that fundamentally alter earth's climate, but they also participate in the intersectional injustices that divide people, prop up systems of domination, and make cooperation and community more difficult.

Extracting Christianity

The sins of the fossil fuel industry also have something particular to teach those of us who are in or interested in learning from Christian communities because Christianity has long been used to defend and justify the extraction of coal, methane, and oil.[47]

This connection comes across clearly in Barbara Freese's history *Coal.* She quotes an 1850 story published by Charles Dickens that she describes as a "Christmas Carol of Carbon." A man who disdains coal is visited in the night by a spirit who emerges from the ashes of his fire. That spirit teaches him about the noble sacrifice of coal miners, convincing him the substance was put on earth so that "many may hereafter live, not merely a savage life, but one civilized and refined, with the sense of a soul within—of God in the world, and over it, and all around it."[48]

Six years later, an American author wrote in the *Christian Review* that God had made coal abundant in Europe and the United States precisely so Christians could be "leaders in the onward march of humanity" through the "treasure" of coal. That treasure, "if used aright, must secure to them a controlling influence on the affairs of the world." Coal, Freese summarizes, was believed to be the key to "raise up not only our civilization but our very souls."[49]

Oil inspired similar religious rhetoric, as chronicled by historian Darren Dochuck's *Anointed with Oil.* He describes the book as a "religious biography of a natural resource with an outsized—and seemingly otherworldly—importance." Dochuck argues that Christianity and the oil industry were essential, and interrelated, in shaping North America in the nineteenth, twentieth, and twenty-first centuries.[50] For example, the deals that led to the creation of enormous oil fields in the tar sands of Alberta, where Kate Beaton worked, were made possible in part by the friendship between the provincial premier Ernest Manning and the oil executive J. Howard Pew, who were introduced to one another by evangelist Billy Graham. Manning, a devout Christian, believed that oil engineers were molding the world "into a shape that God had intended for it." His thought on the subject "shaped the way millions of Christians in [Canada and the United States] thought about energy and their place in the world."[51]

These theological celebrations of fossil fuels continue today. One of the most prominent examples is a group called the Cornwall Alliance, a self-described network of "nearly 70 theologians, scientists, economists, and other scholars and leaders" that promotes "Biblical stewardship" and "economic development for the world's poor." Their website argues that the world is "permeated by an environmental movement whose worldview, theology, and ethics are overwhelmingly anti-Christian, whose science and economics are often poorly done, whose policies therefore often do little good for natural resources but much harm to the world's poor, and whose religious teachings undermine the fundamental Christian doctrines of God, creation, humanity, sin, and salvation."[52] To oppose this threat, the Alliance releases statements, books, and videos while funding scholars who defend the coal, oil, and gas economy on Christian terms.

In a 2009 statement titled "A Renewed Call to Truth, Prudence, and Protection of the Poor," the Cornwall Alliance echoed industry talking points. Just as fossil fuel companies have long cast doubt on widely accepted climate science, the Alliance insisted that "global warming alarmism . . . exaggerates the influence of greenhouse gases on global temperature." Just as the companies insist that governments cannot solve problems with laws, the Alliance critiqued proposals for climate legislation as "laden with regulations and provisions that make achieving the target much more expensive" and "lock the economy into potentially inefficient investments." Just as ExxonMobil insisted that the demand for its product is inevitable, the Cornwall Alliance dismissed proposals to substitute renewable energy as "simply not rooted in reality."[53]

Added to these industry talking points is an insistence that fossil fuels are necessary to respond to global poverty. The Renewed Call reasonably asserts that "care for the poor is a high priority throughout Scripture" but then makes a logical leap by asserting that anyone who wants to restrict or eliminate fossil fuels is trying to take energy away from impoverished communities.[54] No mention is made of proposals to replace subsidies currently given to fossil fuel companies with assistance for energy transition and electrification projects in marginalized communities. No explanation is given for why, if fossil fuels are so liberating, almost 10 percent of the world's population lives in poverty 250 years after the Industrial Revolution began. No attention is given to the enormous wealth extracted from the Global South by fossil fuel companies.

Against the claims that climate change is real and causing damage to God's world and God's people, the Cornwall Alliance responds that "God is sovereign, and it seems unlikely that man can thwart His purposes. Consequently, there is no need to adopt anti-global warming policies."[55] It is hard to square this strong assertion of faith with the money and energy the Cornwall Alliance spends arguing against such policies. If God is sovereign enough that we need not worry about climate change, why should we be worried about legislation to stop climate change?

Like many organizations that advocate for fossil fuels, the Cornwall Alliance does not disclose its sources of funding. However, journalists have traced connections between the Alliance and the Committee for a Constructive Tomorrow, which received substantial donations from ExxonMobil and a foundation associated with the family that inherited wealth from Gulf Oil.[56] I do not know how much this funding influences their work, but the basic argument of the Alliance—that God wants people to use fossil fuels and does not want the government to regulate extraction—certainly serves the industry's interests.

Christians who care about climate justice have a duty to publicly disagree with the theology and the politics of the Cornwall Alliance. The myth of the Powers offers a way to do so, an explanation for how the world is damaged by the fallen fossil fuel companies that degrade ecosystems, exploit human and nonhuman communities, and spread misinformation to justify their actions. The Cornwall Alliance is more indebted to the myths of human exceptionalism, radical individualism, and infinite expansionism than to the loving vision of Christianity. It serves and spreads the lies of the Domination System. It is an ally of the fossil fuel industry.

The God who seeks harmonious communities of liberation and justice calls Christians to treat the fossil fuel industry as an enemy. Following Jesus in the contemporary world means believing that the time of fossil fuel extraction can and should end. Atmospheric defilement is sinful; a more loving world is possible.

Potential Enemies, Potential Allies

Some readers may have been frustrated by this chapter so far, thinking, as you read, about other institutions that could be seen as equally bad or worse than fossil fuel companies. Perhaps there are other enemies, other fallen Powers, that deserve as much attention?

Those of us who want to resist climate change and build a more just world must carefully discern who our enemies are and who our allies might be. Resisting the Domination System requires identifying those who are caught most deeply in its thrall and naming them as enemies. But resistance requires assistance; we must be able to work with communities and institutions that are not perfect.

The myth of the Powers teaches that all human institutions and communities are fallen in some way. So we cannot expect purity in our allies; we cannot hold our partners to impossible standards. None of us can be perfect, and none of us need to be.

There are many institutions that the climate movement could consider its enemies, but I argue that most could—and should—also be seen as potential allies. For example, it would be easy to see politicians and governments as the enemy of climate justice. Nations that continue to subsidize fossil fuel extraction and block international agreements have fallen from the ultimate purpose of uniting and healing communities. But I have hope for their redemption. Indeed, my hope for the future depends on a belief that democratic governments can serve the common good.

When Greta Thunberg traveled across Europe and North America in 2018 and 2019, most of her exhortation was directed to political leaders. She chastised their inaction but also held out the possibility that they could redeem themselves. She shamed the US Congress by telling members that their nation is "the biggest carbon polluter in history. It is also the world's number one producer of oil." But she also asked them to be inspired by the political effectiveness of Martin Luther King Jr. and John F. Kennedy and to "unite behind the science" and "take action."[57] She called for political action because she believed governments can, if they change, be part of the solution.

Others suggest that the true enemy is not the fossil fuel industry but capitalism, that all profit-driven corporations are the enemy. This, too, is a reasonable position worth taking seriously. Kate Aronoff subtitled her excellent book *Overheated* with "How Capitalism Broke the Planet—and How We Fight Back." But within the book, Aronoff particularly critiques the extractive capitalism of the fossil fuel industry and insists she is not arguing that capitalism as a whole "has to end before the world can deal with the climate crisis."[58] Capitalism will, she argues, continue to be a key tool for producing solar panels and windmills and batteries. Markets and economics can, if properly regulated, be allies.

Perhaps other industries that have cooperated closely with fossil fuel companies are also enemies. Private utilities, industrialized agriculture companies, and cement producers have contributed billions of tons of GHG emissions to the atmosphere. The Domination System is certainly exerting its influence when utilities neglect the basic needs of their customers while defiling ecosystems;[59] when Big Agriculture prioritizes production over the long-term health of animals, people, and the planet;[60] and when every pound of cement produced releases a pound of CO_2 into the atmosphere.[61] But again, amid the villainous behavior in each sector, there are potential allies. Utilities can support rather than block renewable energy, particularly when informed and regulated by democratic processes. The production of food and cement can improve, and some companies are working to make this possible. Even within these industries, we have allies.[62]

Is the media an enemy on par with the fossil fuel industry? George Monbiot implies this, arguing that newspapers, magazines, radio, and television are "most responsible for the destruction of life on Earth." He insists that none of the destructive and dominant forces defiling the atmosphere "could continue to operate as they do without the support of" the media, which "is the engine of persuasion that allows our Earth-destroying system to persist."[63] Monbiot notes that even when media coverage takes the injustices of climate change seriously, it rarely mentions fossil fuel corporations except as partners in solutions. This is a fair critique and a profound problem. But Monbiot's solution is better media, like the newspaper for which he writes, the *Guardian*. Many media institutions have fallen, but many can be allies.

Another approach vilifies not fossil fuel corporations but the people who lead them. In October 2021, climate justice activist Lauren MacDonald told the CEO of Shell Oil, "You should be absolutely ashamed of yourself. . . . Every single day that you fail to stop making evil decisions is a day that the death toll of the climate crisis rises. You are one of the most responsible people for this crisis in the world and in my view that makes you one of the most evil people in the world."[64] MacDonald's passion is powerful, her courage is admirable, and she succinctly expressed an anger that many of us feel. But we also have reason to be angry—angrier, I would argue—with the systems that constrain leaders and all of the rest of us. Focusing too much on individual people—even CEOs—ignores the power of institutions. Whoever runs Shell or any other fossil fuel company, the corporation is set up to extract oil, coal, and methane and to encourage other people to burn it. Whoever is in charge, these corporations have profound inertia in a business model that defiles the atmosphere. The real problem is not a person; it is the industry. The real problem is the corruption of the fossil fuel Powers. I have hope that even CEOs can be allies. But they can only do so if they stop being CEOs of the fossil fuel industry as it currently exists. That industry is fallen and broken; it corrupts us all.

The least constructive enemy for the climate movement is the human race as a whole. Some who care about climate imply a sweeping critique, suggesting that the crisis is caused by something fundamental in our species' nature. For instance, in his book *We're Doomed. Now What?*, Roy Scranton insists that "thinking about climate change forces us to face the fact that nobody's driving the car, nobody's in charge, nobody knows how to 'fix it.' And even if we had a driver, there's a bigger problem: no car. There's no mechanisms for uniting the human species to move together in one direction."

This inability to come together is, Scranton insists, "the human way."[65] Here, we see a pernicious extension of the logic that "we have met the enemy and he is us," suggesting not only that everyone is responsible for the injustices of climate change but that it would be impossible to do better. This suggests that humanity itself is the enemy of climate justice and organized change is not worth imagining. That thinking is dangerously aligned to the rhetoric of the fossil fuel industry, which blames each of us for the problem and so insists there is no collective solution.

Scranton and others who blame human nature for climate change ignore important truths. Most of history unfolded without the gargantuan fossil fuel emissions of recent centuries, so clearly humans are not defined by our contributions to atmospheric defilement. Most people on earth today contribute very little to the problem, so it is obviously possible to live without oil, methane, and coal. Scranton fails to consider that perhaps his own study and life experience do not offer him a comprehensive understanding of our species. Perhaps his reluctance to work with others to solve this problem does not reveal a universal flaw shared by every person.

Other human beings are potential allies in the work of climate justice. So are the media, other companies, markets, and governments. None is perfect, and all are constantly tempted by myths of domination. But all can help us resist our real enemy, the fossil fuel industry.

This book is a response to the climate movement, following the lead of protests against the "fossil fuel industry" where activists chant "leave it in the ground" about coal, oil, and methane. The movement is explicitly organized against the extraction, transport, and selling of fossil fuels. And they are right to do so because the fossil fuel industry has aligned itself with the Domination System.

Journalist Nathaniel Rich writes that the fossil fuel industry "in recent decades has committed to playing the role of villain with comic-book bravado."[66] These companies are not only directly responsible for the extraction of methane, coal, and oil; they have also actively campaigned against others' attempts to educate the public about what those substances do to the atmosphere, they have resisted new technologies that would reduce demand for their product, and they have lied to the public and the government.

The Future of Fossil Fuel Companies

Those of us who are open to learning from Christianity must remember that we are called to "not only have enemies but have them well."[67] What might we learn from Christian traditions about how to do a good job at treating the Powers of the fossil fuel industry as enemies?

These traditions remind us that not even fossil fuel companies are purely evil and corrupt. These companies do invest in renewable energy projects, even if it is not nearly as much as they could or should. They sponsor local soccer leagues. They provide livelihoods for hundreds of thousands of employees. They can and do bring good into the world. They do not need to be purely evil to be our enemies.

Having enemies well also means focusing our energy as much as possible on the institutions we oppose rather than the people within them. Fossil fuel executives and employees are not the enemy; the institutions that shape them are. This distinction is fundamental to the myth of the Powers. Villainizing particular people distracts us from the Domination System and the ways it corrupts whoever it encounters. When we focus on individuals, we forget that the real damage comes from the institutions they work for. Our enemies are the companies that outlive and outlast every person they hire and fire.

Having enemies well means believing it is possible for them to be redeemed, which will be a topic in chapter 6. But before concerning ourselves with that, we must remind ourselves that fossil fuel companies are causing, exacerbating, and encouraging atmospheric defilement. Any redemption would require their fundamental transformation. They are currently in service to and warped by the Domination System, dependent on destructive extraction for their very being. To redeem them would be to make them something very different from what they are.

Unless and until they fundamentally change, fossil fuel companies are our enemies. And having an enemy well calls for opposing them, resisting them, fighting them without joining their tactics of domination and destruction. Coalitions of activists, leaders, and neighbors are already doing that, and we can join them.

Part III

RESISTING THE POWERS

ONE WAY TO learn how to have enemies well is to study those who have gone before us, Christians who named and opposed their enemies while still seeking to love them as children of God.

Consider Bayard Rustin (1912–1987), a Quaker activist who devoted his life to racial reconciliation, economic justice, and gay rights. In the 1970s, an interviewer asked Rustin how he felt about President Richard Nixon placing him on a list of "enemies" because of his political activism. Without hesitating, Rustin replied, "Well, I'm delighted to be an enemy of Nixon. Anyone who has his policies on the poor, on the homeless, on those who need medical care, I hope that I shall eternally be an enemy of a man who takes this view. Furthermore, I never like liars and I want to be an enemy of liars."[1]

Over a lifetime of advocacy, Rustin practiced the art of having enemies well. Working for the American Friends Service Committee, he wrote an influential text on Quakers' "search for an alternative to violence," the title of which has become a guiding principle for many movements since: *Speak Truth to Power*. There, Rustin outlined nonviolent strategies of resistance against the Powers, seeking ways to "confound" an enemy with truth and defeat them "without destroying our values and our world."[2]

Rustin also advised Martin Luther King Jr. and other civil rights leaders, helping to shape signature strategies that revealed the violence of segregation and racism by contrasting it with the nonviolence of protesters. He led the organization of the March on Washington in 1963, which remains one of the largest political rallies in US history.

After the Civil Rights Act passed in 1964, Rustin wrote an influential essay, "From Protest to Politics," arguing that the future of the racial justice movement required a shift in tactics: "We need allies. The future of the Negro struggle depends on whether the contradictions of this society can be resolved by a coalition of progressive forces which becomes the *effective* political majority in the United States."[3] To help build such a coalition, he spent decades working for the AFL-CIO, building connections between unions and advocates for racial and economic justice. As he did so, Rustin also engaged in international politics, serving as an election monitor and speaking up in solidarity with poor and struggling people across the world.

Rustin was a Black man in a segregated world. He often told people that when he was born in West Chester, Pennsylvania, there was not a single restaurant where a Black person was allowed to eat and no movie theater where Black people were allowed to sit on the main floor. He was also an openly gay man in culture that rarely accepted him. He did not put his name on *Speak Truth to Power* for fear that his sexuality would lead people to dismiss it. He advised Martin Luther King Jr. mostly from the background, partly because King was reluctant to be publicly associated with a homosexual man. Bayard Rustin knew oppression and suffering, and he spent his life developing creative ways to resist them.

While Rustin died before climate change was widely considered a political or an activist issue, he nevertheless has much to teach those of us who want to resist atmospheric defilement. He drew on the resources of his Christian faith to protest, to make political change, and to reach out to other people in need. He built intersectional coalitions and thought strategically about how to resist domination without becoming a dominator himself. He called out his enemies for their lies and destruction, and he spent his life opposing them.

As far as I know, Rustin did not read Walter Wink's work on the Powers, but their visions of Christian life are deeply compatible. Rustin demonstrates how the Christian tradition can help us have enemies well, resisting them without losing a commitment to a harmonious future of cooperation and care.

Fossil fuel companies have repeatedly, shamelessly lied about the effect of their work on the planet. They have made life harder for people who are poor and marginalized. They are our enemies, and we should not hesitate to name them as such and resist them bravely and creatively.

This section will focus on three components of such resistance: protest movements, political transition, and cultivating mercy in ourselves. As chapter 5 will demonstrate, the legacy of the civil rights movement and other nonviolent struggles continues to inspire climate justice activists today with nonviolent protest, political organizing, and creative disruption. Each of these methods resists the domination of fossil fuel corporations while working to avoid or limit participation in the process of domination.

Chapter 6 will then turn to the Powers that can be redeemed, focusing on the transitions required to build political systems that support clean-energy technologies. Inspired by the biblical story of manna in the desert, this chapter will argue that renewable energy can not only replace fossil fuels but also support democratic coalitions that bring people together with less domination and injustice. We can nurture the best aspects of the Powers that govern our lives, bringing citizens together to regulate and control the fossil fuel companies that defile the atmosphere.

As we fight for such transition, we must also attend to our own emotional lives. Chapter 7 will focus on the "inner work" of climate resistance. Inspired by the parable of the prodigal son, this chapter will particularly attend to the reality of shame and guilt among privileged people; the power of anger on behalf of those who suffer; and the importance of mercy for ourselves, our neighbors, and our enemies.

Learning from Rustin and other activists from and beyond the Christian tradition, those of us concerned about climate change will find many resources for resistance. Naming fossil fuel companies as our enemy helps us see the many ways they can be opposed. Each of us can find a path to resistance based on our abilities and places in the world. This section offers some possibilities, hoping to inspire more ideas and more resistance. We can be delighted to be an enemy of destructive companies, to expose their lies, and to build empowering coalitions for a new world.

5

STRATEGIES OF RESISTANCE

A FRIEND RECENTLY asked me what this book is about. I told her I'm making an argument about what Christian traditions can offer to the global movement for climate justice. She thought about it and then, skeptically, asked, "Are you going to tell people that the earth is burning, but they should just turn the other cheek?"

A good question.

My friend was referencing Matthew 5:38–9: "You have heard that it was said, 'An eye for an eye and a tooth for a tooth.' But I say to you, Do not resist an evildoer. But if anyone strikes you on the right cheek, turn the other also."

The most common interpretation of this text teaches that the best response to violence is passivity. In this view, Jesus asks his followers to nobly accept oppression. When they hit us, we take it and hope that our sacrifice will ensure our reward in heaven. Christians, in this view, should be the willing victims of violence.

However, luckily for me—if not for my friend, who got to hear all about it—Walter Wink has an alternative interpretation of this text. He insists there is nothing passive about Jesus's call to turn the other cheek. His analysis begins with important, practical context: In the ancient world, the left hand was used only for unclean and private tasks, and so the fact that Jesus specifies that the first hit is to "the right cheek" is important. When someone uses their right hand to hit another person's right cheek, it is a backhand slap. It is a dismissal, an expression of dominance, "not administered to an equal, but to an inferior. Masters backhanded slaves; husbands, wives; parents, children; Romans, Jews."[1]

So if Jesus had wanted followers to simply accept being hit, he wouldn't have specified which cheek was hit; he wouldn't have given instructions specifically for how to respond to a dismissive slap. He didn't say, "If someone hits you, invite them to do the exact same thing again." He didn't call for passivity or acceptance; he didn't tell followers to avoid eye contact and hope not to be hurt too badly.

He also didn't say, "If someone hits you, hit them back." A world of slavery and empire makes such open, aggressive defiance dangerous. Most oppressors are well protected. They backhand those they view as inferior precisely because they are confident they have the resources and protection to win a violent competition. Jesus lived in that context; he was a member of a colonized people in a land occupied by a powerful and vicious empire. His audience was not equipped to win a fight with the Roman army.

So Jesus created a "third way," a response to violence that neither passively accepted it nor met it with equal violence. If someone dismisses you with a backhand slap, turn your left cheek toward them. Again, the side matters: to be hit on the left cheek with an attacker's right hand is to be punched. Turning the cheek like this is an insistence that, if they want to hit you again, they will be treating you as an equal rather than an inferior. The goal is not to get hit again but to disrupt the unquestioned violence and hierarchy. The goal is to actively insist on one's own dignity. This upends the power dynamics of the empire, reveals the lie that some people should have the right to dismiss and dominate others, and empowers the victim. It refuses to passively accept violence while also refusing to use violence.

Wink argues that turning the other cheek was a strategy Jesus proposed to empower an occupied people. This was one among many approaches Jesus offered to "recover the initiative and assert their human dignity in a situation that cannot for that time being be changed."[2] Jesus's strategies of nonviolent resistance revealed the lies and division at the heart of oppression.

That is the kind of thinking that Christian traditions can contribute to the global movement for climate justice. We will never be better at domination than the fossil fuel industry. They have learned from the System, which teaches them to hoard all the best tools for violence. We need other tactics, creative strategies that build up community and connection rather than tear them down.

Literally turning our cheeks will not roll back rising seas or protect the people driven from their homes by floods and fires. But we can follow in the spirit of Jesus's advice by finding ways to assert the dignity of those who suffer from atmospheric defilement while revealing the lies of the Powers that perpetuate it.

I explained all this to my friend who had asked about "turning the other cheek." It's possible that I offered more details than she wanted. But she politely followed up with questions about both the ancient world and contemporary strategies of resistance. She keeps asking me skeptical questions in a very helpful way, but she is, I think, a little more open to the idea that ancient traditions have something to teach contemporary movements. I'm heartened by this because the world needs a climate justice movement that can learn from the creativity of the past. The world needs movements that keep asking questions about how to resist.

This chapter will present three strategies for resistance and learn from contemporary exemplars of each. The first, which aligns most closely to Walter Wink's work, is the creative protest of nonviolent resistance. The second is political activism, focusing on intersectional democracy as a path to concrete change. The third is the most radical: sabotage and property destruction that demand attention by literally disrupting extraction.

The good news is that there are thousands of people resisting the fossil fuel Powers in thousands of ways. So, this chapter offers only a sampling of contemporary climate justice activism, learning from a few of the many who do this work across the world.[3]

Nonviolent Resistance

When we think of protest and activism, we often picture people marching in the streets, passing out flyers, asking the rest of us to sign petitions. This approach to resistance calls attention to problems that are neglected by leaders, builds support for solutions, and unifies coalitions of those who are concerned. By telling the truth through signs, slogans, and statements, these protesters hope to reveal systems of domination while demonstrating alternatives for a better world. Such protests often include civil disobedience, the deliberate and open breaking of laws in order to draw attention to the failures of the political system. By trespassing on restricted property or marching without permits, activists hope to reveal the corruption of a government that sometimes protects corporations rather than human and ecological health.

Turning the Other Cheek

In theological terms, nonviolent resistance is an attempt to expose the lies of the Domination System while presenting the possibility of a more collaborative and restorative world. Protesters use this strategy to demonstrate what can happen when coalitions of cooperation resist separation and hierarchy.

The myth of the Powers offers a theological foundation for such nonviolent resistance. Consider, for example, Jesus's first instruction in Matthew 5:39, "Do not resist an evildoer." Walter Wink argues that those of us who read the text in its common English translations miss something important. The Greek word *antistenai* is narrower than the English word *resist*, which is the most frequent translation. *Antistenai* refers specifically to violence in war. Thus, Wink suggests that better translations of Jesus's sentence are "Do not repay evil for evil" or "Don't react violently against the one who is evil."[4] When resisting the Domination System, Jesus instructs, find methods that do not dominate.

This is the "third way" of nonviolence, which rejects both passivity and violence. It resists both the oppression of the System and the domination of the System's methods. This means focusing on ways to nurture goodness rather than punish fallenness, seeking to stir the conscience of one's opponents and the rest of the population. This is how those of us concerned about climate change can put on "the whole armor of God" to stand against the wiles of the devil.

The fallen Powers assert that resisting them is futile, that companies with as much money and clout as Exxon and Aramco cannot possibly be brought down. We may lament the damage these institutions do, the System tells us, but it is naive to believe anything can be done about it. Nonviolent protesters insist otherwise, showing through the progress of their activism that no institution is invulnerable, and no one is completely powerless.

For example, in 2015, a group of protesters in Colorado Springs staged a nonviolent protest outside their utility board to oppose the continued operation of the town's coal-fired power plant. Drawing satirical attention to the kind of thinking needed to justify burning coal so close to a city, they waved signs saying "I love asthma" and "Pollution makes me feel good." Later that day, the board voted to phase the plant out by 2035.[5] Continued pressure ensured that the plant stopped burning coal early in 2022. These protesters helped close a plant and demonstrated that progress is possible. Their tactics simultaneously made the logic of the fossil fuel industry ridiculous and reminded people that government should prioritize human health over corporate profits.

Wink writes that nothing deflates the Powers "faster than deft lampooning." He goes on: "By refusing to be awed by their power, the powerless are emboldened to seize the initiative, even where structural change is not possible. This message, far from being a counsel of perfection unattainable in this life, is a practical, strategic measure for empowering the oppressed."[6] Jesus empowered oppressed people by teaching them to stand up for themselves, to turn the other cheek as an expression of dignity in the face of dehumanizing empire. Nonviolent climate protesters empower those who are oppressed by teaching them to find the gaps and the limits in fossil fuel corporations' power, resisting destructive defilement.

Such tactics may be pacifist, but they are not passive. Wink writes that nonviolence is, in fact, "highly aggressive, and Jesus is the best example of it. He attacks his accusers with the truth. He forces them either to accept the truth or to silence him."[7] When the Roman Empire silenced Jesus, it fueled a movement that has so far lasted two thousand years and spread to every nation across the world. Inspired by this, when the fossil fuel industry tries to silence activists, we are called to ensure that the truth keeps spreading.

The fallen Powers assume that the world can only be as it is, that domination is inevitable. They assert that the demand for fossil fuels must continue, that defiling extraction and consumption are inevitable. By contrast, Jesus repeatedly insisted that the world could be better than he found it. He reached out to children and women and outcasts in a culture that excluded and ignored them. He promised rewards to those who are dismissed by conventional wisdom: the "poor in spirit," the "meek" and "merciful," the "pure in heart," those who make peace and "hunger and thirst for righteousness," those who "mourn," and those who are "persecuted for righteousness' sake." He insisted that "the last will be first, and the first last" (Matthew 5:3–10; 20:16). Jesus disagreed with the *kosmos* that suggested only those who are wealthy, strong, and morally compromised can thrive. Those of us open to learning from Jesus today should similarly disagree with the *kosmos* that suggests only continued atmospheric defilement can support human flourishing.

350.org

Some of the most prominent global protests for climate justice have explicitly used nonviolent tactics, inspired by the civil rights movement in the United States and other activists across the world to expose the domination of the fossil fuel industry while refusing its strategies.

Many of these protests were organized by 350.org, whose slogan as I write is "We fight for a world beyond fossil fuels." The organization describes its work as "moving forward into the world we want to see, leaving no one behind. And we are doing this with the urgency the climate crisis demands of us." They work toward three goals: "stop fossil fuel projects everywhere," "halt fossil fuel finance, invest in renewable solutions," and "power up campaigns for energy justice."[8] They create international networks to organize public protests, educate the public about the dangers of fossil fuels, and lead campaigns pressuring schools and churches to divest.

350.org was founded in 2008 by a group of students at Middlebury College and Bill McKibben, their professor and a journalist, who increasingly devoted his life to activism as the organization grew. McKibben writes that the founders saw the power of climate protests across the world but wanted some way to organize and publicize them: "all we were lacking for a real movement was the movement part, the surge of people that produces respect and maybe even a little fear in leaders."[9] Seeking to build that movement, they chose a name that would be recognizable across the world and in all languages. They took "350" from the atmospheric parts per million of CO_2 deemed safe by the best science of the time.

After studying the civil rights movement and other traditions of protest, in 2011, the organizers led a huge, public civil disobedience action opposing the extension of the Keystone oil pipeline from Alberta, Canada, to Nebraska.[10] 350.org called on protesters to trespass at the White House to emphasize that the president could revoke the permit. Across multiple weeks, over 1,200 people were arrested, attracting media attention and raising public awareness. Citing the example of leaders like Bayard Rustin, Martin Luther King Jr., and Nelson Mandela—all of whom also went to jail for just causes—the climate protesters used their imprisonment to speak about the dangers of extending the fossil fuel economy. Eventually, President Obama delayed the pipeline extension, and that delay lasted long enough that the owner abandoned the project.[11]

In 2016, 350.org built on that success to lead what they called "the largest civil disobedience in the world," building coalitions between activists all over the planet who agreed to break the law in opposition to the fossil fuel industry. Dozens planted themselves on train tracks to prevent oil from being shipped across the United States. Three hundred people occupied a coal mine in South Wales and shut down its operations for a day. Two thousand people in Australia blocked the world's largest coal port for a day. Three thousand participated in a whistle demonstration to call Indonesia's president's attention to the dangers of extractive capitalism. Again, many people were arrested, and media attention to climate increased. This time, the impact was worldwide. Protesters waved banners that encouraged political leaders to "Break Free" from fossil fuels, to listen to Indigenous people and other communities who oppose fossil fuel infrastructure, and to take drastic action on climate change.[12]

350.org is founded on the belief that creative protests can motivate people toward "a world beyond fossil fuels." Against the industry propaganda that suggests no recognizable civilization could possibly endure without coal, oil, and methane, the climate justice movement insists that careful governance, existing technologies, and cultural change are all we need to develop a better world.

Preventing a pipeline extension and delaying some coal exports do not, of course, solve atmospheric defilement. After and around these protests, the fossil fuel industry continued extracting, selling, and burning unconscionable tons of oil, gas, and coal. But 350.org used their protests to call attention, to change discourse, and to build coalitions. They helped build a network that responded when Indigenous leaders called for support at Standing Rock. They helped make climate policies seem more reasonable and necessary to voters and political leaders. They helped make it clear that fossil fuel companies are enemies to be opposed. They helped inspire a local chapter to protest that coal plant in Colorado Springs, which closed.

Protest and civil disobedience are strategies for making an argument in public. Their goal is not to immediately solve a problem but to reveal the stagnation and violence of the status quo by contrasting it with the creative nonviolence of protesters. Organizers of nonviolent protests train participants to resist temptations to be violent or rude to the authorities that police them. When nonviolent activists break the law, they do so openly, and they willingly go to jail to demonstrate their respect for rules and the system they are trying to save.

In 1963, Martin Luther King Jr. explained this strategy in a masterful letter written from jail, where he had been locked up for protesting in Birmingham, Alabama: "In no sense do I advocate evading or defying the law, as would the rabid segregationist. That would lead to anarchy. One who breaks an unjust law must do so openly, lovingly, and with a willingness to accept the penalty. . . . We must never forget that everything Adolf Hitler did in Germany was 'legal' and everything the Hungarian freedom fighters did in Hungary was 'illegal.'"[13]

By carefully adhering to every legal standard and punishment when he paraded without a permit, King sought to draw attention to the "rabid segregationists" who cared more about division and domination than the law. By leading meticulously planned, peaceful protests, he exposed the system that would turn fire hoses and attack dogs on nonviolent marchers.

350.org was designed in that tradition. The echoes of King's letter are clear in what Bill McKibben wrote about his time jailed for trespassing at the White House in 2011:

> There's nothing radical about what we're doing here. *We're just Americans, interested in preserving a country and a planet that looks and feels something like the ones we were born on.*
>
> *Radicals? They work at oil companies and coal companies and gas companies. They're willing to alter the chemical composition of the atmosphere to make money. No one has ever done anything more radical than that.*[14]

As McKibben and King demonstrate, nonviolent protest calls attention to the violence of the System. This is a direct application of Jesus's methods of resistance.

Political Organizing

Many of 350.org's most iconic protests have taken place just outside of political spaces: in front of the White House, near the Indonesian president, outside a utility board meeting. Other strategies focus more on getting into such spaces, seeking to collaborate with politicians to directly rewrite laws and regulations. Political organizing, developing legal language, and lobbying legislators are also ways to build a more harmonious and just world.

Toward Democratic Powers

At the heart of the myth of the Powers is the idea that God created not just human beings but the institutions and systems that connect us. Those systems can be good; they can work. So political advocacy and political engagement are ways of seeking to redeem the Powers, of advocating that they do the work for which they were created.

Many Christians in my country have a troubling habit of assuming that Jesus and God are explicitly and always on the side of the United States, that our nation is specially favored by God. I have heard no convincing theological or biblical justification for that belief. However, I do think the Christian tradition teaches that God is supportive of any structures that bring people together, any institutions that help communities cooperate without domination. In other words, God is not on the side of a particular government, but God is on the side of good governance.

Walter Wink's theology supports this idea. He insists that the goal of a nonviolent protest is to make enough change that protests are no longer required: "Ideally, democracy is nonviolence institutionalized. It is the only political order that rejects domination in principle and grounds itself in equality before the law. . . . When democracies work, nonviolence is simply the modus operandi of the entire system. Nonviolence is expressed through voting, legislative debates, community organization, and voluntary associations for changing public policy or meeting social needs."[15]

This does not mean that any existing democracy is perfect, or consistently nonviolent, or even adequately equipped to respond to the challenges of climate change.[16] The Powers are fallen; the Powers are limited. Every government I know of is deeply, frustratingly flawed. Some government leaders are corrupted by the Domination System and so lead people away from democracy and cooperation. But an important way to resist such corruption is to insist that it is not inevitable, that good and democratic governance is possible.

The ideal of democracy, the goal of effective and collaborative government, matches the ideal that comes from the myth of the Powers: a world of cooperation rather than domination, a world where people work together honestly and openly to solve challenges, even one as big as the defilement of the global atmosphere.

As chapter 4 discussed, the fossil fuel industry and its allies have been trying to shrink and weaken democratic governments for decades. They have insisted that government-sponsored research about the problem should not be trusted, they have resisted regulations that could temper their behavior and their profits, and they have championed unregulated capitalism as the only reasonable way to connect people from different communities and families. They have argued against the basic principles of governance, against government. As I write these words, the largest fossil fuel companies in the world are funding and propping up antidemocratic regimes in China, Saudi Arabia, Russia, and Iran.[17]

Those of us who are concerned about climate change should pay attention to this. Our enemy consistently sets itself up against democratic governance. The enemy of our enemy is our potential ally. Democracy is a tool for resistance.

The climate movement in the United States recognized this when it named its signature policy proposal in the late 2010s the "Green New Deal." This title harkened back to a time in the nation's history when most people seemed to believe that government could solve big problems. The twentieth-century New Deal was, of course, flawed and limited, tainted by the racism and sexism and colonialism of its political context. But it is nevertheless an example of a constructive politics that brought people together to build new systems. It is an example of a democratic government taking on the systemic injustice of poverty and making progress. As labor leader Bob Master puts it, "The Green New Deal reminds us that our nation has grappled with massive social and economic crises in the past and that we can do it again, if we are willing to shed ideological constraints and undertake the massive social mobilization needed to preserve the planet."[18]

The Sunrise Movement

At a 2018 town hall in Pennsylvania, college student Rose Strauss asked gubernatorial candidate Scott Wagner why he refused to act on climate change and whether his position had "anything to do with the $200,000 you have taken from the fossil fuel industry?" Wagner responded, "You're eighteen years old. You know, you're a little young and naïve."

Activists working with Strauss made sure that a video of the exchange went viral immediately. This led to national coverage, including an editorial by Strauss in *Teen Vogue* about the importance of political action on climate change. "#YoungAndNaive" became a mark of pride for some organizers.[19] Wagner lost his race for governor, as did many other candidates across the country who opposed climate action in 2018.

Strauss and those working with her were part of the Sunrise Movement, a youth-led climate organization that proudly brands itself with the words "We are the climate revolution" and advocates for "government action that actually meets the scale, scope, and urgency of the climate crisis."[20] It was founded in 2017 by Sara Blazevic and Varshini Prakash, recent college graduates with training in community organizing. They started a national movement that focuses on mobilizing and empowering young people to make political change.

Sunrise's most famous action was a sit-in that occupied the office of US Speaker of the House Nancy Pelosi in 2017 to demand serious climate legislation. Over two hundred protesters entered the office with letters describing their fears about climate change. On the outside of the envelopes holding those letters was printed "What's Your Plan?"

Dyanna Jaye, the first to speak at that protest, wrote later that sitting in the Speaker's office was a way to move beyond despair to constructive action. Explaining her motivations, she appealed directly to the ideal of democracy and the language of the Powers: "Even in our grief at the state of the world, we knew we had to be stronger and louder and bigger to bring down the powers that be, to transform our country. *When the people rise up, the powers come down.*"[21]

Fifty protesters were arrested in Pelosi's office that day. Their civil disobedience drew media attention and increased political pressure. Like 350.org, the Sunrise Movement learned from, used, and adapted the tactics of nonviolent resistance. They adopted nonviolence as one of their core principles, they modeled their training and planning on successful practices from the civil rights movement, and they used protests and hunger strikes strategically.[22]

The Sunrise Movement is distinct from 350.org, though, with its clear and consistent focus on US politics. While 350.org was founded to create a global movement rallying thousands of people and inspiring a range of local actions, Sunrise was founded to influence the politics in one country, leading targeted protests deemed likely to directly influence politicians. While 350.org focused on global conversations, Sunrise focused on national laws.

For example, when protesters asked the Speaker of the House, "What's your plan?" they were ready with their own. They had helped develop the Green New Deal and ensured they already had support from key legislators in both the House and the Senate. They continued to advocate that legislation until many of its principles were included in the Inflation Reduction Act, which became law in 2022.

While many environmental and climate organizations work to be nonpartisan and to bring politicians from all parties to the negotiating table, the Sunrise Movement is explicit in organizing voters against the Republican Party and trying to score partisan victories. After the passage of the Inflation Reduction Act, they turned their focus to the 2022 midterm elections and contacted over three million voters. The movement claimed partial credit for "our generation being the largest voting bloc for the Democratic Party" and for the primary victories of many "Green New Deal champions."[23]

At the core of Sunrise's organizing has been a belief that government can be a force for good, that the future requires democratic systems monitoring, regulating, and advocating for a healthier climate.[24]

The fossil fuel industry is an enemy of good governance. Sunrise cofounder Varshini Prakash recounted one of her formative moments as an activist in college, when she yelled across her campus quad, "The fossil fuel industry's business plan is incompatible with a livable future." Following this logic, the movement introduced a "No Fossil Fuel Money Pledge," asking candidates for office "not to take contributions over $200 from oil, gas, and coal industry executives, lobbyists, and PACs and instead prioritize the health of our families, climate, and democracy over fossil fuel industry profits."[25] The powers of democratic government can be redeemed, Sunrise suggests, if they are separated from the corrupting influence of fossil fuel companies.

Monkeywrenching

The strategies of nonviolent resistance and democratic organizing are powerful, but they are not as fast or as effective as some believe we need to match the urgency of atmospheric defilement. So other protesters turn to more secretive and immediate tactics that destroy and disrupt fossil fuel infrastructure.

This approach has a long history in the environmental movement. It came to broad consciousness with Edward Abbey's 1975 novel, *The Monkey Wrench Gang*, a fictionalized account of protesters who sabotage roads, construction, and a dam to preserve wilderness in the western United States.[26] Based on that book, *monkeywrenching* now serves as a name for environmentally motivated property destruction. While their work is never as public or as organized as the Sunrise Movement or 350.org, the climate movement includes monkeywrenchers who deserve to be understood and included as part of the coalition of resistance.

Climate Saboteurs

Monkeywrenching is inherently clandestine, so there is no organized movement to explain its mission and strategy to the world. While other climate justice organizations place themselves in the legacy of nonviolent activists for whom publicity is an important strategy, most monkeywrenchers do their work as quietly as possible.

One partial exception is the work of Jessica Reznicek and Ruby Montoya, who conducted a campaign of sabotage against the Dakota Access Pipeline in 2016 and 2017 while living at a Catholic Worker house in Des Moines, Iowa. Both had been involved in peaceful protests and civil disobedience against the pipeline, including locking themselves to a backhoe to delay construction. But when those protests failed to stop the pipeline, they began a different kind of activism.[27]

On the night Donald Trump was elected president in 2016, Montoya and Reznicek set 6 fires in a pipeline construction site, causing an estimated $2.5 million in damage to bulldozers and other equipment. They continued this work for months and eventually learned to use blowtorches to damage pipeline valves. They were careful to focus their efforts on destroying only company equipment, and they worked hard not to endanger human lives, including their own. When they found oil in the pipes, they stopped. An anonymous collective that researches monkeywrenching estimates that Reznicek and Montoya did a total of $6 million in damage and delayed pipeline construction by 2 months.[28]

These women were never caught in the act, but in May 2017, they admitted their crimes and turned themselves in outside the Iowa Utilities Board, which authorized the pipeline in their state. In their statement, they insisted they had worked to keep their actions nonviolent: "We acted from our hearts and never threatened human life nor personal property. What we did do was fight a private corporation that has run rampant across our country seizing land and polluting our nation's water supply. You may not agree with our tactics, but you can clearly see their necessity in light of the broken government."[29]

This statement was published by the Catholic Worker house where both had lived. In the same publication, an activist who had been arrested almost fifty years earlier for pouring blood on draft files during the Vietnam War saluted their action, insisting that "some property has no right to exist."[30]

Since their arrest, Montoya and Reznicek have explained their motivations in many interviews. Montoya, a preschool teacher, insists she acted out of love for the next generation: "We're not leaving them anything. It's scary, it's scary what everyone is going through . . . How do we effectively stop this desecration that continues day in and day out?" Reznicek argues that their action should be understood as fundamentally creative: "I like to focus on the property improvement that we've made versus the property destruction. At every turn, we were acting from our hearts and from our spirits and with all life on this planet in mind. Absolutely no life was in jeopardy while we were acting, and in fact our goal was to save lives."[31]

These two activists have paid a steep price for their work. In 2019, they were indicted on federal charges that labeled their crimes "terrorism." In 2021, Jessica Reznicek was sentenced to eight years in prison. In 2022, Montoya was sentenced to six years. As I write this, both are in federal prison.

Geographer Andreas Malm praises Reznicek and Montoya and many other climate-motivated saboteurs in his book *How to Blow Up a Pipeline*. The book, which inspired a fictionalized film, argues that governments have failed to prohibit the growth of fossil fuels, and so more direct action from citizens is required. Malm calls on people to "announce and enforce" an immediate "prohibition" on fossil fuels:

"Damage and destroy new CO_2-emitting devices. Put them out of commission, pick them apart, demolish them, burn them, blow them up. Let the capitalists who keep on investing in the fire know that their properties will be trashed."[32]

Malm argues that the climate movement should learn less from publicly nonviolent movements and more from the violent slave revolt of US preacher Nat Turner and the window-smashing campaign of the British suffragette Emmeline Pankhurst.[33] Such militant figures made historical change by destroying and endangering property, and Malm insists their tactics should be part of the contemporary climate movement.

Like Reznicek and Montoya, Malm suggests that damaging property is different from violence against human beings and other living creatures.[34] He hopes for a climate movement that includes property destruction whenever it is deemed necessary, but he argues against violence that directly endangers human health or life.

While *How to Blow Up a Pipeline* spends considerable time arguing against nonviolent protest,[35] I find the most convincing argument to be more open to multiple strategies, accepting that some people will organize peaceful and public protests while others take different paths. The climate justice movement as I understand it is a coalition that can include monkeywrenching, protest, and politics, with plenty of room for many other tactics besides. When they turned themselves in, Montoya and Reznicek said they hoped their announcement would "inspire others to act boldly, with purity of heart, to dismantle the infrastructures which deny us our rights to water, land and liberty."[36] There are many ways to do this, and every tactic that meaningfully resists our enemies while avoiding harm to living beings should be included in a coalition for climate justice.

Drawing Lines and Building Coalitions

Walter Wink's interpretation of the myth of the Powers emphasizes the power of public, nonviolent resistance; monkeywrenching moves well outside of that sphere. It requires secretive actions that go against the spirit of openness and honesty in nonviolent campaigns. It damages property more directly than other forms of civil disobedience. It risks injury and serious prison time in ways that many in the movement deem unacceptable.

But Christian traditions certainly include many people who destroyed property to call attention to or solve a problem. All four Gospels include a story of Jesus "cleansing" the temple in Jerusalem, driving merchants and consumers away from the most important house of worship in his tradition. Mark narrates it this way: "He entered the temple and began to drive out those who were selling and those who were buying in the temple, and he overturned the tables of the money changers and the seats of those who sold doves; and he would not allow anyone to carry anything through the temple" (11:15–16).

Was Jesus being violent? It depends on how we define the word of course, but it's hard to deny that he disrupted other people's property, stood in the way of commerce, and physically drove people out of a space they had a legal right to occupy. We cannot call his actions peaceful.

Walter Wink admits that Jesus's behavior could be seen as violent but emphasizes—like Reznicek, and Montoya did about their monkeywrenching—that no human beings or other creatures seem to have been harmed. Still, Wink admits, this story reveals that Jesus's strategies of resistance "may be a good deal more aggressive than certain idealists might like."[37] He also describes the cleansing of the temple as an "exorcism," which he directly compares to the burning of draft cards by Vietnam protesters. The point of these acts, he writes, is "revelation: the unveiling of unsuspected evil in high places."[38]

Wink takes instruction from Mahatma Gandhi on this subject and frequently quotes what Gandhi wrote in 1920 as the Indian independence movement was taking shape: "I do believe that where there is a choice only between cowardice and violence, I would advise violence. . . . I would rather have India resort to arms in order to defend her honor than that she should in a cowardly manner become or remain a helpless witness to her own dishonor."[39]

Of course, Gandhi believed that there was a third option, that India could defend its honor with nonviolent resistance. But his moral stance is clear: if there is no way to peacefully oppose a violent Power, it should still be opposed. It is better to give up on peace than to accept injustice.

Reading Montoya and Reznicek's statement and watching them interviewed, one sees they tried peaceful tactics first and moved to monkeywrenching out of deep frustration when it did not work. They saw the damage and dangers of the Dakota Access Pipeline, and they could think of no other peaceful way to resist it. Other protesters went home or moved on to another issue; Reznicek and Montoya turned to arson and sabotage. They used any means they could—short of hurting someone—to defend the honor of the land, the atmosphere, and the future.

Dana Fisher, a sociologist who studies social movements, writes about the "radical flank" of the climate justice movement, which steadily employs increasingly disruptive tactics. Nonviolent protesters were once the radical flank, but as their methods have become widely accepted, more radical actions are being tried on the margins. Fisher insists this follows the pattern of other movements in history, for which extreme tactics served to gain attention and normalize more mainstream strategies. She predicts, "As the climate crisis worsens and more and more concerned activists lose confidence that institutional politics can adequately address the problem, the radical flank will grow."[40]

I have never destroyed the property of a fossil fuel corporation, and I don't advocate that anyone else do so. My ultimate hope for the future lies with democratic action, and I believe that the bulk of a movement toward climate justice should focus on political and nonviolent methods to keep the goodwill of others on our side. I am not on the radical flank that uses monkeywrenching as a tactic. But those who are on that flank are not my enemies, and as long as they do not hurt any living creatures, I will not spend my time criticizing them or their methods.[41] I focus my negative judgment on those who support fossil fuel companies rather than the allies who oppose them.

Even those of us who will not follow in their footsteps can admire Ruby Montoya and Jessica Reznicek's bravery, commitment, and willingness to sacrifice their freedom for a vital cause. We can respect Malm's arguments and agree with him that climate protesters have much to learn from past movements that included property destruction.

I hope that monkeywrenchers will help more people see the depth of atmospheric defilement. Those who engage in such actions safely, responsibly, and willingly are part of the broad and intersectional coalition of the climate resistance movement. They remind the rest of us that there is no passive solution to atmospheric defilement. The climate justice movement needs to form coalitions of people willing to create tension, test limits, and loudly insist on change. That may include some who secretly, cautiously damage the property of fossil fuel companies.

Toward Coalitions of Climate Justice

It may be tempting to pass judgment among the three groups just discussed, to decide whether nonviolent resistance, political influence, or monkeywrenching is the best strategy for the contemporary climate movement. We should resist that temptation.

The movement for climate justice needs a broad range of strategies; it needs to include many different people willing to take different kinds of actions against fossil fuel companies. Our best hope is a broad coalition that welcomes diverse people and diverse strategies, all working toward stronger democracies that take meaningful action toward a healthy, just, and sustainable future.

On an individual level, discriminating among these approaches is important. Each of us who cares about climate change needs to decide how we will try to influence our neighbors and our leaders, whether we are willing to break a law and risk arrest doing so, and how far we are willing to go. Those of us who can afford to support others need to figure out where we send resources and whose stories we will tell our family, friends, and neighbors.

But we do not need to dismiss or disparage other viable strategies. Those who want to work through entirely legal means for political change should be grateful that others risk arrest to increase public awareness and media attention. Those engaged in protests that risk vilification and imprisonment should trust that others in the movement will support them and spread their messages when they are jailed or silenced.

This work is complicated, but coalitions are possible when we articulate common goals. Organizations that focus on nonviolent protest build international connections and demonstrate a groundswell of public support. Organizations that focus on political organizing develop concrete legislation and empower the candidates most likely to pass it. Monkeywrenchers offer an outlet and an expression for the frustration that our political systems have so far proven inadequate to the seriousness of atmospheric defilement. These are all paths to the same goal of opposing the fossil fuel industry.

Every person and every movement that exposes the violence and domination of fossil fuel industry is doing important work. Walter Wink writes, "When anyone steps out of the system and tells the truth, lives the truth, that person enables *everyone else* to peer behind the curtain too. That person has shown everyone that it is possible to live within the truth, despite the repercussions."[42]

The activists and organizers discussed in this chapter have stepped outside the Domination System, creatively exposing truth, peeling back the curtain. It is up to the rest of us to face the truths they are telling us and then to discern how we will join their coalitions of resistance.

6

TRANSITIONING AWAY

AT THE TIME of this writing, the international community has committed to "transitioning away from fossil fuels in energy systems, in a just, orderly, and equitable manner."[1] This agreement was made at the 2023 Conference of the Parties in Dubai. The final document was approved by consensus among all the nations that signed the Paris Agreement, in which they had officially agreed on the goal of limiting global temperature increase to 1.5°C eight years before.

While preparing for the Dubai conference, many had emphasized the importance of a bold agreement. UN Secretary-General António Gutteres declared the task urgent because with unabated climate change, "humanity has opened the gates of hell." He cited heat waves, floods, and fires as evidence of the harm done by atmospheric defilement. But, he insisted there was still hope of limiting warming to1.5 degrees. "We can," he stated, "still build a world of clear air, green jobs, and affordable clean power for all."[2] He praised governments that were already working to "stamp out fossil fuels" and resisting "the naked greed of entrenched interests raking in billions" while urging others to do the same. During the conference, he was even more specific, asserting that success would mean "a consensus on the need to phase out fossil fuels."[3]

In his speech opening COP28, conference president Sultan Al Jaber declared limiting warming to 1.5°C his "North Star" and his "laser focus." He encouraged global leaders to help him "restore faith in multilateralism and let's deliver some good news to a world that really needs it." However, Al Jaber was far less strident than Gutteres in articulating the costs of climate change and the potential of renewable energy sources. He avoided language about "the gates of hell," and he did not talk about "stamping out" or "phasing out" fossil fuels. Instead, he emphasized that the conference had "made a bold choice to proactively engage with oil and gas companies." He called for a collaborative spirit and urged activists and politicians to be flexible.[4] The final result was a compromise, more ambiguous than what Gutteres had called for. The commitment to "transition away from" fossil fuels is gentler than a "phase out," and the limitation of this goal to "energy systems" leaves open the possibility of long-term continued use of fossil fuels in transportation, agriculture, and plastic production.

Many critics blame the softening of this language on the inclusion of oil and gas companies, noting that Al Jaber was not only president of the conference but also the chief executive of the United Arab Emirates' national oil company, Adnoc. Critics had been arguing for months before the conference that the fossil fuel industry's interest in selling its product was in direct conflict with the conference's goals. They see the conference's compromised conclusion as evidence that the industry as it currently exists cannot be a partner in meaningful climate negotiations.

At one of the most revealing discussions during the conference, Al Jaber rejected the premise that limiting warming to 1.5°C would require ending the use of oil and gas, protesting, "I'm not in any way signing up to any discussion that is alarmist. There is no science out there, or no scenario out there, that says that the phase-out of fossil fuel is what's going to achieve 1.5° C." He went on to suggest there is no "roadmap for a phase-out of fossil fuel that will allow for sustainable socioeconomic development, unless you want to take the world back into the caves."[5]

This is a common message from the industry: any attempt to end the use of fossil fuels will end industrialized life as we know it. For example, earlier in 2023, the podcast *The Other Side of the Story* produced an episode titled "The End of Oil Would Be the End of

Civilization." The hosts began by insisting that "there are no replacements" for plastics and jet fuel and that "the elimination of fossil fuels is a sure path to human extinction." Their guest was Ronald Stein, a consultant for oil refineries and an adviser at the Heartland Institute, which receives considerable funding from the fossil fuel industry. Stein said, "We have no plans to replace the crude oil that's manufactured into our daily lives and brought us through the industrial revolution," concluding that contemporary life depends completely on oil-derivative technologies. No replacements are possible.[6]

That podcast, Sultan Al Jaber, and many other advocates for oil, gas, and coal suggest a stark choice: twenty-first-century humanity can either continue to extract fossil fuels or move back to preindustrialized life. While the fossil fuel Powers are willing to entertain rhetoric of "transitioning away" from burning their product to produce electricity, they insist on keeping the timeline for that transition vague, and they even more stridently argue that there are no substitutes for fossil fuels in transportation or plastic production.

They are wrong. Alternatives to fossil fuels already exist, and they are becoming more and more viable. There is a third way, an alternative to the false choice of continued fossil fuel usage or apocalypse. Those of us who understand the injustices of atmospheric defilement can support technologies that build a better future rather than continuing the rampant degradation of the present. We can and should believe there is enough energy and material to support everyone without defiling the atmosphere. And we can embrace this transition technologically, politically, and spiritually.

This chapter will reflect on transition in conversation with the biblical story of manna from heaven. In this story, manna is a resource from the natural world that falls freely from the sky, provides enough for all to meet their needs, and discourages hoarding and selfishness. If we can learn to treat energy and other resources like manna, we will help build a better world.

Technological Transition to Energy from Heaven

When António Gutteres referred to the use of fossil fuels as "opening the gates of hell," he demonstrated the power of spiritual metaphors for understanding technology. Muslim environmentalist Ibrahim Abdul-Matin makes a similar point when he distinguishes between two kinds of energy. He labels fossil fuels "energy from hell," which is "extracted from the Earth, it is dirty, and it is a major cause of pollution and climate change. Energy from hell is nonrenewable; it takes away from the Earth without giving back." By contrast, Abdul-Matin celebrates "energy from heaven," the power of wind and sun that "is not extracted from the Earth, and it is renewable." Energy from hell causes "imbalance," consuming its own basis. Clean energy, by contrast, "is like a gift from heaven," regularly renewed.[7]

While Abdul-Matin's duality does not account for some complexities in energy production, or for hydro- or geothermal power, its theological insight is profound. It insists that people thrive when their sources of energy and material are renewable, sustainable, and just. It also teaches that energy can be honored as a gift from God: "We need to start seeing energy as a blessing. You don't squander blessings."[8]

As discussed in chapter 4, many Christians who first extracted fossil fuels saw coal and oil as blessings from God. But given what these products have done to the atmosphere and the world, we cannot reasonably see them that way now. It is past time to transition away from dirty, extractive energy.

"God Gives Manna for All"

Another spiritual model for transition comes from the book of Exodus, shared by Jews and Christians as a sacred text. Exodus recounts the Israelites' escape from slavery in Egypt, their life in the desert wilderness, and then their settling into a land of promise.[9]

The story of manna comes after the community has escaped from slavery and find themselves homeless, hungry, and scared. They lament, "If only we had died by the hand of the Lord in the land of

Egypt, when we sat by the fleshpots and ate our fill of bread." Then they lash out at their leader, Moses, "For you have brought us into this wilderness to kill this whole assembly with hunger." Still suffering the traumas of slavery while fearing for the future, the biblical Israelites see only two possibilities: enslavement in Egypt or death in the wilderness. They lack food, the most basic energy required for life, and they cannot imagine any way to get it that doesn't involve returning to the Domination System.

But God offers a third way: "I am going to rain bread from heaven for you, and each day the people shall go out and gather enough for that day. In that way I will test them, whether they will follow my instruction or not. On the sixth day, when they prepare what they bring in, it will be twice as much as they gather on other days."

Each morning thereafter, the Israelites found a "flaky substance, as fine as frost on the ground," and "the taste of it was like wafers made with honey." This was manna from heaven, and it nourished them throughout their time in the desert. It was reliably there every morning for six days every week; on that sixth day, they gathered double and preserved it for the next day, making a sabbath rest possible. However, if anyone took more than they needed on other days, the manna "bred worms and became foul" (Exodus, ch. 16).

Pastor and theologian Dan Erlander suggested in his book *Manna and Mercy* that this myth should be central to Christian life. He called Christians to work toward an "ideal manna society," one that rejects oppression and and refuses to let anyone go hungry. His book offered three lessons for such a society: First, "God gives manna for all." Believers should trust that human needs will and can be provided for, that everyone can "live in sufficiency—with neither too much nor too little." Second, "hoarding stinks." When anyone gathered more manna than they needed for the day, it spoiled. The path of accumulation, of taking more than one's share, "brings rot, decay, and death." The third lesson is "the gift of sabbath." Meeting basic human needs does not require endless work and strain. God's creation is made so that it is "possible for humans and animals and earth to rest."[10]

Erlander finds these lessons not only in the sixteenth chapter of Exodus but throughout the Christian Bible. In his interpretation, Jesus's ministry is a reaffirmation of the same three lessons. Jesus feeds those who are hungry and shares his power, insisting there is enough for all. Jesus resists the hoarding of the empire, of merchants who sell at the temple, and of disciples who want to be first in line. Jesus affirms the value of pause and reflection, celebrating the gift of the sabbath. Erlander concludes that Christians are called to demonstrate the potential of "a universal manna society—a world where all receive, thank, and share. . . . where humans live in harmony with all creation, each part living for the good of the whole."[11]

When the biblical Israelites believed they had only two terrible choices, death or servitude to an empire, God offered a third way. God demonstrated that creation provides for human needs without systems of domination and destruction.

A too literal reading of Exodus would suggest that humanity's energy future depends on God speaking from heaven, announcing a new miracle. But this is not what we need. The myth of manna in the wilderness is not about waiting for God to solve problems; it is instead a call to gather what is already abundant, what can sustain us every day. God's instruction was not to wait passively for salvation but to use and share what is freely available to all.

Renewable Energy Technologies

Sunlight, wind, and rain fall from the sky every day. They can provide the energy human beings need. A better future is possible if we believe there is enough to go around, if we focus our technological innovation on gathering what we can and focus our politics on sharing what we gather. The story of manna in the wilderness offers a spiritual foundation for technological transition, encouraging us to gather the energy heaven provides. God gives manna for all.

The twenty-first century has seen rapid growth in technological capacities to gather energy from sun and wind. At the time of this writing, the cheapest way to produce electricity almost anywhere in the world is with solar panels, which are becoming more efficient and less expensive every year. In many places with good conditions, wind turbines are also more cost-effective than fossil fuels. According to a report by the Rocky Mountain Institute, these two sources of electricity are on an "exponential growth path." Between 2012 and 2022, the cost of solar-produced electricity dropped by 80 percent, the cost of onshore wind by 57 percent.[12]

These technologies were rapidly deployed across Europe in 2021, when Russia's invasion of Ukraine cut off important sources of natural gas that had been used for electricity generation across the continent. That energy transition was sudden and scary, but it brought benefits. The International Energy Agency estimated that consumers in Europe saved a cumulative €100 billion between 2021 and 2023 because of increased use of wind and solar technologies.[13] Europe reduced its dependence on fossil fuels, but civilization did not end. Instead, people worked together to gather energy that comes from heaven each day.

Solar and wind are also "distributed, clean, and universal."[14] In other words, it is easier to share them than to hoard them. While oil, coal, and methane are dug up from the ground and lend themselves to stockpiling, the sun's radiation and the blowing wind are hard to contain within borders or property lines. The technologies used to gather them need not be centralized or proprietary. So the more people trust in energy from heaven, the harder it will be for hoarders—like the Russian authorities under Putin's dictatorial leadership—to influence geopolitics.[15]

Of course, solar and wind power are not perfect.[16] Nothing on earth is. Our enemies are quick to point out that photovoltaic cells and windmills currently require fossil fuels for their construction and shipment. This is true, and it is a problem. But the more we build these technologies, the more solutions we will find. The more we put political and economic energy into transition, the more incentives there will be to do better. Similarly, the more we look for alternatives to the plastics in these technologies, the better chance we have of designing panels and turbines made of something other than petroleum.

Our enemies are also quick to point out that the sun goes down every day, that it can be obscured by clouds, and that sometimes the wind doesn't blow. For example, a Heartland Institute policy expert writes, "Wind and solar are unreliable intermittent, weather dependent sources that can't be scheduled to provide power when needed most."[17] This is not a serious argument. Just as manna could be gathered on the sixth day to save up for the seventh, we know how to save what we gather when the wind blows and the sun shines. Batteries and heat storage systems can store and distribute energy.[18] Hydropower and geothermal power also offer important supplements that do not require extracting and burning and can back up solar and wind energy.

We know how to produce electricity without fossil fuels. Homes and buildings currently heated with natural gas can be switched over to heat pumps, which regulate temperature more efficiently without burning anything. The power plants that today burn thousands of tons of coal or methane can be retired and replaced with fields of solar panels and windmills. Workers in the fossil fuel industry can be trained to transition into a clean-energy economy, in healthier conditions that do not defile the atmosphere. This transition is possible, and it is vitally important.

So, too, is a rapid transition of transportation systems to electric power. Critics are right that the transportation to which privileged people are currently accustomed depends on fossil fuels. Most private cars still carry around their own supply of flammable gas. Jet travel requires fossil fuels. But we can live without these conveniences, and we can live better. Battery-powered cars are becoming more and more efficient. Even better are electric bicycles, buses, trains, and ships.

The binary presented by the fossil fuel industry—either we allow them to continue extracting fossil fuels, or we go without all technology created in the last two centuries—should remind us of the binary choice that Jesus's contemporaries were told they faced in the Roman Empire. Occupied people were taught they could either passively accept the empire's oppression or lose everything. Jesus offered the "third way" of upending power dynamics. He refused to accept only two options. Those of us concerned about climate change in the twenty-first century must similarly seek a third way for energy, refusing to accept that we either allow energy from hell or give up on lights, refrigerators, and hospital machinery.[19] God gives energy for all.

Political Transitions Away from Hoarding

Dan Erlander's second lesson from the story of manna in the wilderness is that, because God's world has enough for everyone's needs, no one should hoard. No one needs more than their share, and the system breaks when some take too much. Erlander traces the sin of hoarding throughout the villains and enemies of the Bible: Pharaoh's Egypt was based on stockpiling food; the Roman Empire was based on monopolizing power. Similarly, rich people in early Christian communities who refused to feed hungry neighbors were criticized for hoarding.

The same lesson applies to the fossil fuel industry. It hoards, and its hoarding defiles the atmosphere. This makes it the enemy of anyone who wants a just and cleaner future. The best path toward that future is for fossil fuels to be managed by democratic politics rather than for-profit corporations.

"Hoarding Stinks"

The business model of oil, methane, and coal corporations depends on stockpiling resources, consolidating ownership, and using that consolidation to control prices. As discussed in chapter 4, these companies actively campaigned against renewable energies and declined to invest in them even after the realities of atmospheric defilement were undeniable. A 2023 report from the International Energy Association revealed that less than 1 percent of global investment in clean energy comes from oil and gas companies. The Agency concludes that "oil and gas companies are watching energy transitions from the sidelines."[20] But even that analysis is too charitable. These companies' minuscule investments in solar and wind power are far outweighed by their extensive lobbying for and enormous expenditures on continued extraction of fossil fuels. They are not on the sidelines; they are the opposition, competing against clean energy. They are resisting the transition, protecting their hoarded power and wealth.

The most literal hoarding comes in stockpiles of oil, methane, and coal. These materials are incredibly expensive to extract, and so only the already rich and powerful can afford to claim them. They then sell what they dig up at a premium, increasing their wealth. They also work to manipulate the price of their product, holding back what they own when the price is lower than they want. The fossil fuel industry is based on, and requires, hoarding.

In fact, the net worth of fossil fuel companies is calculated in part based on their "proven reserves" of their product found but still buried under the earth's surface. In 2023, the Organization of the Petroleum Exporting Countries (OPEC) estimated there were over 1.5 trillion barrels of proven oil reserves globally and over 200 trillion cubic meters of methane.[21] An earlier report from the US Energy Information Administration estimated the world's reserves include 1.1 trillion short tons of coal.[22] These are stockpiled resources. While they are currently underground, they are claimed by fossil fuel companies as property, as profit waiting to be made.

If those reserves are extracted and burned, they will further defile the atmosphere. One study suggests that for even a 50 percent chance of limiting global warming to 1.5°C, over half the proven reserves of oil and gas and 90 percent of coal must remain where it is.[23] These materials should not be treated as hoarded wealth but as a part of the natural world best left undisturbed. As it currently exists, the fossil fuel industry is not equipped to make such a transition. It is devoted to profit above all else and so can only consider methane, oil, and coal as economic resources.

The story of manna in the wilderness teaches that "hoarding stinks," that those who take more than they need and hide it away cause trouble for the entire community. A resource that is stockpiled "brings rot, decay, and death." It defiles the atmosphere. Furthermore, when energy from heaven is available, hoarding is unnecessary. The sun, wind, and water provide enough to meet everyone's needs. A just and healthy future requires more sharing, less hoarding.

The fossil fuel Powers could be part of this change. They are participants in God's creation; they have always had the potential to bring good into the world. Their most fundamental mission—to provide energy that helps humanity thrive—is noble and worthwhile. But they have fallen; they seek profit and domination instead of community and justice. The industry would have to change dramatically to be part of a manna society.

Walter Wink writes, "The goal is not only becoming free *from* the Powers, however, but *freeing* the Powers; not only reconciling people to God despite the Powers, but reconciling the Powers to God."[24] It is hard to imagine freeing and redeeming fossil fuel companies, but the theology of the Powers encourages us to try.

Such reconciliation would mean that fossil fuel companies turn their attention to building loving connection rather than profiting from domination. They would have to enthusiastically embrace not only a genuine and rapid transition away from fossil fuel energy but also a dramatic global phase-out of all fossil fuel extraction. They would need to stop paying people to insist that technology is impossible without their product and instead genuinely invest their vast resources into innovative substitutes for oil, methane, and coal.

In the report cited above, the International Energy Agency suggests that fossil fuel companies could use the expertise they have developed to reverse their process of extraction, building and operating machines that capture CO_2 from the atmosphere and bury it underground. If this was an actual substitute for extraction and burning—rather than merely a way to excuse the continued use of fossil fuels—it would contribute to a healthier world. Fossil fuel companies also have drilling and exploration expertise that could assist with geothermal energy, pulling heat from deep underground in far more renewable and less destructive ways than the extraction of fossil fuels.[25]

The fossil fuel industry can be redeemed; it can be reformed to exist without hoarding. But it will require that these companies fundamentally change, that their spiritual Powers genuinely repent and convert to a different and better purpose.

Making Fossil Fuels Political

Sociologist Holly Jean Buck argues that the most plausible scenario for such a change would be for fossil fuel companies to be controlled by democratic governments: "What we need to do with the fossil fuel industry is put it under public ownership."[26] Government is, at least potentially, equipped to focus on the common good rather than profit, to see fossil fuels as something other than a resource to hoard.

Former US Department of Energy official William Becker also advocates that the US government take control of fossil fuel companies. He argues, "The government has nationalized strategically many times when it was necessary, most recently to rescue the savings and loan industry in 1989 and to bail out banks, investment houses, insurers, and the US auto industry in 2008. Political leaders considered these industries 'too big to fail.' Now the Earth and civilization itself are too big to fail."[27]

Becker argues the federal government could afford to buy controlling ownership of ExxonMobil, Chevron, and ConocoPhillips and could then use that interest to "do what's best for humanity" rather than for private shareholders. At present, those companies' "mission is to make profits for shareholders," and so they hoard fossil fuels. Decisions about when and whether to extract resources should, instead, be in the hands of the government, whose mission is to serve citizens.[28]

As I write, this seems like a distant possibility. Few democratic governments in the wealthy world are interested in nationalizing oil companies or treating fossil fuels as something other than a profit source. In fact, most nations with privatized energy companies offer subsidies, incentivizing continued exploration and extraction. In 2022, the International Monetary Fund estimated governments across the world subsidized the fossil fuel industry with $1.2 trillion.[29] Furthermore, there are democratic nations with nationalized oil companies—Norway, in particular—that continue to extract and export oil and gas at ever-increasing rates.

So politics will also need to be reformed. Politicians will need to be willing to tell people hard truths about the importance of phasing out fossil fuels, they will need to lead bold action toward a better world. Citizens will need to defend democratic institutions and vote based on hope for what can be rather than fear of change. The myth of individualism, which teaches people they do not need governments, will have to be soundly rejected.

In other words, the spiritual Powers of the nations will need to be redeemed. This will not be easy, but it is more plausible than a reform of the profit-obsessed Powers of fossil fuel companies. Governments can do better than they are doing. The Powers of private corporations that extract and sell energy from hell have fallen too far; they are too corrupted to be left to their own devices. Other Powers must direct them, and the Powers of democratic governance are our best hope.

In 2023, Pope Francis released *Laudato Deum*, an apostolic exhortation on climate change written primarily to influence COP28 negotiations in Dubai. In it, he insisted that the best available responses to climate change require good governance. He called for a "framework for effective cooperation" that is truly "multilateral," making binding agreements between nations in a way that is both more open and more influential than the current process. He hoped that government leaders would come together in "spaces for conversation, consultation, arbitration, conflict resolution, and supervision, and, in the end, a sort of increased 'democratization'" of decisions about climate justice. That democratic process should, he argued, lead to agreements for an "efficient, obligatory and readily monitored" energy transition. Such "drastic, intense action" is, he suggested, the only way the international community can "recover its credibility."[30]

I suspect the pope was not satisfied with the result of the negotiations at COP28. But he was also probably not surprised. Inherent in his argument is the assumption that, up to now, the world's political leaders have failed to respond adequately and justly to climate change. People in government too often focus on short-term profits rather than long-term sustainability, so most countries continue to subsidize fossil fuels despite the clear evidence of atmospheric defilement. Our politics as it currently exists is inadequate.

But Pope Francis did not give up on politics. He continued to advocate for democratic negotiation and multilateral work across nations. He insisted a more open, binding, and effective global politics is possible. He insisted the energy transition depends on genuine cooperation among the world's nations.

Similarly, the activists discussed in the previous chapter of this book all expressed deep frustration with politics, but nevertheless continued to work for political change. 350.org organized to increase the number of people voting for, advocating, and prioritizing climate across the world. The Sunrise Movement appealed even more directly to democratically elected leaders. Even Jessica Reznicek and Ruby Montoya, despite deep disillusionment with their government's failure to stop the Dakota Access Pipeline, turned themselves in with the hope of exposing the problem and thereby inspiring change. As she was being handcuffed, Reznicek said the Iowa Utilities Board "needs to start protecting the people of Iowa, not the oil."[31] Her hope was for better government, more democratic processes.

Using the language Walter Wink has taught us, we can see these activists and Pope Francis are committed to redeeming the Powers of government. The failure of our collective institutions, the lack of a sufficient democratic response to the problem of climate change, does not mean government should be abandoned. Democratic governments are not our enemies. They are imperfect; the spirits that animate them are fallen. But commitment and work from their citizens, from those with influence, can strengthen the best aspects of these Powers.

There will always be reasons to be cynical about politics. It will always be tempting to tune out the next election or wave our hands and insist the system is too broken to do any good. When we do this, we allow corrupting forces to retain control of our political systems and stifle our hopes for the future. The fossil fuel industry has spent decades arguing against government action precisely because it knows that government could meaningfully disrupt their status quo. We can call our governing institutions to do exactly that, to live up to their mission of building a better future for all.[32]

Those of us privileged enough to have the right to vote, to have voices that political leaders listen to, can use our power. We can remind democratic institutions of their purpose; we can insist they prioritize renewable energy and climate justice. Those of us with time can volunteer for political campaigns or protest movements that influence politicians. Those of us with leadership skills should consider service in public office. When we lose these struggles, we can mourn and lament, and then we can strategize about how to build stronger coalitions and get back to work.

Politician Kate Knuth gives language for this by suggesting people in the twenty-first century should understand ourselves as "climate citizens," committed to action as full members of our local communities, our nations, and the earth as a whole: "At its core, citizenship is a sacred trust between the individual and collective. As we face the climate crisis, this trust—and how we understand and act on it—is more critical than ever."[33] Citizenship means we are part of the institutions that shape our lives and that we can shape those institutions through our participation. Citizenship means we can shape the Powers of our political systems, helping renew the energy within them toward collaboration and community.

Cultural Transitions

Meaningful technological and political change is only possible if people in the industrialized world change the ways we relate to energy. The fossil fuel industry has not only defiled the atmosphere but also taught us to understand energy as something that should be available to anyone who can afford it, at any time, for any reason. It has taught those of us who can afford energy to want evermore.[34] So, theologian Terra Rowe argues, an energy transition requires cultural change, "alternative embodied, affective, habitual energies that can, in turn, inform the kinds of technologies, sciences, and energy systems pursued."[35]

I argued in chapter 2 that culture is shaped by myths, by stories that express deep truths about the world and human nature. Many industrialized cultures are currently animated by myths of domination, which all insist the world cannot be fundamentally different than it is. These dangerous myths teach us that we will always need, and deserve, ever-more energy.

When the advocates of fossil fuels suggest that oil, methane, and coal are essential to human civilization, that the alternative to extraction and burning is to go "back into the caves," that people should keep using more energy and more plastic, they demonstrate the myth of infinite expansionism. They assume that if their profits do not grow, everything will fall apart. When they insist that greed is the only way to motivate people, they demonstrate the myth of individualism. When they refuse to accept responsibility for the ways their resistance to change exacerbates atmospheric defilement, they demonstrate the myth of exceptionalism.

For culture to change, people need better myths. This book has focused on one, the myth of the Powers, which offers language for naming our enemies, taking on those enemies without embracing their bad habits of domination, and believing that every part of God's good world can be redeemed. However, in a diverse and pluralistic world, one myth will never be enough. We need many myths to guide many people forward in the direction of justice and health.

"The Gift of Sabbath"

Manna in the wilderness is another powerful myth for cultural transformation. The third lesson Dan Erlander draws from the story, about sabbath, demonstrates how this myth contrasts with the Domination System and points to a new kind of hope.

Sabbath is often thought of as an individual choice, with people deciding to take a day off or to regularly focus on worship in their religious community. But the sabbath tradition of the book of Exodus was bigger than one day per week and bigger than any one person or community. The "gift of sabbath," the truth that human beings do not need to work every day to survive, is revolutionary and liberative. The truth at the heart of sabbath is not about what people cannot do but what is possible: God has made a world not only with enough to go around but with enough for people to rest, enjoy, and relax in community with one another and other creatures.

Biblical scholar Richard Lowery argues that the story of manna in the wilderness suggests a "sabbath economics," a worldview that "overturns modern assumptions of scarcity and unlimited needs and wants." He emphasizes that the sabbath tradition in the text is about not just taking one day off each week but also allowing land and animals to rest every seventh year, preventing the abuse of the nonhuman world. Sabbath also means tempering our list of what we "need" to survive, living more simply so that hoarding is unnecessary. Along these lines, the Bible also includes sabbath customs of canceling debts every seventh or forty-ninth year and so preventing the hoarding of wealth over time.[36]

The Hebrew Bible's sabbath traditions are an explicit reaction against slavery and domination.[37] In contrast to the Domination System that exploits people for their labor, the sabbath tradition celebrates the chance to be part of a community without always having to earn one's keep or prove one's worth. In contrast to the System that insists human beings exist outside of the natural world's rules, sabbath celebrates a harmonious cooperation that includes time for every creature to rest and heal. In contrast to individualistic competitions that pit people against one another, sabbath asserts a level of equality: all God's creations deserve enough to eat and a break from work.

Industrialized societies have spent centuries hoarding fossil fuel wealth based on assumptions that there is not enough to go around, that unceasing extraction from the nonhuman world has no costs, that some people deserve more than others. The myth of manna in the wilderness insists another world is possible. There is enough, hoarding is counterproductive, everyone deserves a way to gather what they need and to rest.

When critics suggest "civilization" is not possible without fossil fuels, they demonstrate a failure of imagination. The important parts of life as we know it can continue with new technologies and better politics. If done well, the world we transition into will be more just and healthier than the one we live in now.

It is possible, as advocates of fossil fuel companies insist, that a world without oil will find no viable substitutes for jet fuel and plastic. In that case, we will need to learn to travel a bit more slowly, though trains and ships can still cover long distances very quickly. We may have to learn to live with fewer disposable and cheap objects in our lives. But these changes are conceivable. We could all find ways to thrive in a world with less plastic and fewer jets. The sabbath offers a model of this, insisting the world does not fall apart if we pause to take a breath, slow the pace of life, and focus on what people truly need.

The sabbath tradition insists the civilization we want is not defined by hoarding, extraction, and exploitation. God's people in the wilderness could not gather as much manna as they wanted whenever they wanted. But there was enough for all when it was responsibly collected and shared. Similarly, we do not need access to unlimited energy. If we all take only what will get us through each day, allowing for rest, there will be enough to go around.

The story of manna in the wilderness offers an ideal and a hope. Since it is included in the sacred texts of Muslims, Jews, and Christians, I hope many people can embrace its hope that the world has enough for all, that hoarding is destructive, and that rest is a basic right. Those of us who believe in a God who ensured that refugees in the wilderness would not starve should also believe that God will make a bright future possible as industrialized civilization transitions away from fossil fuels.

Myths of Transition

In a diverse world, the myth of manna in the wilderness and the myth of the Powers will not work for everyone. This is okay. Myths unite communities, but the response to atmospheric defilement requires coalitions of many communities, motivated by many stories. If we can identify common hopes that unite our stories and communities, the diversity of human stories and myths is a strength that builds and empowers coalitions.

The story of manna in the wilderness offers one myth of transition. It tells the story of a people going through a deeply challenging time, freeing themselves from an oppressive enemy, and finding their way to a better future. It is not a perfect story, in part because the book of Exodus goes on to recount the community's achieving the land "promised" to them by violently taking it from other people.[38] But no story is perfect, and we can work to interpret our myths in ways that help us avoid such domination going forward.

Those of us who value the story of manna in the wilderness can tell it to others who come from other communities. We can offer interpretations to express our beliefs and hopes for humanity and the energy transition. Then we can ask about the stories and myths that help them imagine just transitions toward a better future.

As discussed above, Muslim organizer Ibrahim Abdul-Matin applied imagery and principles from the Qur'an to argue for a sustainable future. A core idea in his work, quoted from the Prophet Muhammad, was that "the Earth is a Mosque" and can, if people learn to act with discipline, be respected as such.[39] Buddhist activist Joanna Macy frequently appeals to stories from her tradition about "turning the wheel of the Dharma" and characterizes the reality of climate change as a "Great Turning" that can be embraced and celebrated even as people also honor the pain and fear that come with transition.[40] Penobscot Lawyer and teacher Sherri Mitchell draws on the creation stories of her Indigenous tradition to insist all living beings can learn to live in balance with the earth and one another.[41] Physicist Kate Marvel demonstrates that we can develop new myths, using the tropes of a fairy tale in a story about dragons that advocates limiting global warming to 1.5°C.[42] These are all myths of transition.

As we share these stories and find intersections and connections among them, we build and strengthen coalitions. Celebrating our different ideas while building on our commonalities, we make democratic change possible. We strengthen and affirm the Powers that seek to knit the world together in justice.

Hope in Transition

If future generations of human beings are to thrive on earth, industrialized cultures need to transition away from domination toward community. This is possible. Those of us who care about climate change can build global coalitions that support renewable energy, oppose the hoarding of fossil fuels, and respect the rights of all to live, thrive, and rest. These coalitions are the best way to advocate that future international meetings about climate change take bolder stances and more decisive action against atmospheric defilement. Coalitions can reform nations so that they will hold the fossil fuel industry accountable. Coalitions can find the way toward a world that completely phases out the extraction of oil, methane, and coal.

Imagining a world where people come together this way upends Pogo's suggestion that each of us is "the enemy." We are not the enemy. We are all potential allies. Essayist Mary Annaïse Heglar puts this well: "Yes it's true that you can't solve the climate crisis alone, but it's even more true that we can't solve it without you. It's a team sport."[43] Solutions come when people ban together, when we use stories and politics and every other tool available to create communities focused on justice and equality.

7

THE INNER WORK OF CLIMATE RESISTANCE

IN THE GOSPEL of Luke, Jesus tells the story of a family tested to the breaking point. A father had two sons, and the younger asked for his inheritance early. Once he got it, he left the family, with no apparent intention to ever return. This son was prodigal; he "traveled to a distant country, and there he squandered his property in dissolute living." When a famine struck his new home, the son found himself broke and hungry, but "no one gave him anything." He began to long for the abundance of his father's house. After contemplation, "he came to himself," deciding to return and apologize to his father. He planned to request a job as a servant, but before he could, his father saw him and "was filled with compassion; he ran and put his arms around him and kissed him."

The father called on the entire household to celebrate his son's return, but one refused to join. The prodigal son's older brother angrily told his father that he was hurt. He had never been celebrated, even though he stayed and worked hard. The father replied, "Son, you are always with me, and all that is mine is yours. But we had to celebrate and rejoice, because this brother of yours was dead and has come to life; he was lost and has been found" (Luke 15:11–32).

This is a story of selfishness, migration, overconsumption, environmental disaster, remorse, reconciliation, and frustration. I find a lot to relate to in each of its three characters. Like the prodigal son, I have felt bad about my wasteful and foolish choices, and I have been scared to face people I have hurt. Like the older brother, I have felt self-righteous, jealous, and angry when others don't seem to be punished enough for mistakes I avoided. And, at my best moments, I have known how the father must have felt, swept up by compassion and love even for people who have caused me pain.

This parable offers a way to reflect on three emotional responses to atmospheric defilement. Guilt, anger, and mercy are all important in climate resistance; naming and working through them gives us the internal energy we need for the external work of resisting atmospheric defilement. Those of us who feel guilty that our actions contribute to climate change can use that feeling to return to better relationships with others and with the planet's systems. Those of us who feel anger at people and institutions that exacerbate atmospheric defilement can use this energy to demand a better world. Finally, and most importantly, all of us who have glimpsed the deep pain and injustice of our world can strive to react with compassionate mercy.

Previous chapters have outlined actions we might take in response to atmospheric defilement. We can advocate for political and cultural transitions, working against fossil fuels and for a world where energy is shared widely. We can join coalitions of nonviolent protest, political organizing, and creative resistance. We can resist the Powers of fossil fuel companies, name their failures, and devote ourselves to building better, more inclusive, and more sustainable systems. These examples of "outer work" are only possible if we have the inner strength to sustain ourselves. So this chapter focuses on the self-awareness and emotional attention we need to keep resisting.

The activist and teacher Parker Palmer argues that people who want to work for a better world need to acknowledge and address the "shadows" in our own minds and hearts, emotions that can hurt us and limit our effectiveness if they are left unacknowledged. He writes, "Inner work is as real as outer work, and involves skills one can develop. . . . If people skimp on their inner work, their outer work will suffer as well."[1] The "shadows" of our emotions will teach us important lessons if we bring them into the light, work through them, and use them as energy for the vital outer work of climate resistance.[2]

The Guilt of the Prodigal Son

In a Lenten sermon from 2019, Episcopal priest and climate activist Margaret Bullitt-Jonas suggests the prodigal son as a model for industrialized society. He took his inheritance from his father and spent it selfishly and carelessly. Similarly, we have extracted fossil fuels from the earth that gave us life, consuming energy and emitting gases with little regard for the costs to other people and the rest of life. He spent his inheritance incautiously, with no regard for the future. We, too, have been prodigal, believing in the myth of infinite expansionism and ignoring the needs and fears of future generations. He began to pay the price for his shortsightedness, unprepared for tough times and surrounded by strangers who gave him no help. Like him, Bullitt-Jonas writes, industrialized societies have "wandered far in a land that is waste," pulling away from the communities and connections that can support us in tough times.

Having made this comparison, Bullitt-Jonas then finds hope in the fact that the prodigal son "came to himself" and felt remorse for his mistakes. She writes, "He broke through the spell, he remembered who he was: created in love, created for love—love for himself and his neighbor, love for the natural world, and love for God. When we come to ourselves, when we are truly ourselves, we begin the journey home to God."

Like the prodigal son, those of us who live in industrial societies can "come to ourselves." We can recognize that "we don't have to settle for a death-dealing, materialistic society that willy-nilly gobbles up all the land and trees and creatures of this world [and] extracts and burns dirty fossil fuels."[3] We can reject myths of domination and instead return home to the community of life that has always nurtured us and all of humanity. "Coming to ourselves" means living into the loving and just harmony at the roots of creation. It means committing ourselves to redeemed Powers, to systems that serve the loving connections God intended for the world rather than the separation and violence of the Domination System.

But we are not there yet. Living in a world of fallen powers, we must also admit that our actions are complicit; we participate in the dominating failures of our societies. All of us who participate in industrialized society contribute to atmospheric defilement. All of us with a measure of privilege and wealth use an unjust and unsustainable share of earth's resources. In the United States, where I write this, the average person in 2021 was responsible for emitting 19 tons of climate-changing gases. Aside from a brief reduction during the COVID-19 pandemic, this number has continued to rise in recent years, despite increasing technological efficiencies and growing awareness of climate injustice. Those of us in the United States who eat beef support a cattle industry that releases 139 million metric tons of such gases each year. Those of us who drive cars contribute to over a billion metric tons of emissions each year. Those of us who fly in planes are helping to emit another 120 million metric tons.[4] Our actions are part of the problem.

So far, this book has sought to move attention away from individual guilt. In the introduction, I suggested that my student who felt "a lot of anxiety about my own actions and measuring how 'good' of a person I am based on if I recycle" could benefit by focusing on the dominating system of the fossil fuel industry rather than her own small choices. The argument I have been trying to make ever since is that this student, you, and I are not the enemy. Guilt should not distract us from the fact that the fossil fuel industry sets up systems that constrain our actions, putting just and sustainable ways of life virtually out of our reach.

Climate activists Luisa Neubauer and Alexander Repenning make a similar case, arguing that "green guilt" at the individual level is a sign of the distraction created by the fossil fuel industry: "People, no matter what age, should not have to constantly be faced with a decision between products and services that are rarely compatible with human rights and ecological standards, or those that protect the basis of life for future generations." While we struggle with those decisions, they write, "the industry carries on quite undisturbed, using the increased environmental awareness for new outlets for products."[5] It is the fossil fuel industry that should be disturbed and disrupted, not us.

Some people, naming this systemic injustice, move on from "green guilt," leaving behind concerns about individual behaviors and focusing attention on structural change. This is admirable. But others of us still feel guilt. Even as we know that we are not the real source of the problem, we lament our participation in the Domination System.

When we feel such guilt, we need ways to process it. Ethicist Sarah Fredericks has written the definitive work on this topic: *Environmental Guilt and Shame.* She begins by carefully distinguishing between these two emotions. Guilt is a judgment that our actions and those of our society are wrong, while shame is a judgment that we and/or our societies are inherently flawed. She encourages readers to pay careful attention to both feelings, to recognize that "our emotions help us know the world and ourselves and, indeed, help us become who we are. Guilt and shame are some of the many appropriate reactions to anthropogenic environmental degradation including climate change, because individuals and collectives have done and are doing horrible things to each other, other biota, and ecosystems that will have effects long after we stop the actions."[6]

Attending to our guilt and shame helps us understand our involvement with what is happening in the world. It is also a way to build connections with others who share our emotions. Those of us seeking coalitions of resistance have much to gain from naming our negative emotions and reaching out to others who share them. We can also learn from religious communities about rituals and practices that help us process these emotions.[7]

Fredericks notes, however, that shame is dangerous; it is very difficult to make something positive out of a shameful judgment against one's very identity. It is one thing to call our actions, and the actions of others, wrong; it is a different and more troubling thing to call ourselves or others fundamentally wrong.[8] Shame is less constructive than guilt, harder to turn into energy for positive action. So those of us who feel shame will benefit if we can transform it into guilt, focusing on the fact that our actions have been problematic rather than viewing our very selves as the problem.

The parable of the prodigal son offers a model. When he recognizes his wrongdoing, the son practices what he will say to apologize: "Father, I have sinned against heaven and before you. I am no longer worthy to be called your son." He admits guilt here—naming his actions as wrong—and expresses shame, deeming himself no longer worthy. But before he can even speak, his father rejects the shame, immediately identifying him as "this son of mine." The guilt is allowed to stand, but the shame is overwhelmed by love. The prodigal son has done wrong, but he is not wrong in his very being. Indeed, it was "coming to himself" that allowed him to see his mistakes and seek reconciliation. Guilt brought him back to his father, who encouraged him to move past his shame. He must still deal with the consequences of his actions, but those actions do not make him unworthy of love. His father accepts him, no matter what.

Some of us feel shame about atmospheric defilement. Having recognized that our actions are complicit in the defilement of the atmosphere, the suffering of our neighbors, and the degradation of future generations, we worry that the flaw is basic to our very being. We worry that having been born into a broken system, we ourselves are fundamentally broken. We can learn from this shame about the depth of the problem, about the ways we and so many others feel trapped in the Domination System. But we should be cautious not to let this be the only story we tell about ourselves. We are not defined by complicity; we are not the enemy.

Brené Brown writes that shame "thrives on secrecy, silence, and judgment."[9] Those of us who feel shame about climate change should bring it into the open, talk about it, and find others with the same feelings. When the prodigal son presented himself to his father, he learned that he was still beloved. Christians should trust that this story reflects reality, that everyone is worthy of love. Everyone deserves the comfort of a community that accepts them for who they are.

Guilt is a potentially more constructive emotion. Moving past the idea that we are fundamentally complicit in the problem of climate change and therefore wrong, we should sit with the idea that our actions are complicit and we can do better. Such guilt can be a spur to positive action. If you eat meat or food grown far away, you can channel your guilt to find nutrition closer to home and lower on the food chain. If you drive a car, you can try to use it less and better support public transportation and bicycle infrastructure. If you live in an urban area, you can help plant trees to avoid the heat island effect that will become more dangerous as the world continues to warm. If you have considerable financial resources, you can divest from banks that make loans to fossil fuel projects and donate to groups working for systemic change. If you have the right to vote for your leaders, you can commit to supporting candidates who prioritize the challenges of climate change.[10]

If you have family, friends, and neighbors who are open to learning, you can talk to them more about atmospheric defilement. If you belong to a religious community, you can encourage its leaders to teach and advocate for climate justice. If you live in a relatively safe and prosperous place, you can prepare your community to be open and accepting to new members as other areas of the world become more dangerous. Any of these actions could help those of us who feel guilty to see that change is possible, that we are capable of better and less complicit actions.

But none of these actions will solve the problem because we are not the enemy. Those of us who participate in industrialized societies cannot, in the world as it exists today, stop atmospheric defilement. We live in systems that depend on fossil fuels and fossil fuel corporations, and the only way to stop that is to change those systems. The enemy is the Domination System that structures so much of our lives. Our guilt and our shame must be tempered by this incontrovertible fact: we did not create that system, and we do not control it.

The Danger and Power of Anger

The more we see the limits of our guilt and shame, the more likely we will be to feel angry at destructive systems and at people with more power to change those systems than ourselves. And so we must also process and use our anger.

There are many reasons to be angry. The fossil fuel industry continues to prodigally extract and use up the earth's resources, ignoring the dangers they create and the hurt they cause. An estimate in the journal *Nature Medicine* suggests that four million human deaths will have been caused by climate change by the end of 2024.[11] The Intergovernmental Panel on Climate Change reports that almost half of coastal wetlands have been lost in the last hundred years and that 14 percent of species on earth are likely to face extinction at even the lowest levels of anticipated warming in the future.[12]

It is difficult to make sense of numbers like these, but we do not need to fully process them intellectually to feel angry about them. And we may grow even angrier when we remember that these negative impacts are felt most by communities and ecosystems that contribute the least to the problem and that most political leaders who have had access to these facts for decades are still doing very little in response.

In a 2021 study of ten thousand young people, 83 percent were identified as angry about climate change, considerably more than were identified as anxious or sad.[13] A study by Australian psychologists argued this could be a positive development as they determined that anger is "a uniquely adaptive response to the climate crisis," a key "emotional driver of engagement." Anger, they argued, can motivate people to engage solutions to climate change. They encourage those who advocate for climate action to "rely on anger-based messaging."[14]

Those of us who learn from the Christian tradition also have good reasons to recognize and utilize our anger. In the Gospel of Matthew, Jesus expresses his anger by repeatedly calling the enemies of his ministry "vipers" (3:7, 12:34, 23:33). When he saw people turning

God's temple into a marketplace, he turned over their tables and yelled at them. He was angry, and his anger was part of his good work in the world.[15] In a classic text of Christian ethics, Beverly Harrison insists that such anger is a "work of love, a mode of connectiveness to others and it is always a vivid form of caring."[16] When we feel angry about atmospheric defilement, we are reminded that we care; we marshal the energy we need to oppose our enemies.

The older brother in Jesus's parable has reason to be angry. He feels taken for granted, while his wasteful brother is celebrated. It is not fair. But we do not know how the older brother processes that feeling; we meet him and leave him in the same state of anger. Jesus's story leaves the older brother bitter and refusing to participate in the celebration. His father encourages him to change his mind and join the party, but does he? Does he move through his feelings or remain stuck in them? Two possible answers to this question reveal the danger and the power of anger in the climate movement.

Avoiding Destructive Anger

Perhaps the rift between the two brothers was too deep, and the eldest remained angry and deepened the division his brother had created. Perhaps the older brother held his anger more closely than he held his brother and father for the rest of his life. Anger can do that; it can pull communities apart by hardening even those of us with legitimate grievances into inflexibility. Anger can make people more individualistic and greedier, less open to finding and building connections.

It is important for those of us who feel angry about climate change to know that our anger could become divisive and destructive. We can become so frustrated with the institutions defiling the atmosphere and the people who support them that we enter the logic of the Domination System, seeking to control or destroy those who make us angry. We end up hoping for our enemies to lose rather than for their redemption.

There are important lessons to learn from horrific and extreme versions of such warped anger. In 2019, a heavily armed man invaded two mosques in Christchurch, New Zealand, killing fifty-one people and injuring many others. He targeted Muslims because he believed in a fundamental civilizational conflict between those he deemed "white" and the rest of the world. In his manifesto, he called himself an "eco-fascist" and claimed that by "killing the invaders," he was helping to "save the environment." Later the same year, another shooter targeted Hispanic people in El Paso, killing twenty-three. He cited inspiration from the Christchurch shooter after writing, "The environment is getting worse by the year" and asserting that "if we can get rid of enough people, then our way of life can become more sustainable."[17] Both men bought into simplistic narratives of "overpopulation," which warps environmental concern into an assertion that people must compete for scarce resources, that there is not enough to go around. Both men used environmental rhetoric to endorse the anti-immigrant, anti-Islamic, anti-diversity, and ultimately antihuman sensibilities of what has come to be called the "great replacement theory."

These shooters were sick; their actions are utterly reprehensible. I make no attempt to fully explain the psychological and societal failures that allowed them to carry out such horrors. But those of us who are concerned about climate change and sustainability should pay attention to the way they used environmentalist language to justify hate and violence. We should note that these two shooters, and all too many who have moved in their direction, are angry at the state of the climate and use that anger to destroy other people and degrade human communities.[18]

A report from the Centre for Analysis of the Radical Right in the United Kingdom calls further attention to the growth of self-identified "eco-fascists" across the world. Even though far-right political movements often deny the reality of climate change, the stresses and fears of a changing world are nevertheless becoming part of those movements' narratives. Indeed, the Centre's report argues that the simplicity of climate denial—which refuses to accept the complexity of atmospheric defilement—can easily evolve into an insistence that there must be a simple answer to all environmental problems. Eco-fascists search for a familiar victim to blame for all degradation. Extremists "transmit the desire to do something" about climate change "into Islamophobic anti-immigrant fervor and ultraviolent pathology."[19]

The shooters in El Paso and Christchurch were, among other problems, desperate for an answer that felt simple. So they treated innocent people as their enemies. They were so blinded by anger that they believed they could eradicate these enemies and solve environmental problems. Their anger led them to accept and then take extreme actions based on simplistic stories.

By contrast, having enemies well means understanding the complexity of every conflict. Environmental degradation and injustice are not caused by one group of easily dismissed people; they are caused by a broad intersection of systems and historical trends. I hope and pray that no one reading this—and, indeed, no one anywhere—is ever tempted to shoot another person as a solution to atmospheric defilement. Such wanton cruelty and violence only make things worse. Defilement is not resolved by violence or domination.

I have argued that we should not name the people who work for fossil fuel companies as our enemies, focusing instead on the Powers of the fossil fuel industry. It is harder to dehumanize people when we recognize that they, like us, have been shaped by fallen systems. As Walter Wink writes, our human enemies are "also victims of the delusional system." So our anger is most productively directed at "the System itself rather than those who carry out its bidding."[20] When we direct our anger at individuals or groups of people, it becomes too easy to make them into scapegoats and forget their humanity. We fight among ourselves and forget the systemic forces at the root of the problem.

This does not mean we cannot be angry with individuals. Greedy CEOs, corrupt politicians, and family members who refuse to learn about atmospheric defilement will make us understandably upset. We should acknowledge those feelings when they come up. But we should also remind ourselves about the Powers influencing those people, the complex systems that spread domination and destruction. Those Powers are our true enemies, and they deserve even more of our anger and resistance.

We should use our anger, but we should never allow it to keep us from the communities that nourish and support us.

The Power of Righteous Anger

Perhaps, in a happier ending to Jesus's story, the older brother came around. In this version, he finds joy in reunion, realizing that his family is worth more than his legalistic sense of fairness. He accepts his brother's apology and learns to forgive. Perhaps his anger even allows him to help his brother through a process of repentance. And perhaps he is motivated to work for and with his father in a new way that doesn't lead to bitterness and resentment. In that version of the story, the older brother's anger was not only understandable, but also constructive.

In 2019, the climate movement was blessed with an incarnation of righteous anger when Swedish activist Greta Thunberg spoke to the UN General Assembly. She said, "People are suffering. People are dying. Entire ecosystems are collapsing. We are in the beginning of a mass extinction. And all you can talk about is money and fairy tales of eternal economic growth. How dare you!" She continued, "Your generation is failing us. But the young people are starting to understand betrayal. The eyes of all future generations are upon you. And if you choose to fail us, I say we will never forgive you."[21]

In a diary published later, Thunberg recounted the decision she made to express herself this way:

> *I've never been angry in public. I've barely even been angry at home. But this time I've decided that I have to make the most out of the speech. To address the United Nations General Assembly is something you probably only get to do once in your lifetime. So this is it. I need to say things I will be able to stand by for the rest of my life, so that I won't look back in*

> *60–70 years from now and regret that I didn't say enough, that I held back. So I chose to let my emotions take control.*[22]

Thunberg tapped into a vital resource for resisting atmospheric defilement. She captured the world's attention because many people resonated with her anger and frustration. Anger provides energy to those of us who want to protest when people lose their homes to floods but are turned away by neighbors who could afford to shelter them. Anger reminds us not to passively accept that rampant wildfires will destroy ecosystems and habitats and drive species to extinction. Anger helps us to focus on the fallenness of the Powers that structure our lives and to insist they can and should do better.[23]

Thunberg's honest anger also led her to point fingers directly at those she saw as most responsible for the climate crisis. At the United Nations, she told political leaders they were failing to serve their constituents. At the World Economic Forum in Davos, she told powerful and wealthy people that they were too invested in preserving the status quo. She referred to the common claim that all human beings share responsibility for climate change as "just another convenient lie," insisting "if everyone is guilty, then no one is to blame."[24]

These expressions of anger are constructive because they are not dismissive. Thunberg calls out those she sees as failing, but she makes it clear they can change. World leaders can still choose to respond to climate change. The wealthy investors at Davos can still choose to use their money constructively. Thunberg does not seem to have given up on those who made her angry. She wants them to do better; she wants them to listen to her and respond.

Thunberg's anger is also constructive because she has been honest with herself and others about it. Working through her angry feelings and being deliberate about deploying them helped her respond deftly when then-President Trump accused her in a 2019 tweet of having an "anger management" problem and suggested she should "go to a good old-fashioned movie with a friend."[25] In the context of

Thunberg's Asperger's diagnosis, this joke was ableist, characterizing Thunberg with the loneliness and volatility that are too often associated with the autism spectrum. But she responded with aplomb, wryly copying Trump's phrasing to criticize his anger months later at the results of the November 2020 election. She drew a contrast between her own righteous, self-aware anger and his less strategic emotional outbursts.

Most importantly, Thunberg's anger is constructive because she uses it to motivate action. She protests, writes, and advocates for a better world. She lives out what the radical poet and librarian Audre Lorde articulated decades before in a speech about the "Uses of Anger": "Anger expressed and translated into action in the service of our vision and our future is a liberating and strengthening act of clarification, for it is in the painful process of this translation that we identify who are our allies with whom we have grave differences, and who are our genuine enemies."[26]

Greta Thunberg demonstrates what it looks like to be angry with our enemies, and those who serve them, in constructive, healthy ways. She demonstrates how we can recognize our frustrations and use them to build rather than degrade community. She also demonstrates that anger can produce the energy needed for genuine, meaningful resistance. Those of us who want to work for climate justice have much to learn from her.

The Importance of Mercy in a World of Atmospheric Defilement

We also have much to learn from the father in Jesus's parable. He responds with compassion when he has every right to instead be judgmental. His son asked him to divide his property and then left the family to foolishly squander what he took. The father must have been sad and angry. When his son returned, the father had every right to reject him or treat him as he asked by hiring him as a servant. He had every right to test the honesty of his son's remorse before embracing him. But the father exercised none of those rights. Instead, he reacted as a loving parent, welcoming his son and spreading joy throughout his entire household.

Life on earth has always been challenging. Just to survive is often exhausting. Caring about others is stressful. No one's safety or health is ever guaranteed. Atmospheric defilement has increased this struggle, stress, and uncertainty for many of us, and it promises to increase them for all people in the future. It will be tempting, in the face of these challenges, to harden and close ourselves off. It will be tempting to hoard our resources for those closest to us and build walls to keep others away. It will be especially tempting to push away those who cause us harm or come from far away.

Jesus's parable offers a different response to hardship: welcoming others, sharing abundance, celebrating joys even amid hardship. This is possible for the prodigal son's father because he is merciful, because he chooses to embrace his son instead of—or perhaps before—chastising him. The father chooses to act on his love and happiness rather than his bitterness and pain.

Learning from this parable, those of us who care about atmospheric defilement should cultivate mercy and compassion toward all people, even for those who do not deserve it. We should learn to be merciful to ourselves, despite our imperfections. We should learn to be merciful to our neighbors, even when they exacerbate the injustices and causes of climate change. We should even aspire to be merciful to our enemies, to hope for their redemption. Perhaps most importantly, we should learn to be merciful to those in desperate need, driven from their homes by a changing climate and seeking refuge and assistance.

Our Neighbors, Ourselves, and Our Enemies

One of Jesus's most powerful moral teachings is that there are inherent connections among a person's relationships to themselves, to their neighbors, and to the divine. When asked about the most important commandment, he quoted two verses from the Hebrew Bible: "You shall love the Lord your God" and "You shall love your neighbor as yourself" (Mark 12:30–31).[27] Jesus consistently asserts that a person's relationship to God—the foundational force of love in the universe—is connected to their relationship with themselves and to the ways they relate to other people. All of these relationships, Jesus teaches, should be based in love.[28]

Such love calls Christians to extend mercy to ourselves and everyone else. It asks us to remember, when we are tempted to lash out at people who have failed us or broken the rules, that we have also occasionally failed and trespassed. When asked whether a woman caught in adultery should be stoned, Jesus paused thoughtfully and then said, "Let anyone among you who is without sin be the first to throw a stone at her." The accusers walked away, and Jesus declined to condemn the woman (John 8:7). He insisted that his God forgives, and so he called on his followers to forgive one another and their enemies. He insisted that God loves us even though we are not perfect, and so we should try to love others even when we inevitably learn they are not perfect either. With the father in the parable of the prodigal son as a template of what he means when he calls God "father," Jesus called followers to "be merciful, just as your Father is merciful" (Luke 6:36).

To care about climate change and recognize the reality of atmospheric defilement is to constantly see sin all around us. People do foolish, destructive things. Drivers who generally travel alone with very little cargo buy huge, gas-guzzling trucks. Political leaders consistently downplay the threat of climate change to justify their inadequate responses. Our fellow citizens continue to vote for candidates who deny the problem and make it worse. It is tempting to condemn these people, to wish ill on them. But Jesus advises us to love our neighbors despite their failings, to extend forgiveness to them just as we hope we will be forgiven when we fall short.

My own mercy is particularly tested by very wealthy people who fly on private jets for brief diversions. They burn an enormous amount of jet fuel and release incredible amounts of CO_2 for the sake of minor convenience. I have never been on a private jet. Using them seems not just selfish but ridiculously extravagant, so I feel angry at the people who consume resources so recklessly. But I fly on commercial planes a few times a year. That, too, consumes fuel and releases CO_2. I may be doing less damage than very rich vacationers on private jets, but there are many people in the world who will never buy a plane ticket and would see my flights as wildly extravagant. They would have every right to judge me for my choices, for my excess contribution to the defilement of our shared atmosphere. I hope those people, if they ever think of me, do so with mercy. With that hope, I get a little better at extending mercy to those flying in private jets.

Mercy is part of being in community. Anyone who has ever lived with another human being knows we must be willing to work around the imperfections of others, to forgive and move past at least small mistakes and slights. We also need to extend that openness to our neighbors if we want to live in communities resilient enough to manage the challenges of a changing climate. Bill McKibben writes, "When people ask me where they should move to be safe from climate change, I always tell them anyplace with a strong community. Neighbors were optional the past fifty years, but they'll be essential in the decades to come."[29] I would add only that such a community depends on mercy, on a willingness to continue working together even when we or our neighbors make mistakes.

Most of us will fail at being merciful sometimes. Even those of us who aspire to the deep compassion Jesus taught will find our limits. This is okay. If there are people we cannot forgive, or can forgive but cannot live in community with, we should be honest about that and find ways to move forward. We can focus our energy on the communities in which we can be merciful, and we can try to build communities that train us to become more merciful. We can try to channel our anger at the systems that make such mercy difficult.

Christian mercy teaches people not to make enemies too casually. It reminds us not to dismiss others who are trapped in destructive systems simply because they have made different choices or had different opportunities. It keeps us focused on our real enemies: the fallen Powers of the fossil fuel industry and others that depend on and feed domination and defilement.

Ultimately, mercy can extend even to the Powers themselves. Knowing they were created for and are capable of goodness means we can continue to hope for their redemption too. We can hope that they will become better, that they will help to build a world that makes it easier for people to be good. Walter Wink insists that God wants the redemption of all people and systems: "We must pray for our enemies, because somewhere within them is a profound longing to become synchronized with the divine Source of us both. And deep within them, the Source is trying to stir up the desire to be just."[30]

As discussed in the last chapter, this even includes hope for a redeemed fossil fuel industry. Calling those Powers our enemy does not mean we give up on them. Instead, we hope for their transformation; we hope they can become what the world needs, that they can provide sustainable power and support healthy communities and ecosystems. But we must be clear about how far the fossil fuel industry has fallen from this ideal, how far they are today from their potential to serve the loving community of creation. Our enemies deserve both our mercy and our honesty.

Mercy for Climate Migrants[31]

The inner work of mercy matters to each of us as individuals. It also matters to the world because only those of us who have cultivated our mercy will be ready to compassionately welcome our neighbors in need.

As I write in early 2024, one of the most prominent topics in the political discourse of the United States is immigration. There is widespread agreement among political leadership that thousands of people who would like to enter this nation through the southern border are a problem. Phrases like "out of control," and "chaos," and "flood of migrants" are being used repeatedly to characterize the issue. Human beings are being casually and dismissively referred to as "illegals."

This discourse too rarely acknowledges that every person seeking to cross the border is a human being, a neighbor whom the Christians among us are called to treat with loving mercy. Politicians too rarely ask their constituents to reflect on the fact that people fleeing their homes and leaving their families must have good reasons to do so. In the immigration debate as it stands, it is easy for most of us to act like the older brother in the parable of the prodigal son, to insist that those trying to join our community have no right to be here, that we deserve to keep all our resources to ourselves.

Another thing rarely mentioned in public discourse about immigration is that much of it is driven by climate change. Migrants come to the United States from southern Mexico because of mudslides that wash their homes and livelihoods away, a phenomenon becoming more likely as the atmosphere changes.[32] They come from El Salvador, Guatemala, and Honduras because of long-standing droughts there, exacerbated by global warming.[33] They come from Venezuela because of political unrest driven partly by the concentrated power of fossil fuel income.[34] Many immigrants are motivated by the defilement of the atmosphere in their countries of origin, changes that—when combined with other political and economic factors—make it hard for them to care for their families. Most seek entry into the United States—which has contributed far more than any of their home countries to the problem of atmospheric defilement—simply to make a living.

Of course, the United States is not the only country seeing increased immigration as the world warms. Rising sea levels are pushing people off islands in the Pacific, floods are driving people from their homes in South Asia, and droughts are increasing migration across West Africa. While there is no reliable estimate of the number migrants driven by climate change each year, it is in the millions, and it is growing.[35] In 2020, over 80 percent of refugees and asylum seekers on the planet were fleeing from countries that the United Nations' High Commissioner on Refugees has identified as having the highest vulnerability to climate change, up from 60 percent ten years before.[36] Climate migration is a growing phenomenon, and no discussion of immigration, or immigration policy, is complete without taking it into account.

One danger of these statistics is that they will inspire fear and division rather than mercy and openness. In his book *Storming the Wall: Climate Change, Migration, and Homeland Security*, journalist Todd Miller chronicles the many ways wealthy countries are preparing for increased climate change by tightening borders and restricting migration. He predicts that "one of the most reliable forecasts for our collective future is that vast numbers of people will be on the move, and vast numbers of agents will be trained, armed, and paid to stop them."[37] This may be true, but I hope that Christians—who seek to love their neighbors and to follow the merciful example of the prodigal son's father—will resist the walls, will work to welcome neighbors in need. Christians should be advocating that their nations, towns, and communities help as many climate migrants as possible rather than keeping them out.

There is international debate about how to refer to migrants who flee climate disasters and seek more sustainable livelihoods in a changing world. Some advocates argue that these migrants should be understood as "climate refugees," seeking sanctuary from danger and deserving the same protections as refugees who flee political persecution.[38] Others argue that the term *refugee* has an important existing political meaning and should not be stretched to include environmental concerns. The latter group frequently also points out that even those currently labeled *refugees* are not consistently given the asylum and support they deserve under international law.[39]

I am less interested in this terminology than in the fact that every person who is driven from home by climate change is, in Christian terms, my neighbor. Every one deserves as much love and as much mercy as I would hope to be shown in their situation. For people who are currently privileged, responding to climate migrants begins with the inner work of cultivating mercy.

The United States and other wealthy nations are complicit in the forces causing climate migration. We have emitted far more than our share of the gases defiling the atmosphere, and this must be part of our consideration when we decide how to respond to climate migration. When we decide whether our nation, our town, or our church will respond with mercy to migrants looking for work, we should remember our own failings, our own need for mercy.

What's more, those of us who are comfortable today should remember that we might be seeking shelter and assistance someday. Rich nations are not spared the travails of global warming; our homes and livelihoods may someday be endangered. Wildfires are increasingly common in North America. Floods are increasingly common on our coasts. In his book *The Waters Will Come*, journalist Jeff Goodell predicts that Miami, Florida, is "a modern-day Atlantis-in-the-making," not only unprepared to deal with rising waters but continuing to invest billions of dollars in seaside construction that will be unviable as floods increase.[40] Journalist Abrahm Lustgarten also calls attention to the drought-prone Great Plains, where a huge portion of food in the United States is grown. This area was the source of one great migration in the twentieth century, when drought contributed to the Dust Bowl, which reduced crop yields by 60 percent and drove millions of people to head west. Yields have since returned and increased in the Great Plains, but Lustgarten predicts that climate-induced droughts are coming back. By 2050, he writes, "Dust Bowl-era yields will be the norm, even as demand for scarce water" increases.[41]

So we should not assume that climate migration is only necessary for other people, in other places. The world is changing. The places we live are threatened, too. We have good reason to treat our neighbors seeking refuge as we would like to be treated because someday we, our children, or our friends might need refuge too. When we can, we should be as merciful as the prodigal son's father because, someday, we may find ourselves in the position of his son. We may be fleeing famine and desperate for sustenance and inclusion. Before the prodigal son went home, "no one gave him anything." We should treat those in need differently.

This book has advocated resistance against our enemies. Part of that means being as welcoming as possible to their victims, our neighbors, near and far. We can try to make our towns and cities, our counties, our states, and our nations as open as possible to migrants in need. We can intervene in dehumanizing rhetoric about immigration and remind those involved that we are talking about human beings who deserve mercy and care. We can volunteer to work with refugees and migrants; we can help them navigate systems of support and advocate for those systems to improve and increase.

Environmental educator Jill Rios offers a powerful example. She is a member of the La Capilla de Santa Maria church in Hendersonville, North Carolina. Many of her fellow congregants are originally from Mexico but left failing crops and now provide for their families by working in the United States. Some are undocumented; some are impoverished. But Rios insists that all are her neighbors and deserve respect. Her church has declared it "will continue to be a sanctuary for human migrants who arrive and resettle in our community." Rios also calls other Christians in the United States to similarly reach out to, learn from, and support immigrant populations. And she insists that privileged Christians can use our political influence to change toxic national discourse: "We must recognize that anti-immigrant policies promote division, not unity, and create problems, not solutions, in our communities."[42]

Rios, like the father of the prodigal son, compassionately welcomes those in need. Such mercy is the best way I know of to build and sustain community in a changing world. May we be merciful, just as the father is merciful.

Joy in Troubled Times

The parable of the prodigal son ends with a party. We do not know if the older brother attends, but we know the father calls the whole household to celebrate. He does not merely feed the one who has returned; he puts his arms around him and kisses him. He calls for music and dancing. Explaining his actions to his other son, the father says, "We had to celebrate and rejoice."

This is a final, crucial lesson to be drawn from the parable: we must find reasons to celebrate and to enjoy one another's company. Even in a harsh world, even in a defiled atmosphere, we can rejoice. It is not a coincidence that the character who represents mercy is also the one who calls for the party. Filled with compassion, the father not only wants his sons to feel safe and fed but also wants everyone around him to share in his joy. His compassion helps him rejoice.

In an interview two years after she spoke to the United Nations, Greta Thunberg emphasized that one change in her life since that time had been an increase in happiness. She found community in the climate movement, connecting with other people her age who shared her passion and her commitment. This strengthened her activism, but it also gave her space to develop elaborate private jokes, to join text threads with people who make her smile. It helped her feel included and loved.

Thunberg continues to work hard to resist the forces of atmospheric defilement, but in 2021, she also wanted the world to know that she has hobbies and loves to spend time with her dogs and her friends: "We are very silly. Maybe people have the idea that climate activists are serious, but that's not the case." The interviewer asked if the best thing to come out of her activism was friendship, and she responded, "Yes . . . Definitely. I am very happy now."[43]

Atmospheric defilement will not be solved in Thunberg's lifetime. There is no guarantee things will even get better, despite the hard work she and so many others are doing. But if she can continue to find a nurturing community and feel happiness, then she will have a vital foundation from which to continue struggling.

Living in the world is hard. It seems to be getting harder. But we can do the inner work required to care for ourselves and others in the face of these realities. Like the father in the parable, we can still celebrate when we see someone we love. Like Jesus on the night before he was betrayed, we can gather with friends over food and drink. Like

Greta Thunberg, we can make sure we are supported by people who care about what we care about and are amused by what amuses us. The Powers are mighty and destructive. But so are the coalitions that resist them. This is reason to celebrate. When we gather with those we love, when we meet those who share our cause, when we offer hospitality to those in need, we can rejoice together.

This chapter has considered three powerful emotions that may be inspired by climate change: guilt, anger, and mercy. We might also feel anxiety or fear about the future ahead. We might feel despair about the possibility that things might get worse. We might feel overwhelmed, numb, or apathetic. However we feel about atmospheric defilement, we need to do the work of recognizing and honoring it. Then, when we can, we should use what we have learned from that self-examination for the outer work resisting the fallen Powers.

We can also nurture our joy. We can gather with those we love and with those we are learning to love, and we can have fun. We can follow the father's final instruction in the parable: celebrate and rejoice.

Conclusion

THOUSANDS OF ANSWERS

THE PARABLE OF the Sower and *The Parable of the Talents*, the most famous books by groundbreaking speculative fiction author Octavia Butler, are set in the United States during the mid-twenty-first century. Writing in the 1990s, Butler imagined a grim life in California, with much of the state made unsafe by wildfires, droughts, drug addiction, and poverty. In her stories, neighboring states have built walls to keep Californians from seeking refuge. She imagined increasing authoritarianism and growing economic disparity, both of which led to reductions in labor and environmental restrictions. Butler described the books as set among "the whole nasty family of problems brought on by global warming."[1] Extrapolating from the world she saw decades ago, she predicted many contemporary realities. Long before most people, she saw the deep, terrifying connections between climate change and injustice.

Butler was also thoughtful about how people should respond to these problems. Her books emphasize the importance of opposing violent and authoritarian institutions, building healthier and more collaborative systems, and educating future generations. Her characters go through terrible traumas but often learn in the process to develop stronger relationships and deeper commitments to one another. They come to accept that transitions in life and civilization are inevitable, but human beings can shape a positive future by taking care of one another in the process. Her main character summarizes this with a simple but powerful lesson: "Kindness eases change."[2]

Butler's books resist quick summary because they provide no easy or simple answers, as she emphasized in an essay from *Essence* magazine. There she recounts the story of a student, troubled by her writings, who asked a version of a question that most people who talk and write about climate change frequently hear: "So what's the answer?"

Butler replied, "There isn't one."

Thinking she might be joking, he asked, "You mean we're just doomed?"

She clarified, "No. I mean there's no single answer that that will solve all of our future problems. There's no magic bullet. Instead, there are thousands of answers—at least. You can be one of them if you choose to be."[3]

There is much to learn here. Butler here outlines the urgency of climate change: We face crises, but there are no simple solutions. We cannot expect ourselves or anyone else to conclusively end atmospheric defilement. There is no magic bullet. But at the same time, we are not doomed. There are many people who are concerned and are trying to make the world better. We can, if we choose, join that group. We can build and join coalitions participating in thousands of answers.

This book has argued that some answers include naming the fossil fuel industry as our enemy and learning from Christian traditions about how to have enemies well. Understanding the intersectional injustices of atmospheric defilement empowers us to oppose those enemies and the dominating myths that make their defilement seem inevitable. The myth of the Powers helps us understand the fossil fuel industry as a fallen system that could contribute to a loving and just world but instead serves domination and defilement. Christians can resist our enemies by forming coalitions of creative protest, advocating political and cultural transitions, and cultivating mercy for ourselves, our neighbors, and our enemies.

None of these ideas is a magic bullet that will end atmospheric defilement. These are just a few among the thousands of possible, partial answers. We must all discern how we can be an answer, and we must all accept that no answer is conclusive.

Octavia Butler's essay about that encounter with a student is called "A Few Rules for Predicting the Future," and it draws lessons from her books about "trying to look ahead to discern possibilities and offer warnings." She insists that such attention to the future is "an act of hope."[4] Taking climate change seriously is such an act of hope, based on the belief that we can make the world better than its current realities and trajectories. Naming our enemies is an act of hope, based on the belief that they can be redeemed. Building coalitions of resistance is an act of hope, based on the belief that the creative energy of human collectives can be stronger than the Domination System.

I wrote this book in 2023 and 2024 as an act of hope. It won't be published for many months after I'm done writing, so you are reading in my future. You know things I don't; you've lived through things I haven't. I offer my ideas hoping they will be relevant to the world you live in and that you will have the power to use them for good.

At my most hopeful, I indulge in a fantasy about a reader encountering these words decades in my future. Perhaps you have found this book on a shelf in a comfortable library where it has sat undisturbed for a long while. Perhaps, in the meantime, the world has changed for the better and some of the problems I've named here are resolved. I hope this is true and that it feels like a strange anachronism to read about a "fossil fuel industry," much less to treat it as an enemy. In this imagined future, oil and coal and methane are no longer extracted from the ground, and the fossil fuels that were extracted in the past are only used very occasionally in urgent circumstances that serve the common good rather than private gain and convenience.

As I hope, I imagine that your culture is less limited than mine by greed, individualism, and inattention to earth's ecosystems. Perhaps your culture invests serious energy in repairing the ecosystems and communities that were damaged by mine. Perhaps your politics is better than mine at helping people wrestle with the long-term implications of their decisions, better at building healthy institutions, better at creating just, sustainable, and intersectional communities.

As I think about these hopes, I am heartened to know they are possible. Perhaps not likely but possible.

Of course, I can also imagine a more challenging future, where the fossil fuel industry continues to extract its products and twist politics and culture to justify its profits. I can imagine readers in such a future who find my words too optimistic. If this is your situation, I am sorry. I hope you find the strength to endure and take care of yourself and the people around you as best you can.

Whenever and wherever you are reading this, I believe we have some things in common. We live in a world where the climate, the earth, and human communities have been defiled by broken systems. If my term for this, *atmospheric defilement*, does not capture the phenomenon well in your context, I hope you will find another term that works for you.

We all need some grounds for hope, some way to believe the world can be better than it is. I have argued that the myth of the Powers offers such grounding, asserting that every part of the world was made for and can contribute to goodness. If that does not help you, I hope you will find other myths, stories, or facts that do.

We all need to name the enemies pulling our world away from community and toward domination. I have argued that the fossil fuel industry is a key enemy that deserves dedicated, focused resistance. If this is not the most important enemy in your context, I hope you will name your own, recognize it as part of a system of domination, and commit to resistance.

We all need communities to support us in such resistance. I have written about the coalitions I see forming and acting in my time, creatively inspiring political and cultural change. If those are not good partners for your struggles, then I hope you will find others that give you strength and help you build a better world.

We all need to take care of ourselves as we do hard work. I have made an appeal to treat ourselves, our neighbors, and our enemies with mercy. If that does not work for you, I hope you will find another way to nurture kindness, at least to yourself, in the face of difficult realities.

This book has offered some answers to the question of how to live in a world of climate change and injustice. But I am under no illusion that every reader should embrace the same ideas. I have presented a few of the thousands of answers available to people who care about this urgent problem. My hope is that you, reading this, will commit to being one such answer.

I hope that you take the time to discern the best way to do so and that this will help you resist our enemies. I hope that, in the process, you find fulfillment, friends, and joy.

NOTES

Introduction

1 For an account of the poster's creation and a critique of its individualistic focus, see especially Finis Dunaway, *Seeing Green: The Use and Abuse of American Environmental Images* (Chicago: University of Chicago Press, 2018), ch. 4.

2 Climate scientist Michael Mann makes a similar critique of the infamous "Crying Indian" advertisement, which taught that bottles and cans littering the countryside "were the result of our bad personal behavior. That's a convenient message to promote if you're an industry whose practices generate massive metal and plastic pollution and you're trying to fight regulations aimed at requiring you to package and process that waste." Michael E. Mann, *The New Climate War: The Fight to Take Back Our Planet* (Washington, DC: Public Affairs, 2021), 59.

3 I am not arguing that individual action and understanding do not matter but that these have been so emphasized that contemporary climate action needs to focus resolutely on structural issues. I have a different approach from the philosophers who advocate a "symbiotic conception of structural and individual reform" rather than either/or thinking on this issue. See Michael Brownstein, Daniel Kelly, and Alex Madva, "Individualism, Structuralism, and Climate Change," *Environmental Communication* 16, no. 2 (2022): 271.

4 Jawanza Eric Clark, *Reclaiming Stolen Earth: An Africana Ecotheology* (Maryknoll, NY: Orbis Books, 2022). Clark convincingly argues that such universal claims are a product of white supremacy and that it is particularly important for people from social locations like mine to be clear and explicit that we do not and should not speak for all.

5 NOAA, "2023 was the Warmest Year in the Modern Temperature Record," accessed March 30, 2024, https://www.climate.gov/news-features/featured-images/2023-was-warmest-year-modern-temperature-record.

6 IPCC, "Summary for Policymakers," in *Climate Change 2023: Synthesis Report. Contribution of Working Groups I, II, and III to the Sixth Assessment Report of the Intergovernmental Panel on Climate Change*, ed. Core Writing Team, Hoesung Lee, and José Romero (Geneva: IPCC, 2023), 1–34.

7 Heather McGhee, *The Sum of Us: What Racism Costs Everyone and How We Can Prosper Together* (New York: One World, 2021).

8 Kevin J. O'Brien, *The Violence of Climate Change: Lessons of Resistance from Nonviolent Activists* (Washington, DC: Georgetown University Press, 2017), 82.

9 All biblical quotations in this book are from the New Revised Standard Version.

10 Melissa Florer-Bixler, *How to Have an Enemy: Righteous Anger and the Work of Peace* (Harrisonburg, VA: Herald Press, 2021), 43.

11 Bill McKibben, "Global Warming's Terrifying New Math," *Rolling Stone*, August 2, 2012.

12 The School of Life, *The School of Life: An Emotional Education* (London: School of Life, 2019), 16.

13 Nicole Seymour proposes that environmentalists need more irony "to disrupt the binarized logic of despair/hope and to dispute mainstream environmentalism's claims to authenticity and straightforwardness." She writes that environmental authors should be wary of comparisons with prophecy because "as anyone who has been dragged to church services in their youth can probably attest, notions of salvation, redemption, and the divine create a tense dynamic in which the virtuous believer is patronizingly positioned as morally correct, thus thrusting the nonvirtuous nonbeliever into shame and (possibly) submission." It humbles me that Seymour here uses Christianity as a key example of shame and sanctimony. I hope the Christian climate ethics in this book suggest another possibility from the tradition, and I hope this book embraces the ironic sensibility she calls for. Nicole Seymour, *Bad Environmentalism: Irony and Irreverence in the Ecological Age* (Minneapolis: University of Minnesota Press, 2018), 5, 16–17.

Part I: The Problem

1 Anthony Leiserowitz et al., *Climate Change in the American Mind, April 2022* (New Haven, CT: Yale Program on Climate Communication, 2022).

2 In his poignant book about becoming an adult in the shadow of climate change, author and activist Daniel Sherrell deals with this issue in a way that is both heartbreaking and playful, referring only to a "Problem" that he does not name. He writes that the protest marches he helped organize were a way to wrestle with the indefinable nature of the issue: "We were trying . . . to bring the Problem into view as a scene of immanent force. To literally embody it, even if just for a couple hours." Daniel Sherrell, *Warmth: Coming of Age at the End of Our World* (New York: Penguin, 2021), 176.

3 Mike Hulme, *Climate Change* (New York: Routledge, 2021), xxix, xxxi. Timothy Morton makes a similar point when he suggests that climate change is a "hyperobject," too vast to be fully comprehended. Timothy Morton, *Hyperobjects: Philosophy and Ecology after the End of the World* (Minneapolis: University of Minnesota Press, 2013).

Chapter 1: Climate Change as Atmospheric Defilement

1 Kimberlé Crenshaw, "Demarginalizing the Intersection of Race and Sex: A Black Feminist Critique of Antidiscrimination Doctrine, Feminist Theory and Antiracist Politics," *University of Chicago Legal Research Forum* 1989, no. 1 (1989): 139–140.

2 Kimberlé Crenshaw, "The Urgency of Intersectionality," 2016, https://www.ted.com/talks/kimberle_crenshaw_the_urgency_of_intersectionality.

3 Anna Kaijser and Annica Kronsell, "Climate Change through the Lens of Intersectionality," *Environmental Politics* 23, no. 3 (2014): 417–433.

4 Kimberlé Crenshaw, "Mapping the Margins: Intersectionality, Identity Politics, and Violence against Women of Color," *Stanford Law Review* 43, no. 6 (1991): 1299.

5 See especially Leah Thomas, *The Intersectional Environmentalist: How to Dismantle Systems of Oppression to Protect People + Planet*

(New York: Voracious, 2022). She defines "intersectional environmentalism (IE) as an inclusive approach to environmentalism that advocates for the protection of both people and the planet. IE argues that social and environmental justice are intertwined and that environmental advocacy that disregards this connection is harmful and incomplete" (31).

6 I am informed by the slogan insisted on by disability activists, "Nothing about us without us," and so try to depend on the expertise of marginalized peoples to understand the injustices of marginalization. For a careful and insightful ethical analysis of this norm, its challenges for some people with intellectual and development disabilities, and implications for ethnography in Christian ethics, see Lorraine Cuddeback-Gedeon, "'Nothing about Us without Us': Ethnography, Conscientization, and the Epistemic Challenges of Intellectual Disability," *Practical Matters Journal* 11 (2018): 70–87.

7 In her powerful exploration of the environmental implications of Eric Garner's death, Melanie Harris writes that Garner "suffered not only because of racially motivated violence, but also because the air in his community robbed him of a normal quality of life: the right to breathe clean." Melanie L. Harris, *Ecowomanism: African American Women and Earth-Honoring Faiths* (Maryknoll, NY: Orbis Books, 2017), 18.

8 Delores S. Williams, "Sin, Nature, and Black Women's Bodies," in *Ecofeminism and the Sacred*, ed. Carol J. Adams (New York: Continuum, 1993), 25.

9 Williams, "Sin, Nature, and Black Women's Bodies," 29. See also "Black Women's Surrogacy Experience and the Christian Notion of Redemption," in *After Patriarchy: Feminist Transformations of the World Religions*, ed. Paula M. Cooey, William R. Eakin, and Jay B. McDaniel (Maryknoll, NY: Orbis, 1991), 12.

10 Williams, "Sin, Nature, and Black Women's Bodies," 24, 29. A similar and complementary argument is well developed in Shamara Shantu Riley, "Ecology Is a Sistah's Issue Too: The Politics of Emergent Afrocentric Ecowomanism," in *Ecofeminism and the Sacred*, ed. Carol J. Adams (New York: Continuum, 1993).

11 Williams, "Sin, Nature, and Black Women's Bodies," 24.

12 Williams writes, "American national consciousness has been structured so that the defilement of black women is invisible due

to the kind of associations made with the color of their black skin . . . put all of this together with the practice of controlling and using nature, which many Christians believed to be their God given right, and it is not difficult to understand why Westerners did not recognize in the early stages of technological development the defilement of nature that could and surely would occur" (Williams, "Sin, Nature, and Black Women's Bodies," 29).

13 Marilyn V. Longmuir, *Oil in Burma: The Extraction of 'Earth-Oil' to 1914* (Banglamun, Thailand: White Lotus Press, 2001). I was pointed to this source by Amitav Ghosh, *The Great Derangement: Climate Change and the Unthinkable* (Chicago: University of Chicago Press, 2016), 100.

14 David Eckstein, Marie-Lena Hutfils, and Maik Winges, "Global Climate Risk Index 2019: Who Suffers Most from Extreme Weather Events? Weather-Related Loss Events in 2017 and 998 to 2017," 2018, 8, https://germanwatch.org/sites/germanwatch.org/files/Global%20Climate%20Risk%20Index%202019_2.pdf.

15 Helene Maria Kyed and Justine Chambers, "Climate Change Actions in Conflict Affected Contexts: Insights from Myanmar after the Military Coup," accessed March 9, 2024, https://reliefweb.int/report/myanmar/climate-change-actions-conflict-affected-contexts-insights-myanmar-after-military-coup.

16 Ghosh, *Great Derangement*, 98–103.

17 Ghosh, *Great Derangement*, 146.

18 Amitav Ghosh, *The Nutmeg's Curse: Parables for a Planet in Crisis* (Chicago: University of Chicago Press, 2021), 60.

19 Ghosh is careful to insist that his indictment is not exclusively directed at "Westerners" but also includes "the urban elites and middle classes of countries like India, China, Indonesia, and so on" who have adopted the standards of success offered by the West. Ghosh, *Nutmeg's Curse*, 165.

20 Ghosh, *Great Derangement*, 135.

21 Ghosh, *Great Derangement*, 162.

22 Kyle Powys Whyte, "Indigenous Climate Change Studies: Indigenizing Futures, Decolonizing the Anthropocene," *English Language Notes* 55, no. 1–2 (2017): 154.

23 Kyle Powys Whyte, "Is It Colonial Déjà Vu? Indigenous Peoples and Climate Injustice," in *Humanities for the Environment:*

Integrating Knowledges, Fording New Constellations of Practice, ed. Joni Adamson, Michael Davis, and Hsinya Huang (New York: Earthscan Publications, 2016), 92.

24 See especially Dina Gilio-Whitaker, *As Long as Grass Grows: The Indigenous Fight for Environmental Justice, from Colonization to Standing Rock* (Boston: Beacon Press, 2019); Nick Estes, "Fighting for Our Lives: #NoDAPL in Historical Context," 2016, https://therednation.org/2016/09/18/fighting-for-our-lives-nodapl-in-context/.

25 Kyle Powys Whyte, "The Dakota Access Pipeline, Environmental Injustice, and U.S. Colonialism," *Red Ink* 19, no. 1 (2017): 162, 167–168. He offers the same interpretation of the disputes over coal export terminals in the Pacific Northwest, which have roots in the confining of Salish peoples to reservations and the degradation of salmon habitats in the Puget Sound, exacerbated by shipping traffic and fossil fuel spills. In an essay on Native responses to the prospect of large-scale climate engineering projects, Whyte further emphasizes this theme of consent, insisting that conversation must begin with the fact that "Indigenous peoples never consented to any of [the] global or local structures of colonial power that have generated the topic of genoengineering in the first place." No attempt to "solve" climate change has credibility unless it begins from the understanding that "climate change impacts are an intensification of entangled processes of colonialism, capitalism and industrialization that continue to inflict violence and harm on indigenous peoples." Kyle Powys Whyte, "Indigeneity in Geoengineering Discourses: Some Considerations," *Ethics, Policy and Environment* 21, no. 3 (2018): 291, 298.

26 For an expansion of this argument in the context of African and African American history and thought, see Jawanza Eric Clark, *Reclaiming Stolen Earth: An Africana Ecotheology* (Maryknoll, NY: Orbis Books, 2022).

27 Whyte, "Is It Colonial Déjà Vu," 97.

28 See especially Celina Harpe, "Effects of the Tar Sands: Fort Mackay, Alberta," 2009, https://www.youtube.com/watch?v=kG2sJAn47QI; Nicholas Kusnets, "The Deep Toll of Tar Sands on Canada's Indigenous People," 2021, https://undark.org/2021/11/22/ecocide-tar-sands/.

29 Kate Beaton, *Ducks: Two Years in the Oil Sands* (Montreal: Drawn and Quarterly, 2022), 21.

30 Beaton, *Ducks*, 113.

31 Andreas Malm, *Fossil Capital: The Rise of Steam-Power and the Roots of Global Warming* (Washington, DC: National Geographic Books, 2016), 11. See also Matthew T. Huber, *Lifeblood: Oil, Freedom, and the Forces of Capital* (Minneapolis: University of Minnesota Press, 2013).

32 Malm also admits that noncapitalist systems have degraded and continue to degrade the atmosphere and earth's systems but insists that capitalism "gave birth to" the fossil economy. To those who ask why he doesn't spend more time criticizing the environmental damage caused by the Soviet Union instead of contemporary capitalism, he replies, "Why concentrate research efforts on cancer rather than smallpox? Both can be fatal! But only one still exists" (Malm, *Fossil Capital*, 278).

33 Beaton, *Ducks*, 323–328.

34 Beaton, *Ducks*, 433.

35 Beaton, *Ducks*, 165.

36 Beaton, *Ducks*, 434.

37 Greta Thunberg et al., *Our House Is on Fire* (New York: Penguin Books, 2020), 131.

38 For more on youth climate activism, see especially Gayle Kimball, *Climate Girls Saving Our World: 54 Activists Speak Out* (Lincoln, NE: Equality Press, 2021).

39 Thunberg, *Our House Is on Fire*, 28.

40 Greta Thunberg, "Six Months on a Planet in Crisis: Greta Thunberg's Diary from the U.S. to Davos," *Time Magazine*, July 10, 2020. She offers a similar satirical point in another way: "Everyone is so accustomed to the idea that everything should be adapted to their own needs. People are like spoiled children. And then they complain about us children being lazy and spoiled. I know that those of us with Asperger's can't perceive irony because it says so in the manual that all the old psychiatrists have written about people like me—but I don't think that irony can be described better than this" (Thunberg, *Our House Is on Fire*, 111). Making a related point, comedian Hannah Gadsby in her special *Douglas* describes having autism as "like being the only sober person in a room full of drunk people."

41 Greta Thunberg, *No One Is Too Small to Make a Difference* (New York: Penguin, 2019), 103.
42 Eli Clare, *Brilliant Imperfection* (Durham, NC: Duke University Press, 2017), 38.
43 See Tom Shakespeare, *Disability: The Basics* (New York, Routledge, 2017), Ch 1. For this reason, many people with impairments prefer to be referred to as "disabled people" rather than "people with disabilities." The former emphasizes that disabling is something done to people rather than something inherent in themselves.
44 Clare, *Brilliant Imperfection*, 12–13. It is important to note that while he embraces the social model over the medical model of disability, Clare is also cautious to insist that disability activism should pay careful attention to the embodied experience of disabled people. He argues that focus on social structures and systemic injustices should not detract from the importance of the physical embodiment of all persons. See especially Eli Clare, "Stolen Bodies, Reclaimed Bodies: Disability and Queerness," *Public Culture* 13, no. 3 (2001): 359–366.
45 Clare, *Brilliant Imperfection*, 6.
46 Clare, *Brilliant Imperfection*, 175.
47 Clare, *Brilliant Imperfection*, 60, 87.
48 Clare, *Brilliant Imperfection*, 59. It is also important to note that Clare and many other disability activists only carefully make metaphorical comparisons between disability and problems like climate change and have deep concerns about simple connections between the two. For example, Clare savagely critiques a Sierra Club campaign that connected coal plants to birth defects and so treats disabilities as merely "symbols for environmental damage," appealing to and enhancing ableist assumptions (Clare, *Brilliant Imperfection*, 56).

Chapter 2: Myths of Domination

1 This definition is derived from two others: Karen Armstrong writes that myths refer "beyond the chaotic flux of historical events to what is timeless in human life, helping us to glimpse the stable core of reality." Karen Armstrong, *Sacred Nature: Restoring*

Our Ancient Bond with the Natural World (Washington, DC: National Geographic Books, 2022), 24. Walter Wink writes that a myth is "an incredibly condensed story that depicts, through the indirect language of narrative, the nature of ultimate reality." Walter Wink, *Naming the Powers: The Language of Power in the New Testament* (Minneapolis: Augsburg Fortress, 1984), 142.

2 Armstrong, *Sacred Nature*, 24.

3 Melanie Challenger provocatively begins her book *How to Be Animal* with the sentence: "The world is now dominated by an animal that doesn't think it's an animal. And the future is being imagined by an animal that doesn't want to be an animal." Melanie Challenger, *How to Be Animal: A New History of What It Means to Be Human* (New York: Penguin, 2021), 1.

4 For a classic and still relevant indictment of this attitude, see Herman E. Daly and John B. Cobb Jr., *For the Common Good: Redirecting the Economy toward Community, the Environment, and a Sustainable Future* (Boston: Beacon Press, 1994).

5 E. Calvin Beisner, *Where Garden Meets Wilderness: Evangelical Entry into the Environmental Debate* (Grand Rapids, MI: The Acton Institute for the Study of Religion and Liberty, 1997), 55, 103, xv. When he wrote that book, Beisner denied that climate change was happening and insisted that human activity was not driving warming temperatures. Now his rhetoric instead stresses that climate action will have a negative impact on poor people and says little about the consequences of ignoring climate change. See https://cornwallalliance.org.

6 Robin Wall Kimmerer, *Braiding Sweetgrass* (Minneapolis: Milkweed, 2013), 57.

7 Kimmerer offers an alternative worldview from the Potawatomi language, which uses "the same words to address the living world as we use for our family. Because they are our family." She calls readers to learn a "grammar of animacy" that will help us democratically relate to the rest of the world rather than hierarchically separating ourselves from it. Kimmerer, *Braiding Sweetgrass*, 55.

8 As Rebecca Solnit puts it, "If you regard women as an undifferentiated part of nature, their bodies are just another place a man has every right to go." Rebecca Solnit, *Call Them by Their True Names: American Crises (and Essays)* (London: Granta, 2018), 44.

9 See especially Aph Ko, *Racism as Zoological Witchcraft: A Guide for Getting Out* (Brooklyn, NY: Lantern Books, 2019).

10 This point is made well by Amitav Ghosh, whose argument about the connections between empire and climate change was discussed in chapter 1. He argues that one of the biggest mistakes of Western colonialism is the association of "civilization" with the belief that "the Earth is inert and machine-like." Those who believe in the "vitality of natural and celestial objects" were dismissed by much of the colonial world as "savages." Ghosh argues that the only way for a culture to respond to the deep violence of climate change is to understand that "the Earth teems with other beings who act, communicate, tell stories, and make meaning." He calls those of us in colonizing cultures to learn "that nonhumans can, do, and *must* speak. It is essential now, as the prospect of planetary catastrophe comes ever closer, that those nonhuman voices be restored to our stories." Amitav Ghosh, *The Nutmeg's Curse: Parables for a Planet in Crisis* (Chicago: University of Chicago Press, 2021), 87, 197, 257.

11 See, for example, Sarah Jaquette Ray, *The Ecological Other* (Tucson: University of Arizona Press, 2013).

12 Christopher Carter, *The Spirit of Soul Food: Race, Faith, and Food Justice* (Chicago: University of Illinois Press, 2021), 103.

13 Eric C. Miller, "The Myth of American Individualism: Interview with Alex Zakaras," *Religion and Politics*, February 21, 2023. In his book, Zakaras suggests that the individual of the "American political imagination" is in fact a set of three overlapping myths: the "independent proprietor," the "rights-bearer," and the "self-made man." He also argues, in some tension with my thesis in this chapter, that progressive movements are wisest to use rather than fight against this myth. See Alex Zakaras, *The Roots of American Individualism: Political Myth in the Age of Jackson* (Princeton, NJ: Princeton University Press, 2022).

14 The classic and still relevant analysis of individualism as the "first language" of US culture is Robert Bellah et al., *Habits of the Heart: Individualism and Commitment in American Life* (Berkeley: University of California Press, 1996).

15 Douglas Keay and Margaret Thatcher, "Interview for *Women's Own*," 1987, https://www.margaretthatcher.org/document/106689.

16 W. E. B. Du Bois, *Black Reconstruction in America* (New York: Russell & Russell, 1935), 602.

17 Kate Aronoff, "We Didn't Start the Fire," in *Winning the Green New Deal: Why We Must, How We Can*, ed. Varshini Prakash and Guido Girgenti (New York: Simon & Schuster, 2020), 15.

18 For an account of the earliest US political responses to global warming during the Reagan administration, see Nathaniel Rich, *Losing Earth: A Recent History* (New York: MCD Books, 2019).

19 See especially Dan M. Kahan, Hank Jenkins-Smith, and Donald Braman, "Cultural Cognition of Scientific Consensus," *Journal of Risk Research* 14, no. 2 (2011): 147–174. Robin Veldman also found this trend in her ethnographic work with Christian evangelicals whom she categorizes as "climate skeptics." Robin Globus Veldman, *The Gospel of Climate Skepticism* (Oakland: University of California Press, 2019).

20 For example, Calvin Beisner uses the Parable of the Talents to insist that inequality is not inherently unjust, which is important to him in part because he suggests that economic growth is the best way to improve environmental well-being and that economic growth depends on inequality (Beisner, *Where Garden Meets Wilderness*, 40).

21 For some of the classic evidence, analyses, and critiques of the growth inherent to capitalism as currently practiced, see especially Donella H. Meadows, *Limits to Growth* (New York: Signet, 1972); E. F. Schumacher, *Small Is Beautiful: Economics as If People Mattered* (New York: Harper & Row, 1973); Daly and Cobb, *For the Common Good*. For more contemporary critiques, see Bill McKibben, *Deep Economy: The Wealth of Communities and the Durable Future* (New York: Macmillan, 2007); Chris Doran, *Hope in the Age of Climate Change: Creation Care This Side of the Resurrection* (Eugene, OR: Wipf and Stock Publishers, 2017); Cynthia D. Moe-Lobeda, *Resisting Structural Evil: Love as Ecological-Economic Vocation* (Minneapolis: Fortress Press, 2013).

22 Sallie McFague, *A New Climate for Theology: God, the World, and Global Warming* (Minneapolis: Fortress Press, 2008), 83.

23 See especially Rich, *Losing Earth*, 161–204; Naomi Oreskes and Erik M. Conway, *Merchants of Doubt: How a Handful of Scientists Obscured the Truth on Issues from Tobacco Smoke to Global Warming* (New York: Bloomsbury Press, 2010), ch 6. George

H. W. Bush is widely reported to have responded to critiques of consumption in the United States with the statement, "The American way of life is not up for negotiations. Period," but I have been unable to find a primary source for that quote.

24 Thunberg's address is at Greta Thunberg, "Our House Is Still on Fire and You're Fueling the Flames," January 21, 2020, https://www.weforum.org/agenda/2020/01/greta-speech-our-house-is-still-on-fire-davos-2020/. Mnuchin's response is reported in Heather Long, "Treasury Secretary Mnuchin Says Climate Activist Greta Thunberg Should Go Study Economics," *Washington Post*, January 23, 2020.

25 Naomi Klein, *This Changes Everything: Capitalism vs. the Climate* (New York: Simon & Schuster, 2014), 86–89.

Part II: The Fossil Fuel Powers

1 Donna Jeanne Haraway, *Staying with the Trouble: Making Kin in the Chthulucene* (Durham, NC: Duke University Press, 2016), 37. In other work, I have focused on climate change as a "wicked" problem, which is a different way of articulating the dangers of one-dimensional, emergency responses. See Kevin J. O'Brien, *The Violence of Climate Change: Lessons of Resistance from Nonviolent Activists* (Washington, DC: Georgetown University Press, 2017); Whitney Bauman and Kevin James O'Brien, *Environmental Ethics and Uncertainty: Wrestling with Wicked Problems* (New York: Routledge, 2019).

2 Amitav Ghosh, *The Nutmeg's Curse: Parables for a Planet in Crisis* (Chicago: University of Chicago Press, 2021), 221.

3 Kendra Pierre-Louis, "Wakanda Doesn't Have Suburbs," in *All We Can Save*, ed. Ayana Elizabeth Johnson and Katharine K. Wilkinson (New York: One World, 2020), 141, 144.

4 See especially Jennifer Price, *Stop Saving the Planet!: An Environmentalist Manifesto* (New York: W. W. Norton, 2021).

Chapter 3: Powers That Be

1 The most systematic attempt to observe and celebrate environmental religion that moves past Christianity and other Western monotheisms is Bron Raymond Taylor, *Dark Green Religion:*

Nature Spirituality and the Planetary Future (Berkeley: University of California Press, 2010).

2 Science fiction writer N. K. Jemisin explores this idea by imagining the major cities of the world creating avatars of themselves who are responsible for representing and protecting the basic character of each city. While I do not know of any influence of the Bible or Wink on her work, she offers a fascinating and insightful depiction of something a lot like the myth of the Powers as I understand it. N. K. Jemisin, *The City We Became* (New York: Orbit, 2021).

3 While this chapter and book focus on Wink's work, he is not the only thinker to reflect on the implications of the Bible's discussion of Powers. See especially also Jacques Ellul, *The Presence of the Kingdom* (Colorado Springs: Helmers & Howard Publishing, 1989); Hendrik Berkhof, *Christ and the Powers,* trans. John Howard Yoder (Waterloo, ON: Herald Press, 1977); William Stringfellow, *An Ethic for Christians and Other Aliens in a Strange Land* (Eugene, OR: Wipf and Stock Publishers, 2004); Bill Wylie Kellermann, *Principalities in Particular: A Practical Theology of the Powers That Be* (Minneapolis: Fortress Press, 2017).

4 Walter Wink, *The Powers That Be: Theology for a New Millennium* (New York: Doubleday, 1998), 4.

5 Walter Wink, *Unmasking the Powers: The Invisible Forces That Determine Human Existence* (Minneapolis: Augsburg Fortress, 1986), 1.

6 Walter Wink, *Naming the Powers: The Language of Power in the New Testament* (Minneapolis: Augsburg Fortress, 1984), 137.

7 In the ancient world, Walter Wink argues, all created things were assumed to have a "numinous interiority" by virtue of their ongoing relationship with God. Wink, *Unmasking the Powers*, 169.

8 Wink's most extensive engagement with environmental issues, which I have worked to summarize and expand here, is in Wink, *Unmasking the Powers*, ch 7. In addition, his autobiography briefly uses climate change as the quintessential of example of "divine forbearance, whereby God 'gives us up' to the consequences of our folly (Rom 1:18–32)." Walter Wink, *My Struggle to Become Human* (Minneapolis: Fortress Press, 2017), 5.

9 Walter Wink, *Engaging the Powers: Discernment and Resistance in a World of Domination* (Minneapolis: Fortress Press, 1992), 51.

For another articulation of the distinction between the biblical *kosmos* and contemporary discussions of the "cosmos," see Cherice Bock, *A Quaker Ecology: Meditations on the Future of Friends* (Newberg, OR: Barclay Press, 2022).

10 Wink discusses the "angels of the nations," these texts, and many others in Wink, *Unmasking the Powers*, ch 4.

11 Whether the angels of nature and the natural world are also "fallen" is beyond the scope of my study here. One thoughtful reflection on related questions is Christopher Southgate, *The Groaning of Creation: God, Evolution, and the Problem of Evil* (Louisville, KY: Westminster John Knox Press, 2008).

12 Wink, *Unmasking the Powers*, 87.

13 David Loy argues, compellingly, that "the Market" is "the most successful religion of all time." David Loy, "The Religion of the Market," *Journal of the American Academy of Religion* 65, no. 2 (1997): 276. Laura Hartman and I wrote about the importance of this essay in Laura M. Hartman and Kevin J. O'Brien, "Teaching against the 'False Religion' of the Market: Toward Explicitly Anticapitalist Teaching and Research in Religion and the Environment," *Religions* 14, no. 8 (2023): 975.

14 While Wink focused more on politics than on economics, I believe he would agree with this diagnosis. He wrote, "What characterizes our society is the unique value ascribed to money. . . Our entire social system has become an 'economy'; no earlier society would have characterized itself thus. Profit is the highest social good. Consumerism has become the only universally available mode of participation in modern society" (Wink, *Engaging the Powers*, 54).

15 Ron Rude insightfully and amusingly suggests that the "poster child" for the Powers could be Jabba the Hut from the *Star Wars* franchise: "Ravenous day and night, Jabba never has enough. His belly bellows and belches for more and more, even as such gluttony renders him less satisfied and less secure." Ron Rude, *(Re) considering Christianity: An Expedition of Faith Joining Science, Ancient Wisdom, and Sustainability* (St. Paul, MN: Beavers Pond Press, 2012), 91, n 65.

16 Wink, *Engaging the Powers*, 9.

17 Wink, *The Powers That Be*, 39.

18 Wink writes that most managers in business are "to a very high degree interchangeable and replaceable" because their choices matter far less than those of the system. "What *motivates* them is almost irrelevant. They need not be greedy for profit at all: *the system is greedy on their behalf*" (Wink, *Engaging the Powers*, 78).

19 Walter Wink, *When the Powers Fall: Reconciliation in the Healing of Nations* (Minneapolis: Augsburg Fortress, 1998), 53–54.

20 Wink seems to have agreed, writing that though he thought of the Powers as "impersonal entities," he knew "of no sure way to settle the question" and so left the "independent existence" of the Powers "for the reader to decide." Wink, *The Powers That Be*, 27.

21 Wink, *Naming the Powers*, 137.

Chapter 4: The Fallen Fossil Fuel Industry

1 Christiana Figueres, "I Thought Fossil Fuel Firms Could Change. I Was Wrong," *Al Jazeera*, July 6 2023.

2 Krista Tippett, "Interview with Christiana Figueres," 2023, https://onbeing.org/programs/christiana-figueres-ecological-hope-and-spiritual-evolution/#transcript.

3 Christine Shearer, *Kivalina: A Climate Change Story* (Chicago: Haymarket Books, 2011).

4 United States District Court for the Northern District of California Oakland Division, "C 08-1138 SBA," *Native Village of Kivalina v. ExxonMobil Corporation et al*, https://climatecasechart.com/wp-content/uploads/case-documents/2009/20090930_docket-408-cv-01138-SBA_order.pdf.

5 Jessica Grady-Benson, "Fossil Fuel Divestment: The Power and Promise of a Student Movement for Climate Justice" (bachelor thesis, Pitzer College, 2014).

6 Bill McKibben, "Global Warming's Terrifying New Math," *Rolling Stone*, August 2, 2012.

7 "Global Fossil Fuel Divestment Commitments Database," 2022, https://divestmentdatabase.org/.

8 Indigenous Environmental Network, "Talking Points on the AOC-Markey Green New Deal (GND) Resolution," 2019, https://www.ienearth.org/talking-points-on-the-aoc-markey-green-new-deal-gnd-resolution/.

9 Greta Thunberg et al., "At Davos We Will Tell World Leaders to Abandon the Fossil Fuel Economy," *Guardian*, January 10, 2020.

10 Jeff Goodell, *Big Coal: The Dirty Secret behind America's Energy Future* (New York: Houghton Mifflin, 2006), 253.

11 Steve Coll, *Private Empire: ExxonMobil and American Power* (New York: Penguin, 2012).

12 Kate Aronoff, *Overheated: How Capitalism Broke the Planet—and How We Fight Back* (New York: Bold Type Books, 2021), 28. See also Ross Gelbspan, *The Heat Is On: The Climate Crisis, the Cover-Up, the Prescription* (Boston: Addison Wesley, 1997); Christopher Leonard, *Kochland: The Secret History of Koch Industries and Corporate Power in America* (New York: Simon & Schuster, 2019); Alexandra Gillies, *Crude Intentions: How Oil Corruption Contaminates the World* (New York: Oxford University Press, 2020).

13 Naomi Oreskes and Erik M. Conway, *Merchants of Doubt: How a Handful of Scientists Obscured the Truth on Issues From Tobacco Smoke to Global Warming* (New York: Bloomsbury Press, 2010). See also Oreskes and Conway, *The Big Myth: How American Business Taught Us to Loathe Government and Love the Free Market* (New York: Bloomsbury Publishing, 2023); Geoffrey Supran and Naomi Oreskes, "Assessing ExxonMobil's Climate Change Communications (1977–2014)," *Environmental Research Letters* 12 (2017): 084019.

14 Michael E. Mann, *The New Climate War: The Fight to Take Back Our Planet* (Washington, DC: Public Affairs, 2021), 3.

15 Andreas Malm, *Fossil Capital: The Rise of Steam-Power and the Roots of Global Warming* (Washington, DC: National Geographic Books, 2016).

16 Holly Jean Buck, *Ending Fossil Fuels: Why Net Zero Is Not Enough* (Brooklyn, NY: Verso Books, 2021). See also Matthew T. Huber, *Lifeblood: Oil, Freedom, and the Forces of Capital* (Minneapolis: University of Minnesota Press, 2013); Imre Szeman and Dominic Boyer, *Energy Humanities: An Anthology* (Baltimore: Johns Hopkins University Press, 2017).

17 See Paul Griffin, *The Carbon Majors Database: CDP Carbon Majors Report 2017* (London: CDP, 2017). This work is based

on the initial research and methods of Richard Heede, "Tracing Anthropogenic Carbon Dioxide and Methane Emissions to Fossil Fuel and Cement Producers, 1854–2010," *Climatic Change* 122, no. 1–2 (2014):229–241.

18 Leonard, *Kochland.*

19 Influence Map, "The Carbon Majors Database: Launch Report," 2024, https://influencemap.org/site//data/000/027/Carbon_Majors_Launch_Report.pdf.

20 Oil Sands Action, "Life without Oil and Petroleum Products? Not So Simple," (2016), https://www.facebook.com/OilSandsAction/videos/life-without-oil-and-petroleum-products-not-so-simple/1058773337581878/.

21 Carol Linnit, "'Grassroots' Oil and Gas Advocacy Group Canada Action Received $100,000 from ARC Resources," June 24, 2020, https://thenarwhal.ca/canada-action-received-100-thousand-from-arc-resources/.

22 Quoted in Coll, *Private Empire*, 534. It is important to note that Tillerson also opened the door to a tax on carbon in this speech, but context suggests that this was a strategic attempt to argue against the cap-and-trade system that was at that time a more likely prospect. A key public project of his, and of almost all US-based fossil fuel executives, has been to resist any government's efforts to slow or hold institutions accountable for the defilement of the atmosphere.

23 Kate Aronoff makes the point well: "One might argue—as executives like Tillerson do—that these corporations are simply producing their supply to meet our demand. That argument, though, ignores how central they've been to keeping that demand high and growing it, despite every shred of evidence suggesting that their business model—to dig up and burn as many fossil fuels as possible—is driving the world off a climate cliff." KateAronoff, "We Didn't Start the Fire," in *Winning the Green New Deal: Why We Must, How We Can*, ed. Varshini Prakash and Guido Girgenti (New York: Simon & Schuster, 2020), 17.

24 Quoted in Geoffrey Supran and Naomi Oreskes, "Addendum to 'Assessing ExxonMobil's Climate Change Communications (1977–2014)'," *Environmental Research Letters* 15 (2020): 119401.

25 Yutong Si et al., "Fossil Fuel Companies' Climate Communication Strategies: Industry Messaging on Renewables and Natural Gas," *Energy Research and Social Science* 98 (2023): 103028.
26 Aronoff, *Overheated*, 140.
27 Aronoff, *Overheated*, 178.
28 Daniel J. Weiss, "Anatomy of a Senate Climate Bill Death," 2010, https://www.americanprogress.org/article/anatomy-of-a-senate-climate-bill-death/.
29 Aliya Haq, "Peabody Coal's Unprecedented Support for Climate Denial," 2016, https://www.nrdc.org/bio/aliya-haq/peabody-coals-unprecedented-support-climate-denial.
30 Mark Kaufman, "The Carbon Footprint Sham: A 'Successful, Deceptive' PR Campaign," 2020 https://mashable.com/feature/carbon-footprint-pr-campaign-sham; Abrahm Lustgarten, *Run to Failure: BP and the Making of the Deepwater Horizon Disaster* (New York: W. W. Norton, 2012), ch. 5.
31 John Kenny, "Beyond Propaganda," *New York Times*, August 14, 2006.
32 See especially Lustgarten, *Run to Failure*.
33 Neela Banerjee, Lisa Song, and David Hasemyer, "Exxon's Own Research Confirmed Fossil Fuels' Role in Global Warming Decades Ago," 2015, https://insideclimatenews.org/news/16092015/exxons-own-research-confirmed-fossil-fuels-role-in-global-warming. See also Supran and Oreskes, "Assessing ExxonMobil's Climate Change Communications (1977–2014)." Steve Coll notes that ExxonMobil's efforts to deny climate change after the 1980s were frequently conducted in secret through organizations like the Cato Institute, the American Enterprise Institute, and the Heritage Foundation. Coll, *Private Empire*, 184.
34 Benjamin Franta, "Early Oil Industry Disinformation on Global Warming," *Environmental Politics* 30, no. 4 (2021): 663–668.
35 James Hoggan and Richard Littlemore, *Climate Cover-Up: The Crusade to Deny Global Warming* (Vancouver: Greystone Books, 2009).
36 For excellent reporting on these campaigns of denial, see especially the podcast *Rigged* (https://drilled.media/podcasts/rigged) and seasons 1 and 3 of the podcast *Drilled* (https://drilled.media/podcasts/drilled).
37 Gelbspan, *The Heat Is On*, 5.

38 Walter Wink, *Engaging the Powers: Discernment and Resistance in a World of Domination* (Minneapolis: Fortress Press, 1992), 94.

39 See especially Christian Azar, "Bury the Chains and the Carbon Dioxide. Review of *Bury the Chains: Prophets and Rebels in the Fight to Free an Empire's Slaves* by Adam Hochschild," *Climatic Change* 85, no. 3–4 (2007): 473–475; Marc D. Davidson, "Parallels in Reactionary Argumentation in the US Congressional Debates on the Abolition of Slavery and the Kyoto Protocol," *Climatic Change* 86, no. 1–2 (2008): 67–82; Jean-François Mouhot, "Past Connections and Present Similarities in Slave Ownership and Fossil Fuel Usage," in *Energy Humanities: An Anthology*, ed. Imre Szeman and Dominic Boyer (Baltimore: Johns Hopkins University Press, 2017).

40 Chris Hayes, "The New Abolitionism: Averting Planetary Disaster Will Mean Forcing Fossil Fuel Companies to Give Up at Least $10 Trillion in Wealth," *The Nation*, April 22, 2014.

41 See especially Jade Begay, "An Indigenous Systems Approach to the Climate Crisis," in *Not Too Late: Changing the Climate Story from Despair to Possibility*, ed. Rebecca Solnit and Thelma Young-Lutunatabua (Chicago: Haymarket Books, 2023), 66–72.

42 Darren Dochuk, *Anointed with Oil: How Christianity and Crude Made Modern America* (New York: Basic Books, 2019), 212–13.

43 As will be discussed in chapter 6, one of the most promising characteristics of wind and solar power is that they are more difficult to hoard, and so could counteract the resource curse.

44 Farhana Sultana, "Decolonizing Climate Coloniality," in *Not Too Late: Changing the Climate Story from Despair to Possibility*, ed. Rebecca Solnit and Thelma Young-Lutunatabua (Chicago: Haymarket Books, 2023), 58.

45 For an account of ExxonMobil's investment in Guyana and the ways it continues colonial trends and warps politics, see the eighth season of the podcast *Drilled* at https://drilled.media/podcasts/drilled.

46 Cara Daggett, "Petro-Masculinity: Fossil Fuels and Authoritarian Desire," *Millennium: Journal of International Studies* 41, no. 1 (2018): 25–44. See also Shannon Elizabeth Bell, Cara Daggett, and Christine Labuski, "Toward Feminist Energy Systems: Why Adding Women and Solar Panels Is Not Enough☆," *Energy Research and Social Science* 68 (2020): 101557.

47 An insightful account of these connections can be found in Terra Schwerin Rowe, *Of Modern Extraction: Experiments in Critical Petro-Theology* (London: Bloomsbury, 2022).
48 Barbara Freese, *Coal: A Human History* (New York: Basic Books, 2003), 11.
49 Freese, *Coal*, 12.
50 Dochuk, *Anointed with Oil*, 9.
51 Dochuk, *Anointed with Oil*, 351.
52 "What We Do," accessed September 28, 2023, https://cornwallalliance.org/about/what-we-do/.
53 Cornwall Alliance, "A Renewed Call to Truth, Prudence, and Protection of the Poor," 2009, 2, 56, 67, http://www.cornwallalliance.org/docs/a-renewed-call-to-truth-prudence-and-protection-of-the-poor.pdf.
54 Alliance, "A Renewed Call to Truth," 20.
55 Alliance, "A Renewed Call to Truth," 7.
56 "The Oily Operators behind the Religious Climate Change Disinformation Front Group, Cornwall Alliance," 2010, https://thinkprogress.org/the-oily-operators-behind-the-religious-climate-change-disinformation-front-group-cornwall-alliance-536175fe5e04/.
57 Greta Thunberg, *No One Is Too Small to Make a Difference* (New York: Penguin, 2019), 91, 94.
58 Aronoff, *Overheated*, 9.
59 Katherine Blunt, *California Burning: The Fall of Pacific Gas and Electric—And What It Means for America's Power Grid* (New York: Penguin, 2022).
60 Philip Lymbery, *Sixty Harvests Left: How to Reach a Nature-Friendly Future* (London: Bloomsbury Publishing, 2022).
61 Mark Fischetti, Nick Bockelman, and Wil V. Srubar, "Solving Cement's Massive Carbon Problem," *Scientific American*, February 1, 2023.
62 The automobile industry might be a harder one to deem an ally as it is difficult to imagine a just and sustainable future that continues to sell private cars to every individual. But even that industry is, at the time of this writing, showing more willingness to embrace a new, electrified future than fossil fuel companies.
63 George Monbiot, "Changing the Media Narrative," in *The Climate Book*, ed. Greta Thunberg (New York: Penguin, 2023), 369.

64 "Decarbonizing Fossil Fuels," 2021, https://www.ted.com/talks/countdown_summit_decarbonizing_fossil_fuels.
65 Roy Scranton, *We're Doomed. Now What?: Essays on War and Climate Change* (New York: Soho Press, 2018), 48–49. For a sharp critique of Scranton's position, see Malm, *Fossil Capital*, ch. 3.
66 Nathaniel Rich, *Losing Earth: A Recent History* (New York: MCD Books, 2019), 6. This criticism is even more pointed in the context of Rich's book, which broadly works to temper criticisms of the fossil fuel industry by arguing that "everyone knew" about climate change and that the failure to act in the 1980s was collective rather than the sole responsibility of the industry. For a critique of his approach, see Mann, *New Climate War*, 64–65. The fact that even Rich concedes that the industry has been villainous throughout the twenty-first century is a profound indictment.
67 Melissa Florer-Bixler, *How to Have an Enemy: Righteous Anger and the Work of Peace* (Harrisonburg, VA: Herald Press, 2021), 43.

Part III: Resisting the Powers

1 Nancy D. Kates and Bennett Singer, directors, *Brother Outsider: The Life of Bayard Rustin* (Berkeley: Question Why Films, 2003), 1:23.
2 American Friends Service Committee, *Speak Truth to Power* (Philadelphia: American Friends Service Committee, 1955), 64.
3 Devon W. Carbado and Don Weise, *Time on Two Crosses: The Collected Writings of Bayard Rustin* (New York: Cleis Press, 2015), 125.

Chapter 5: Strategies of Resistance

1 Walter Wink, *The Powers That Be: Theology for a New Millenium* (New York: Doubleday, 1998), 101.
2 Wink, *The Powers That Be*, 107.
3 Some activist groups that are particularly important as I write but won't be discussed in this chapter are Fridays for Future (https://fridaysforfuture.org/), Extinction Rebellion (www.rebellion.global), and the Climate Justice Alliance (https://climate

justicealliance.org/). Three excellent organizations that bring religious perspectives to this work are Earth Ministry (https://earthministry.org/), GreenFaith (https://greenfaith.org/), and Interfaith Power and Light (https://interfaithpowerandlight.org/).

4 Walter Wink, *Engaging the Powers: Discernment and Resistance in a World of Domination* (Minneapolis: Fortress Press, 1992), 186; Wink, *The Powers That Be*, 101.

5 Billie Stanton Anleu, "Protestors Turn to Humor in Plea for Drake Closure," *The Gazette*, 2015.

6 Walter Wink, *Jesus and Nonviolence: A Third Way* (Minneapolis: Fortress Press, 2003), 21.

7 Wink, *Engaging the Powers*, 227.

8 350.org, Home, accessed October 10, 2023, https://350.org/.

9 Bill McKibben, *Oil and Honey: The Education of an Unlikely Activist* (New York: Times Books, 2013), 11.

10 For a legal analysis of the use of civil disobedience and analogies to slavery and civil rights in climate movements, see Maxine Burkett, "Climate Disobedience," *Duke Environmental Law and Policy Forum* 27, no. 1 (2016): 1–50.

11 McKibben tells the story of this protest in detail in McKibben, *Oil and Honey*.

12 350.org recounts this work at "This Is What the Largest Civil Disobedience in the History of the Environmental Movement Looks Like in Europe," 2016, https://350.org/this-is-what-the-largest-civil-disobedience-in-the-history-of-the-environmental-movement-looks-like-in-europe/.

13 Martin Luther King Jr., *Why We Can't Wait* (New York: Penguin, 1964), 83–84.

14 McKibben, *Oil and Honey*, 44. Emphasis in original. McKibben is not only a student of King and the civil rights movement but also a devout Christian whose faith informs his protest. While 350.org is not affiliated with any religious tradition, he has written extensively about how his Christian faith contributes to his activism. See especially Bill McKibben, *The Flag, the Cross, and the Station Wagon: A Graying American Looks Back at His Suburban Boyhood and Wonders What the Hell Happened* (New York: Henry Holt, 2022); McKibben, *The Comforting Whirlwind: God, Job, and the Scale of Creation* (Grand Rapids, MI: Eerdmans, 1994).

15 Wink, *Engaging the Powers*, 171.

16 In his book about South Africa, Wink writes, "Democracy . . . is not the equivalent of God's reign. As countries move toward more democratic forms, it is important to stress that democracy as we know it is far from adequate. . . . 'Representative' democracy has, in countries like the United States, become more and more unrepresentative. Business interests overwhelm parliaments, people do not bother to vote, corruption is rife, and oligarchies of the rich run the show from backstage." Walter Wink, *When the Powers Fall: Reconciliation in the Healing of Nations* (Minneapolis: Augsburg Fortress, 1998), 64.

17 Paul Griffin, *The Carbon Majors Database: CDP Carbon Majors Report 2017* (London: CDP, 2017).

18 Bob Master, "Reviving Labor, in New Deals Old and Green," in *Winning the Green New Deal: Why We Must, How We Can*, ed. Varshini Prakash and Guido Girgenti (New York: Simon & Schuster, 2020), 263. In the same book, legal scholar Ian Haney López justifies the Green New Deal in part by arguing that racist "dog whistle politics" was used "to break New Deal commitments—the belief that government should actively work for people rather than for concentrated wealth." Ian Haney López, "Averting Climate Collapse Requires Confronting Racism," in *Winning the Green New Deal: Why We Must, How We Can*, ed. Varshini Prakash and Guido Girgenti (New York: Simon & Schuster, 2020), 44.

19 Emily Rolen, "Gubernatorial Candidate Scott Wagner Called This 18-Year-old 'Young and Naive' When She Asked Him about Climate Change," *Philly Voice*, July 25, 2018.

20 Accessed October 10, 2023, https://www.sunrisemovement.org/.

21 Sara Blazevic et al., "We Shine Bright: Organizing in Hope and Song," in *Winning the Green New Deal: Why We Must, How We Can*, ed. Varshini Prakash and Guido Girgenti (New York: Simon & Schuster, 2020), 168. Emphasis in original.

22 One Sunrise activist talks explicitly about her nonviolence training in Gayle Kimball, *Climate Girls Saving Our World: 54 Activists SpeakOut* (Lincoln, NE: Equality Press, 2021), 273.

23 Accessed November 4, 2023, https://www.sunrisemovement.org/report/2022-electoral-impact/.

24 The Sunrise website argues, "For the first time in decades, most Americans now see the U.S. government as a major force in our lives. Especially as a result of the COVID pandemic, most of us realize the government is needed to survive a crisis, for better or worse" https://www.sunrisemovement.org/theory-of-change/our-story/ (accessed November 4, 2023).

25 Varshini Prakash, "People Power and Political Power," in *Winning the Green New Deal: Why We Must, How We Can*, ed. Varshini Prakash and Guido Girgenti (New York: Simon & Schuster, 2020), 139, 161.

26 Edward Abbey, *The Monkey Wrench Gang* (Philadelphia: Lippincott, 1975).

27 Julia Shipley, "'You Strike a Match': Why Two Women Sacrificed Everything to Stop the Dakota Access Pipeline," *Grist Magazine*, May 26, 2021.

28 Stop Fossil Fuels, "Ruby Montoya & Jessica Reznicek: DAPL Ecosaboteurs," accessed October 11, 2023, https://stopfossilfuels.org/ecosabotage/ruby-montoya-jessica-reznicek-dapl-ecosaboteurs/.

29 Jessica Reznicek and Ruby Montoya, "Why We Acted," *Via Pacis* 41, no. 3 (2017): 1.

30 David Eberhardt, "A Reflection on the DAPL 2," *Via Pacis* 41, no. 3 (2017): 9.

31 "Interview With DAPL Eco-Saboteurs Ruby Montoya and Jessica Reznicek," August 2, 2017, https://dgrnewsservice.org/resistance/direct-action/property-destruction/interview-dapl-eco-saboteurs-montoya-reznicek/.

32 Andreas Malm, *How to Blow Up a Pipeline* (Brooklyn, NY: Verso Books, 2021), 67.

33 Malm, *How to Blow Up a Pipeline*, 39–41.

34 There is, however, a distinction. Reznicek and Montoya argue that property destruction, at least the destruction of corporate property, is not violence. Malm, by contrast, argues that "property destruction is violence, insofar as it intentionally exerts physical force to inflict injury on a thing owned by someone who does not want it to happen." Malm, *How to Blow Up a Pipeline*, 102.

35 He most pointedly critiques McKibben's work, suggesting it represents a "Gandhian climate movement," the time for which he suggests has passed. See especially ch. 1 and pp. 152, 161.

36 Reznicek and Montoya, "Why We Acted."
37 Wink, *Engaging the Powers*, 128.
38 Walter Wink, *Unmasking the Powers: The Invisible Forces That Determine Human Existence* (Minneapolis: Augsburg Fortress, 1986), 65.
39 Gandhi and Louis Fischer, ed., *The Essential Gandhi: His Life, Work, and Ideas* (New York: Vintage Books, 1983), 156–157.
40 Dana R. Fisher, *Saving Ourselves: From Climate Shocks to Climate Action* (New York: Columbia University Press, 2024), 96.
41 Montoya and Reznicek reported that they stopped their activities when they discovered that oil was flowing through a pipe, deciding that sabotaging an active pipeline was too dangerous to their own and others' safety.
42 Wink, *Engaging the Powers*, 98.

Chapter 6: Transitioning Away

1 United Nations Framework Convention on Climate Change, "First Global Stocktake: Draft Decision as of 13 December 2023," 2023, https://unfccc.int/sites/default/files/resource/cma2023_L17_adv.pdf.
2 Antónios Gutteres, "Secretary-General's Opening Remarks at the Climate Ambition Summit," 2023, https://www.un.org/sg/en/content/sg/statement/2023-09-20/secretary-generals-opening-remarks-the-climate-ambition-summit.
3 Kate Abnett and Elizabeth Piper, "Phasing Out Fossil Fuels Is Key to COP28 Success, Says UN's Guterres," 2023, https://www.reuters.com/business/environment/phasing-out-fossil-fuels-is-key-cop28-success-says-uns-guterres-2023-12-11/.
4 Sultan Al Jaber, "Cop28 President Dr. Sultan Al Jaber's Opening Plenary Speech," 2023, https://www.cop28.com/en/news/2023/11/COP28-President-DrSultan-Al-Jabers-Opening--Plenary-Speech.
5 Damian Carrington and Ben Stockton, "COP28 President Says There Is 'No Science' behind Demands for Phase-Out of Fossil Fuels," *The Guardian*, 2023. Al Jaber went on in the conversation to admit that "a phase-down and a phase-out of fossil fuel in my view is inevitable" but resisted any strict timeline and insisted current fossil fuel producers could and should lead the process.

His focus throughout the meeting was to reduce the emissions caused by the extraction of oil and methane without addressing the damage caused when they are sold and burned.

6 Jay Lehr and Tom Harris, "The End of Oil Would Be the End of Civilization," accessed December 3, 2023, https://www.americaoutloud.news/the-end-of-oil-would-be-the-end-of-civilization/page/3/?et_blog.

7 Ibrahim Abdul-Matin, *Green Deen: What Islam Teaches about Protecting the Planet* (San Francisco: Berrett-Koehler Publishers, 2010), 77, 89.

8 Leah Penniman, "All That Breathes Gives Praise: A Conversation with Ibrahim Abdul-Matin and Chris Bolden-Newsome," in *Black Earth Wisdom: Soulful Conversations with Black Environmentalists* (New York: HarperCollins, 2023), 30.

9 I am particularly indebted to Nancy Menning's powerful argument that this narrative can be understood as a "rite of passage" that provides a "hopeful vision" of the transitions required by climate change. Nancy Menning, "Narrating Climate Change as a Rite of Passage," *Climatic Change* 147 (2018): 343–353.

10 Daniel Erlander, *Manna and Mercy: A Brief History of God's Unfolding Promise to Mend the Entire Universe* (Mercer Island, WA: The Order of Saints Martin and Teresa, 1992), 7–8.

11 Erlander, *Manna and Mercy*, 9.

12 Kingsmill Bond et al., *X-Change: Electricity—On Track for Net Zero* (Boulder, CO: Rocky Mountain Institute, 2023), 4, 6.

13 International Energy Agency, *Renewable Energy Market Update: Outlook for 2023 and 2024* (Paris: International Energy Agency, 2023).

14 Bond, *X-Change*, 4.

15 Kate Aronoff cautions, though, that "justice won't fall out of a low-carbon future, and that future isn't guaranteed. As ever, getting either will mean a fight over not just what kinds of power turn the lights on but who holds it" (Kate Aronoff, *Overheated: How Capitalism Broke the Planet--and How We Fight Back* [New York: Bold Type Books, 2021], 249).

16 Much of the information above comes from the newsletter and podcast *Volts*, https://www.volts.wtf/, an invaluable source of conversation and analysis of the technology and politics of decarbonization.

17 Larry Bell, "Wind Unaffordable, Costs Common Sense," 2023, https://www.newsmax.com/larrybell/carbon-fossil-electricity/2023/11/01/id/1140564/.

18 Large-scale batteries currently require metals that are rare enough to cause conflicts and exploitative labor. But, even so, building batteries is far cleaner, more efficient, and more just than extracting, shipping, and burning fossil fuels.

19 For another Christian ethical account of the energy transition, see especially James B. Martin-Schramm, *Climate Justice: Ethics, Energy, and Public Policy* (Minneapolis: Fortress Press, 2010). While I apply different standards, Martin-Schramm's ethics and insights are foundational to this book.

20 International Energy Agency, *The Oil and Gas Industry in Net Zero Transitions* (Paris: International Energy Agency, 2023).

21 OPEC, "Annual Statistical Bulletin," 2023, https://asb.opec.org/.

22 US Energy Information Administration, "Coal and Coke Reserves," 2021, https://www.eia.gov/international/data/world/coal-and-coke/coal-reserves.

23 D. Welsby et al., "Unextractable Fossil Fuels in a 1.5 °C World," *Nature* 597, no. 7875 (2021): 230.

24 Walter Wink, *Engaging the Powers: Discernment and Resistance in a World of Domination* (Minneapolis: Fortress Press, 1992), 319.

25 International Energy Agency, *The Oil and Gas Industry.*

26 Holly Jean Buck, *Ending Fossil Fuels: Why Net Zero Is Not Enough* (Brooklyn, NY: Verso Books, 2021), 177.

27 William S. Becker, "Breaking Policy Gridlocks," in *Democracy in a Hotter Time: Climate Change and Democratic Transformation*, ed. David W. Orr (Cambridge: MIT Press, 2023), 137.

28 Becker, "Breaking Policy Gridlocks," 137.

29 Simon Black et al., *IMF Fossil Fuel Subsidies Data: 2023 Update (Working Paper)* (Washington, DC: International Monetary Fund, 2023). The IMF also calculates the "indirect subsidy" created by governments' failure to charge the energy industry for its environmental harm, which leads to an astonishing total subsidy of seven trillion dollars.

30 Pope Francis, *Laudate Deum* (Vatican City: Apostolic Exhortation, 2023), 42–43, 59.

31 Jessica Reznicek and Ruby Montoya, "Why We Acted," *Via Pacis* 41, no. 3 (2017): 1.
32 Activist and pastor Bill Wylie-Kellerman wrote in 2003 that while many who believed in the myth of the Powers had spent decades struggling against governmental forces, it was becoming increasingly common to see "global corporations" as a more pernicious enemy. So, he suggested, Christians should consider "siding with the nations as a countervailing force." Bill Wylie Kellermann, *Principalities in Particular: A Practical Theology of the Powers That Be* (Minneapolis: Fortress Press, 2017), 189.
33 Kate Knuth, "Becoming a Climate Citizen," in *All We Can Save*, ed. Ayana Elizabeth Johnson and Katharine K. Wilkinson (New York: One World, 2020), 132.
34 Sociologists Richard York and Shannon Bell refer to this as the "displacement paradox," wherein new energy sources have tended not to replace old sources but rather supplement them. In 2019, they argued the growth of solar and wind was better categorized as an "energy addition" than an "energy transition." Richard York and Shannon Elizabeth Bell, "Energy Transitions or Additions?" *Energy Research and Social Science* 51 (2019): 40–43.
35 Terra Schwerin Rowe, *Of Modern Extraction: Experiments in Critical Petro-Theology* (London: Bloomsbury, 2022), 210.
36 Richard H. Lowery, "Biblical Sabbath as Critical Response in an Era of Global Pandemic and Climate Change," *American Journal of Economics and Sociology* 80, no. 5 (2021), 1345.
37 See especially Christopher Spotts, "The Possibilities of the Hebrew Sabbath for Black Theology," *Journal of the Society of Christian Ethics* 33, no. 2 (2013): 41–56.
38 See especially Robert Allen Warrior, "Canaanites, Cowboys, and Indians," *Christianity and Crisis*, September 11, 1989.
39 Abdul-Matin, *Green Deen*.
40 Joanna Macy and Chris Johnstone, *Active Hope: How to Face the Mess We're in without Going Crazy* (Novato, CA: New World Library, 2012).
41 Sherri Mitchell, *Sacred Instructions: Indigenous Wisdom for Living Spirit-Based Change* (Berkeley, CA: North Atlantic Books, 2018).
42 Kate Marvel, "Slaying the Climate Dragon," *Scientific American*, 2018, https://www.scientificamerican.com/blog/hot-planet/slaying-the-climate-dragon/.

43 Mary Annaïsse Heglar, "Here's Where You Come In," in *Not Too Late: Changing the Climate Story from Despair to Possibility*, ed. Rebecca Solnit and Thelma Young-Lutunatabua (Chicago: Haymarket Books, 2023), 23.

Chapter 7: The Inner Work of Climate Resistance

1 Parker J. Palmer, *Let Your Life Speak: Listening for the Voice of Vocation* (Hoboken, NJ: John Wiley & Sons, 1999), 91.

2 Others have done excellent work thinking through the implications and ethics of other emotions. See especially Panu Pihkala, "Toward a Taxonomy of Climate Emotions," *Frontiers in Climate* 3 (2022): 738154; Pihkala, "Anxiety and the Ecological Crisis: An Analysis of Eco-Anxiety and Climate Anxiety," *Sustainability* 12, no. 19 (2020): 7836; Steven Bouma-Prediger, *Earthkeeping and Character* (Ada, MI: Baker Academic, 2019); Chris Doran, *Hope in the Age of Climate Change: Creation Care This Side of the Resurrection* (Eugene, OR: Wipf and Stock Publishers, 2017); Sharon Delgado, *Love in a Time of Climate Change: Honoring Creation, Establishing Justice* (Minneapolis: Fortress Press, 2017).

3 Margaret Bullitt-Jonas, "The Prodigal Son and the Great Turning," 2019, https://revivingcreation.org/the-prodigal-son-and-the-great-turning/.

4 "U.S. Environmental Footprint Factsheet," 2023, https://css.umich.edu/publications/factsheets/sustainability-indicators/us-environmental-footprint-factsheet; "Carbon Footprint Factsheet," 2023, https://css.umich.edu/publications/factsheets/sustainability-indicators/carbon-footprint-factsheet.

5 Luisa Neubauer and Alexander Repenning, *Beginning to End the Climate Crisis: A History of Our Future* (Waltham, MA: Brandeis University Press, 2023), 16–17, 54.

6 Sarah E. Fredericks, *Environmental Guilt and Shame: Signals of Individual and Collective Responsibility and the Need for Ritual Responses* (New York: Oxford University Press, 2021), 3, 10.

7 Fredericks, *Environmental Guilt and Shame*, ch. 9.

8 Fredericks, *Environmental Guilt and Shame*, 116.

9 Brené Brown, *Atlas of the Heart: Mapping Meaningful Connection and the Language of Human Experience* (New York: Random House, 2021), 137.

10 One good guide for individual action, easily accessible but based on careful analysis of data, is Seth Wynes, *SOS: What You Can Do to Reduce Climate Change—Simple Actions That Make a Difference* (Washington, DC: National Geographic Books, 2019).
11 Colin J. Carlson, "After Millions of Preventable Deaths, Climate Change Must Be Treated Like a Health Emergency," *Nature Medicine* 30 (January 2024): 622.
12 IPCC, *Climate Change 2023: Synthesis Report* (Geneva: Intergovernmental Panel on Climate Change, 2023), 46, 71.
13 Caroline Hickman et al., "Young People's Voices on Climate Anxiety, Government Betrayal and Moral Injury: A Global Phenomenon," *SSRN Electronic Journal* 5, no. 12 (2021): 863–873.
14 Samantha K. Stanley et al., "From Anger to Action: Differential Impacts of Eco-Anxiety, Eco-Depression, and Eco-Anger on Climate Action and Wellbeing," *Journal of Climate Change and Health* 1 (2021): 2,4.
15 On the anger of Jesus and the ways it echoes the anger of the Psalms, see Melissa Florer-Bixler, *How to Have an Enemy: Righteous Anger and the Work of Peace* (Harrisonburg, VA: Herald Press, 2021), ch 4.
16 Beverly Wildung Harrison and Carol S. Robb, *Making the Connections: Essays in Feminist Social Ethics* (Boston: Beacon Press, 1985), 14.
17 Graham Macklin, "The Extreme Right, Climate Change and Terrorism," *Terrorism and Political Violence* 34, no. 5 (2022).
18 See especially Sam Moore and Alexandre Roberts, *The Rise of Ecofascism: Climate Change and the Far Right* (New York: Polity, 2022).
19 Alexander Reid Ross and Emmi Bevensee, "Confronting the Rise of Eco-Fascism Means Grappling with Complex Systems," *CARR Research Insight* 3 (2020): 27.
20 Walter Wink, *Engaging the Powers: Discernment and Resistance in a World of Domination* (Minneapolis: Fortress Press, 1992), 273.
21 Greta Thunberg, *No One Is Too Small to Make a Difference* (New York: Penguin, 2019), 96, 98–99.
22 Greta Thunberg, "Six Months on a Planet in Crisis: Greta Thunberg's Diary from the U.S. to Davos," *Time Magazine*, July 10, 2020.

23 In the field of Christian ethics, the best term I know for Thunberg's emotion is "social anger." Michael Jaycox, who developed this concept, defines it as a collective "interruption of the ideological rationalizations for privilege and oppression." Such anger originates among the oppressed, who can use anger to "create a new community of critical discourse capable of deconstructing the ideology of dominant discourse." Jaycox understands social anger as a "symptom of systemic injustice," which ethicists should view as "righteous according to the heuristic of restorative justice." After developing the idea of social anger using examples from the antiapartheid, civil rights, and Black Lives Matter movements, he concludes with the suggestion that this emotion "might be necessary to save the soul of a society that has betrayed its own moral conscience." Michael P. Jaycox, "The Civic Virtues of Social Anger: A Critically Reconstructed Normative Ethic for Public Life," *Journal of the Society of Christian Ethics* 36, no. 1 (2016): 124–126, 133, 140.

24 Thunberg, *No One Is Too Small*, 15.

25 Accessed March 9, 2024, https://www.cnn.com/2019/12/12/politics/greta-thunberg-donald-trump/index.html.

26 Audre Lorde, *Sister Outsider: Essays and Speeches* (Trumansburg, NY: Crossing Press, 1984), 127.

27 Jesus's first answer quotes Deuteronomy 6:5; the second quotes Leviticus 19:18.

28 For a powerful reflection on Christian love in response to systematic climate degradation, see Cynthia D. Moe-Lobeda, *Resisting Structural Evil: Love as Ecological-Economic Vocation* (Minneapolis: Fortress Press, 2013).

29 Bill McKibben, *Oil and Honey: The Education of an Unlikely Activist* (New York: Times Book, 2013), 40.

30 Wink, *Engaging the Powers*, 276.

31 I am grateful to Laura Yordy, whose 2014 presentation, "Environmental Refugees: People of No Place" at the 2014 Annual Meeting of the Society of Christian Ethics helped me begin thinking of migration as an issue of climate justice.

32 Jill Rios, "Faith and Flight: Immigration, the Church and the Climate," in *Sacred Acts: How Churches Are Working to Protect Earth's Climate*, ed. Mallory McDuff (Gabriola Island, BC: New Society Publishers, 2012), 170.

33 Abrahm Lustgarten, "Climate Refugees," in *The Climate Book*, ed. Greta Thunberg (New York: Penguin, 2023), 165–168.
34 Amelia Cheatham and Diana Roy, "Venezuela: The Rise and Fall of a Petrostate," 2023, https://www.cfr.org/backgrounder/venezuela-crisis.
35 Institute for Environment and Human Security, "5 Facts on Climate Migrants," 2015, https://ehs.unu.edu/news/news/5-facts-on-climate-migrants.html.
36 UNHCR, *Focus Area Strategic Plan for Climate Action: 2024–2030* (Geneva: United Nations High Commission on Refugees, 2023).
37 Todd Miller, *Storming the Wall: Climate Change, Migration, and Homeland Security* (San Francisco: City Lights Open Media, 2017), 30. See also Betsy Hartmann, "Rethinking Climate Refugees and Climate Conflict: Rhetoric, Reality and the Politics of Policy Discourse," *Journal of International Development* 22, no. 2 (2010): 233–246.
38 Saverio Bellizzi et al., "Global Health, Climate Change and Migration: The Need for Recognition of 'Climate Refugees,'" *Journal of Global Health* 13 (2023): 03011.
39 Gregory White, "'Climate Refugees'—A Useful Concept," *Global Environmental Politics* 19, no. 4 (2019): 133–138.
40 Jeff Goodell, *The Water Will Come: Rising Seas, Sinking Cities, and the Remaking of the Civilized World* (Boston: Little, Brown, 2017), 9.
41 Abrahm Lustgarten, "Climate Change Will Force a New American Migration," *ProPublica*, September 15, 2020.
42 Rios, "Faith and Flight," 181, 180.
43 Simon Hattenstone, "The Transformation of Greta Thunberg," *Guardian*, September 25, 2021.

Conclusion

1 Octavia E. Butler, "A Few Rules for Predicting the Future," 2000, https://commongood.cc/reader/a-few-rules-for-predicting-the-future-by-octavia-e-butler/.
2 Octavia E. Butler, *Parable of the Sower* (New York: Warner Books, 1993), 167.
3 Butler, "A Few Rules for Predicting the Future."
4 Butler, "A Few Rules for Predicting the Future."

BIBLIOGRAPHY

Abbey, Edward. *The Monkey Wrench Gang*. Philadelphia: Lippincott, 1975.

Abdul-Matin, Ibrahim. *Green Deen: What Islam Teaches about Protecting the Planet*. San Francisco: Berrett-Koehler Publishers, 2010.

Abnett, Kate, and Elizabeth Piper. "Phasing Out Fossil Fuels Is Key to Cop28 Success, Says UN's Guterres." 2023. https://www.reuters.com/business/environment/phasing-out-fossil-fuels-is-key-cop28-success-says-uns-guterres-2023-12-11/.

Al Jaber, Sultan. "Cop28 President Dr. Sultan Al Jaber's Opening Plenary Speech." 2023. https://www.cop28.com/en/news/2023/11/COP28-President-DrSultan-Al-Jabers-Opening--Plenary-Speech.

American Friends Service Committee. *Speak Truth to Power*. Philadelphia: American Friends Service Committee, 1955.

Armstrong, Karen. *Sacred Nature: Restoring Our Ancient Bond with the Natural World*. Washington, DC: National Geographic Books, 2022.

Aronoff, Kate. *Overheated: How Capitalism Broke the Planet—and How We Fight Back*. New York: Bold Type Books, 2021.

———. "We Didn't Start the Fire." In *Winning the Green New Deal: Why We Must, How We Can*, edited by Varshini Prakash and Guido Girgenti, 14–26. New York: Simon & Schuster, 2020.

Azar, Christian. "Bury the Chains and the Carbon Dioxide. Review of *Bury the Chains: Prophets and Rebels in the Fight to Free an Empire's Slaves* by Adam Hochschild, 2005, Houghton Mifflin, 468 Pp." *Climatic Change* 85, no. 3–4 (2007): 473–475.

Banerjee, Neela, Lisa Song, and David Hasemyer. "Exxon's Own Research Confirmed Fossil Fuels' Role in Global Warming Decades Ago." 2015. https://insideclimatenews.org/news/16092015/exxons-own-research-confirmed-fossil-fuels-role-in-global-warming.

Bauman, Whitney, and Kevin James O'Brien. *Environmental Ethics and Uncertainty: Wrestling with Wicked Problems*. New York: Routledge, 2019.

Beaton, Kate. *Ducks: Two Years in the Oil Sands*. Montreal: Drawn and Quarterly, 2022.

Becker, William S. "Breaking Policy Gridlocks." In *Democracy in a Hotter Time: Climate Change and Democratic Transformation*, edited by David W. Orr, 133–150. Cambridge: MIT Press, 2023.

Begay, Jade. "An Indigenous Systems Approach to the Climate Crisis." In *Not Too Late: Changing the Climate Story From Despair to Possibility*, edited by Rebecca Solnit and Thelma Young-Lutunatabua, 66–72. Chicago: Haymarket Books, 2023.

Beisner, E. Calvin. *Where Garden Meets Wilderness: Evangelical Entry into the Environmental Debate*. Grand Rapids, MI: The Acton Institute for the Study of Religion and Liberty, 1997.

Bell, Larry. "Wind Unaffordable, Costs Common Sense." 2023. https://www.newsmax.com/larrybell/carbon-fossil-electricity/2023/11/01/id/1140564/.

Bell, Shannon Elizabeth, Cara Daggett, and Christine Labuski. "Toward Feminist Energy Systems: Why Adding Women and Solar Panels Is Not Enough☆." *Energy Research and Social Science* 68 (2020): 101557.

Bellah, Robert Neelly, Richard Madsen, William M. Sullivan, Ann Swidler, and Steven M. Tipton. *Habits of the Heart: Individualism and Commitment in American Life*. Berkeley: University of California Press, 1996.

Bellizzi, Saverio, Christian Popescu, Catello M. Panu Napodano, Maura Fiamma, and Luca Cegolon. "Global Health, Climate Change and Migration: The Need for Recognition of 'Climate Refugees.'" *Journal of Global Health* 13 (2023): 03011.

Berkhof, Hendrik. *Christ and the Powers*. Translated by John Howard Yoder. Waterloo, ON: Herald Press, 1977.

Black, Simon, Antung A. Liu, Ian Parry, and Nate Vernon. *IMF Fossil Fuel Subsidies Data: 2023 Update (Working Paper)*. Washington, DC: International Monetary Fund, 2023.

Blazevic, Sara, Victoria Fernandez, Dyanna Jaye, and Aru Shiney-Ajay. "We Shine Bright: Organizing in Hope and Song." In *Winning the Green New Deal: Why We Must, How We Can*, edited by Varshini Prakash and Guido Girgenti, 166–196. New York: Simon & Schuster, 2020.

Blunt, Katherine. *California Burning: The Fall of Pacific Gas and Electric—And What It Means for America's Power Grid.* New York: Penguin, 2022.

Bock, Cherice. *A Quaker Ecology: Meditations on the Future of Friends.* Newberg, OR: Barclay Press, 2022.

Bond, Kingsmill, Sam Butler-Sloss, Amory Lovins, Laurens Speelman, and Nigel Topping. *X-Change: Electricity—On Track for Net Zero.* Boulder, CO: Rocky Mountain Institute, 2023.

Bouma-Prediger, Steven. *Earthkeeping and Character.* Ada, MI: Baker Academic, 2019.

Brown, Brené. *Atlas of the Heart: Mapping Meaningful Connection and the Language of Human Experience.* New York: Random House, 2021.

Brownstein, Michael, Daniel Kelly, and Alex Madva. "Individualism, Structuralism, and Climate Change." *Environmental Communication* 16, no. 2 (2022): 269–288.

Buck, Holly Jean. *Ending Fossil Fuels: Why Net Zero Is Not Enough.* Brooklyn, NY: Verso Books, 2021.

Bullitt-Jonas, Margaret. "The Prodigal Son and the Great Turning." 2019. https://revivingcreation.org/the-prodigal-son-and-the-great-turning/.

Burkett, Maxine. "Climate Disobedience." *Duke Environmental Law and Policy Forum* 27, no. 1 (2016): 1–50.

Butler, Octavia E. "A Few Rules for Predicting the Future." 2000. https://commongood.cc/reader/a-few-rules-for-predicting-the-future-by-octavia-e-butler/.

———. *Parable of the Sower.* New York: Warner Books, 1993.

Carbado, Devon W., and Don Weise. *Time on Two Crosses: The Collected Writings of Bayard Rustin.* New York: Cleis Press, 2015.

"Carbon Footprint Factsheet." 2023. https://css.umich.edu/publications/factsheets/sustainability-indicators/carbon-footprint-factsheet.

Carlson, Colin J. "After Millions of Preventable Deaths, Climate Change Must Be Treated Like a Health Emergency." *Nature Medicine* 30 (2024): 622.

Carrington, Damian, and Ben Stockton. "Cop28 President Says There Is 'No Science' behind Demands for Phase-Out of Fossil Fuels." *Guardian*, 2023.

Carter, Christopher. *The Spirit of Soul Food: Race, Faith, and Food Justice*. Chicago: University of Illinois Press, 2021.

Challenger, Melanie. *How to Be Animal: A New History of What It Means to Be Human*. New York: Penguin, 2021.

Cheatham, Amelia, and Diana Roy. "Venezuela: The Rise and Fall of a Petrostate." 2023. https://www.cfr.org/backgrounder/venezuela-crisis.

Clare, Eli. *Brilliant Imperfection*. Durham, NC: Duke University Press, 2017.

———. "Stolen Bodies, Reclaimed Bodies: Disability and Queerness." *Public Culture* 13, no. 3 (2001): 359–365.

Clark, Jawanza Eric. *Reclaiming Stolen Earth: An Africana Ecotheology*. Maryknoll, NY: Orbis Books, 2022.

Climate Accountability Institute. "Carbon Majors." Accessed May 27, 2024. https://climateaccountability.org/carbon-majors/.

Coll, Steve. *Private Empire: ExxonMobil and American Power*. New York: Penguin, 2012.

Cornwall Alliance. "A Renewed Call to Truth, Prudence, and Protection of the Poor." 2009. http://www.cornwallalliance.org/docs/a-renewed-call-to-truth-prudence-and-protection-of-the-poor.pdf.

Crenshaw, Kimberlé. "Demarginalizing the Intersection of Race and Sex: A Black Feminist Critique of Antidiscrimination Doctrine, Feminist Theory and Antiracist Politics." *University of Chicago Legal Research Forum* 1989, no. 1 (1989): 139–167.

———. "Mapping the Margins: Intersectionality, Identity Politics, and Violence against Women of Color." *Stanford Law Review* 43, no. 6 (1991): 1241–1299.

———. "The Urgency of Intersectionality." 2016. https://www.ted.com/talks/kimberle_crenshaw_the_urgency_of_intersectionality.

Cuddeback-Gedeon, Lorraine. "'Nothing about Us without Us': Ethnography, Conscientization, and the Epistemic Challenges of Intellectual Disability." *Practical Matters Journal* 11 (2018): 70–87.

Daggett, Cara. "Petro-Masculinity: Fossil Fuels and Authoritarian Desire." *Millennium: Journal of International Studies* 41, no. 1 (2018): 25–44.

Daly, Herman E., and John B. Cobb Jr. *For the Common Good: Redirecting the Economy toward Community, the Environment, and a Sustainable Future*. Boston: Beacon Press, 1994.

Davidson, Marc D. "Parallels in Reactionary Argumentation in the US Congressional Debates on the Abolition of Slavery and the Kyoto Protocol." *Climatic Change* 86, no. 1–2 (2008): 67–82.

"Decarbonizing Fossil Fuels." 2021. https://www.ted.com/talks/countdown_summit_decarbonizing_fossil_fuels.

Delgado, Sharon. *Love in a Time of Climate Change: Honoring Creation, Establishing Justice*. Minneapolis: Fortress Press, 2017.

Dochuk, Darren. *Anointed with Oil: How Christianity and Crude Made Modern America*. New York: Basic Books, 2019.

Doran, Chris. *Hope in the Age of Climate Change: Creation Care This Side of the Resurrection*. Eugene, OR: Wipf and Stock Publishers, 2017.

Du Bois, W. E. B. *Black Reconstruction in America*. New York: Russell & Russell, 1935.

Dunaway, Finis. *Seeing Green: The Use and Abuse of American Environmental Images.* Chicago: University of Chicago Press, 2018.

Eberhardt, David. "A Reflection on the DAPL 2." *Via Pacis* 41, no. 3 (2017): 9.

Eckstein, David, Marie-Lena Hutfils, and Maik Winges. "Global Climate Risk Index 2019: Who Suffers Most from Extreme Weather Events? Weather-Related Loss Events in 2017 and 1998 to 2017." 2018. https://germanwatch.org/sites/germanwatch.org/files/Global%20Climate%20Risk%20Index%202019_2.pdf.

Ellul, Jacques. *The Presence of the Kingdom*. Colorado Springs: Helmers & Howard Publishing, 1989.

Erlander, Daniel. *Manna and Mercy: A Brief History of God's Unfolding Promise to Mend the Entire Universe*. Mercer Island, WA: The Order of Saints Martin and Teresa, 1992.

Estes, Nick. "Fighting for Our Lives: #NoDAPL in Historical Context." 2016. https://therednation.org/fighting-for-our-lives-nodapl-in-context/

Figueres, Christiana. "I Thought Fossil Fuel Firms Could Change. I Was Wrong." *Al Jazeera*, July 6, 2023.

Fischetti, Mark, Nick Bockelman, and Wil V. Srubar. "Solving Cement's Massive Carbon Problem." *Scientific American*, February 1, 2023.

Fisher, Dana R. *Saving Ourselves: From Climate Shocks to Climate Action*. New York: Columbia University Press, 2024.

Florer-Bixler, Melissa. *How to Have an Enemy: Righteous Anger and the Work of Peace*. Harrisonburg, VA: Herald Press, 2021.

Francis, Pope. *Laudate Deum*. Vatican City: Apostolic Exhortation, 2023.

Franta, Benjamin. "Early Oil Industry Disinformation on Global Warming." *Environmental Politics* 30, no. 4 (2021): 663–668.

Fredericks, Sarah E. *Environmental Guilt and Shame: Signals of Individual and Collective Responsibility and the Need for Ritual Responses*. New York: Oxford University Press, 2021.

Freese, Barbara. *Coal: A Human History*. New York: Basic Books, 2003.

Gandhi, and Louis Fischer, ed. *The Essential Gandhi: His Life, Work, and Ideas*. New York: Vintage Books, 1983.

Gelbspan, Ross. *The Heat Is On: The Climate Crisis, the Cover-Up, the Prescription*. Boston: Addison Wesley, 1997.

Ghosh, Amitav. *The Great Derangement: Climate Change and the Unthinkable*. Chicago: University of Chicago Press, 2016.

———. *The Nutmeg's Curse: Parables for a Planet in Crisis*. Chicago: University of Chicago Press, 2021.

Gilio-Whitaker, Dina. *As Long as Grass Grows: The Indigenous Fight for Environmental Justice, from Colonization to Standing Rock*. Boston: Beacon Press, 2019.

Gillies, Alexandra. *Crude Intentions: How Oil Corruption Contaminates the World*. New York: Oxford University Press, 2020.

"Global Fossil Fuel Divestment Commitments Database." 2022. https://divestmentdatabase.org/.

Goodell, Jeff. *Big Coal: The Dirty Secret behind America's Energy Future*. New York: Houghton Mifflin, 2006.

———. *The Water Will Come: Rising Seas, Sinking Cities, and the Remaking of the Civilized World*. Boston: Little, Brown, 2017.

Grady-Benson, Jessica. "Fossil Fuel Divestment: The Power and Promise of a Student Movement for Climate Justice." Bachelor thesis, Pitzer College, 2014.

Griffin, Paul. *The Carbon Majors Database: CDP Carbon Majors Report 2017*. London: CDP, 2017.

Gutteres, António. "Secretary-General's Opening Remarks at the Climate Ambition Summit." 2023. https://www.un.org/sg/en/content/sg/statement/2023-09-20/secretary-generals-opening-remarks-the-climate-ambition-summit.

Haney López, Ian. "Averting Climate Collapse Requires Confronting Racism." In *Winning the Green New Deal: Why We Must, How We Can*, edited by Varshini Prakash and Guido Girgenti, 38–52. New York: Simon & Schuster, 2020.

Haq, Aliya. "Peabody Coal's Unprecedented Support for Climate Denial." 2016. https://www.nrdc.org/bio/aliya-haq/peabody-coals-unprecedented-support-climate-denial.

Haraway, Donna Jeanne. *Staying with the Trouble: Making Kin in the Chthulucene*. Durham, NC: Duke University Press, 2016.

Harpe, Celina. "Effects of the Tar Sands: Fort Mackay, Alberta." 2009. https://www.youtube.com/watch?v=kG2sJAn47QI.

Harris, Melanie L. *Ecowomanism: African American Women and Earth-Honoring Faiths*. Maryknoll, NY: Orbis Books, 2017.

Harrison, Beverly Wildung, and Carol S. Robb. *Making the Connections: Essays in Feminist Social Ethics*. Boston: Beacon Press, 1985.

Hartman, Laura M., and Kevin J. O'Brien. "Teaching against the 'False Religion' of the Market: Toward Explicitly Anticapitalist Teaching and Research in Religion and the Environment." *Religions* 14, no. 8 (2023): 975.

Hartmann, Betsy. "Rethinking Climate Refugees and Climate Conflict: Rhetoric, Reality and the Politics of Policy Discourse." *Journal of International Development* 22, no. 2 (2010): 233–246.

Hattenstone, Simon. "The Transformation of Greta Thunberg." *Guardian*, 2021.

Hayes, Chris. "The New Abolitionism: Averting Planetary Disaster Will Mean Forcing Fossil Fuel Companies to Give Up at Least $10 Trillion in Wealth." *Nation*, April 22, 2014.

Heede, Richard. "Tracing Anthropogenic Carbon Dioxide and Methane Emissions to Fossil Fuel and Cement Producers, 1854–2010." *Climatic Change* 122, no. 1–2 (2014): 229–241.

Heglar, Mary Annaïse. "Here's Where You Come In." In *Not Too Late: Changing the Climate Story from Despair to Possibility*, edited by Rebecca Solnit and Thelma Young-Lutunatabua, 19–27. Chicago: Haymarket Books, 2023.

Hickman, Caroline, Elizabeth Marks, Panu Pihkala, Susan Clayton, Eric R. Lewandowski, Elouise E. Mayall, Britt Wray, Catriona Mellor, and Lise van Susteren. "Young People's Voices on Climate Anxiety, Government Betrayal and Moral Injury: A

Global Phenomenon." *SSRN Electronic Journal* 5, no. 12 (2021): 863–873.

Hoggan, James, and Richard Littlemore. *Climate Cover-Up: The Crusade to Deny Global Warming.* Vancouver: Greystone Books, 2009.

Huber, Matthew T. *Lifeblood: Oil, Freedom, and the Forces of Capital.* Minneapolis: University of Minnesota Press, 2013.

Hulme, Mike. *Climate Change.* New York: Routledge, 2021.

Indigenous Environmental Network. "Talking Points on the AOC-Markey Green New Deal (GND) Resolution." 2019. https://www.ienearth.org/talking-points-on-the-aoc-markey-green-new-deal-gnd-resolution/.

Influence Map. "Carbon Majors Database: Launch Report." 2024. https://influencemap.org/site//data/000/027/Carbon_Majors_Launch_Report.pdf.

Institute for Environment and Human Security. "5 Facts on Climate Migrants." 2015. https://ehs.unu.edu/news/news/5-facts-on-climate-migrants.html.

International Energy Agency. *The Oil and Gas Industry in Net Zero Transitions.* Paris: International Energy Agency, 2023.

———. *Renewable Energy Market Update: Outlook for 2023 and 2024.* Paris: International Energy Agency, 2023.

"Interview with DAPL Eco-Saboteurs Ruby Montoya and Jessica Reznicek." August 2, 2017. https://dgrnewsservice.org/resistance/direct-action/property-destruction/interview-dapl-eco-saboteurs-montoya-reznicek/.

IPCC. "Summary for Policymakers." In *Climate Change 2023: Synthesis Report. Contribution of Working Groups I, II, and III to the Sixth Assessment Report of the Intergovernmental Panel on Climate Change*, edited by Core Writing Team, Hoesung Lee, and José Romero, 1–34. Geneva: IPCC, 2023.

Jaycox, Michael P. "The Civic Virtues of Social Anger: A Critically Reconstructed Normative Ethic for Public Life." *Journal of the Society of Christian Ethics* 36, no. 1 (2016): 123–143.

Jemisin, N. K. *The City We Became.* New York: Orbit, 2021.

Kahan, Dan M., Hank Jenkins-Smith, and Donald Braman. "Cultural Cognition of Scientific Consensus." *Journal of Risk Research* 14, no. 2 (2011): 147–174.

Kaijser, Anna, and Annica Kronsell. "Climate Change through the Lens of Intersectionality." *Environmental Politics* 23, no. 3 (2014): 417–433.

Kates, Nancy D., and Bennett Singer. *Brother Outsider: The Life of Bayard Rustin*. Berkeley: Question Why Films, 2003.

Kaufman, Mark. "The Carbon Footprint Sham: A 'Successful, Deceptive' PR Campaign." 2020. https://mashable.com/feature/carbon-footprint-pr-campaign-sham.

Keay, Douglas, and Margaret Thatcher. "Interview for *Women's Own*." 1987. https://www.margaretthatcher.org/document/106689.

Kellermann, Bill Wylie. *Principalities in Particular: A Practical Theology of the Powers That Be*. Minneapolis: Fortress Press, 2017.

Kenny, John. "Beyond Propaganda." *New York Times*, August 14, 2006.

Keyd, Helene Maria, and Justine Chambers. "Climate Change Actions in Conflict Affected Contexts: Insights from Myanmar after the Military Coup," accessed March 9, 2024, https://reliefweb.int/report/myanmar/climate-change-actions-conflict-affected-contexts-insights-myanmar-after-military-coup.

Kimball, Gayle. *Climate Girls Saving Our World: 54 Activists SpeakOut*. Lincoln, NE: Equality Press, 2021.

Kimmerer, Robin Wall. *Braiding Sweetgrass*. Minneapolis: Milkweed, 2013.

King, Martin Luther Jr. *Why We Can't Wait*. New York: Penguin, 1964.

Klein, Naomi. *This Changes Everything: Capitalism vs. the Climate*. New York: Simon & Schuster, 2014.

Knuth, Kate. "Becoming a Climate Citizen." In *All We Can Save*, edited by Ayana Elizabeth Johnson and Katharine K. Wilkinson, 129-135. New York: One World, 2020.

Ko, Aph. *Racism as Zoological Witchcraft: A Guide for Getting Out*. Brooklyn, NY: Lantern Books, 2019.

Kusnets, Nicholas. "The Deep Toll of Tar Sands on Canada's Indigenous People." 2021. https://undark.org/2021/11/22/ecocide-tar-sands/.

Lehr, Jay, and Tom Harris. "The End of Oil Would Be the End of Civilization." Accessed December 3, 2023. https://www.americaoutloud.news/the-end-of-oil-would-be-the-end-of-civilization/page/3/?et_blog.

Leiserowitz, Anthony, Edward Maibach, Seth Rosenthal, John Kotcher, J. Carman, L. Neyens, T. Myers, et al. *Climate Change in the American Mind, April 2022*. New Haven, CT: Yale Program on Climate Communication, 2022.

Leonard, Christopher. *Kochland: The Secret History of Koch Industries and Corporate Power in America*. New York: Simon & Schuster, 2019.

Linnit, Carol. "'Grassroots' Oil and Gas Advocacy Group Canada Action Received $100,000 from ARC Resources." June 24, 2020. https://thenarwhal.ca/canada-action-received-100-thousand-from-arc-resources/.

Long, Heather. "Treasury Secretary Mnuchin Says Climate Activist Greta Thunberg Should Go Study Economics." *Washington Post*, 2020.

Longmuir, Marilyn V. *Oil in Burma: The Extraction of 'Earth-Oil' to 1914*. Banglamun, Thailand: White Lotus Press, 2001.

Lorde, Audre. *Sister Outsider: Essays and Speeches*. Trumansburg, NY: Crossing Press, 1984.

Lowery, Richard H. "Biblical Sabbath as Critical Response in an Era of Global Pandemic and Climate Change." *American Journal of Economics and Sociology* 80, no 5 (2021): 1345-1380.

Loy, David. "The Religion of the Market." *Journal of the American Academy of Religion* 65, no. 2 (1997): 275–290.

Lustgarten, Abrahm. "Climate Change Will Force a New American Migration." *ProPublica*, September 15, 2020.

———. "Climate Refugees." In *The Climate Book*, edited by Greta Thunberg, 165–168. New York: Penguin, 2023.

———. *Run to Failure: BP and the Making of the Deepwater Horizon Disaster*. New York: W. W. Norton, 2012.

Lymbery, Philip. *Sixty Harvests Left: How to Reach a Nature-Friendly Future*. London: Bloomsbury Publishing, 2022.

Macklin, Graham. "The Extreme Right, Climate Change and Terrorism." *Terrorism and Political Violence* 34, no. 5 (2022): 979–996.

Macy, Joanna, and Chris Johnstone. *Active Hope: How to Face the Mess We're in without Going Crazy*. Novato, CA: New World Library, 2012.

Malm, Andreas. *Fossil Capital: The Rise of Steam-Power and the Roots of Global Warming*. Washington, DC: National Geographic Books, 2016.

———. *How to Blow Up a Pipeline*. Brooklyn, NY: Verso Books, 2021.

Mann, Michael E. *The New Climate War: The Fight to Take Back Our Planet*. Washington, DC: Public Affairs, 2021.

Martin-Schramm, James B. *Climate Justice: Ethics, Energy, and Public Policy*. Minneapolis: Fortress Press, 2010.

Marvel, Kate. "Slaying the Climate Dragon." October 11, 2018. https://www.scientificamerican.com/blog/hot-planet/slaying-the-climate-dragon/.

Master, Bob. "Reviving Labor, in New Deals Old and Green." In *Winning the Green New Deal: Why We Must, How We Can*, edited by Varshini Prakash and Guido Girgenti, 262–277. New York: Simon & Schuster, 2020.

McFague, Sallie. *A New Climate for Theology: God, the World, and Global Warming*. Minneapolis: Fortress Press, 2008.

McGhee, Heather. *The Sum of Us: What Racism Costs Everyone and How We Can Prosper Together*. New York: One World, 2021.

McKibben, Bill. *The Comforting Whirlwind: God, Job, and the Scale of Creation*. Grand Rapids, MI: Eerdmans., 1994.

———. *Deep Economy: The Wealth of Communities and the Durable Future*. New York: Macmillan, 2007.

———. *The Flag, the Cross, and the Station Wagon: A Graying American Looks Back at His Suburban Boyhood and Wonders What the Hell Happened*. New York: Henry Holt, 2022.

———. "Global Warming's Terrifying New Math." *Rolling Stone*, August 2, 2012.

———. *Oil and Honey: The Education of an Unlikely Activist*. New York: Times Book, 2013.

Meadows, Donella H. *Limits to Growth*. New York: Signet, 1972.

Menning, Nancy. "Narrating Climate Change as a Rite of Passage." *Climatic Change* 147 (2018): 343–353.

Miller, Eric C. "The Myth of American Individualism: Interview with Alex Zakaras." *Religion and Politics* February 21, 2023.

Miller, Todd. *Storming the Wall: Climate Change, Migration, and Homeland Security*. San Francisco: City Lights Open Media, 2017.

Mitchell, Sherri. *Sacred Instructions: Indigenous Wisdom for Living Spirit-Based Change*. Berkeley, CA: North Atlantic Books, 2018.

Moe-Lobeda, Cynthia D. *Resisting Structural Evil: Love as Ecological-Economic Vocation*. Minneapolis: Fortress Press, 2013.

Monbiot, George. "Changing the Media Narrative." In *The Climate Book*, edited by Greta Thunberg, 369–371. New York: Penguin, 2023.

Moore, Sam, and Alexandre Roberts. *The Rise of Ecofascism: Climate Change and the Far Right*. New York: Polity, 2022.

Morton, Timothy. *Hyperobjects: Philosophy and Ecology after the End of the World*. Minneapolis: University of Minnesota Press, 2013.

Mouhot, Jean-François. "Past Connections and Present Similarities in Slave Ownership and Fossil Fuel Usage." In *Energy Humanities: An Anthology*, edited by Imre Szeman and Dominic Boyer, 205–219. Baltimore: Johns Hopkins University Press, 2017.

Neubauer, Luisa, and Alexander Repenning. *Beginning to End the Climate Crisis: A History of Our Future*. Waltham, MA: Brandeis University Press, 2023.

NOAA. "2023 was the Warmest Year in the Modern Temperature Record." Accessed March 30, 2024. https://www.climate.gov/news-features/featured-images/2023-was-warmest-year-modern-temperature-record.

O'Brien, Kevin J. *The Violence of Climate Change: Lessons of Resistance from Nonviolent Activists*. Washington, DC: Georgetown University Press, 2017.

Oil Sands Action. "Life without Oil and Petroleum Products? Not So Simple." 2016. https://www.facebook.com/OilSandsAction/videos/life-without-oil-and-petroleum-products-not-so-simple/1058773337581878/.

"The Oily Operators behind the Religious Climate Change Disinformation Front Group, Cornwall Alliance." 2010. https://thinkprogress.org/the-oily-operators-behind-the-religious-climate-change-disinformation-front-group-cornwall-alliance-536175fe5e04/.

OPEC. "Annual Statistical Bulletin." 2023. https://asb.opec.org/.

Oreskes, Naomi, and Erik M. Conway. *The Big Myth: How American Business Taught Us to Loathe Government and Love the Free Market*. New York: Bloomsbury Publishing, 2023.

———. *Merchants of Doubt: How a Handful of Scientists Obscured the Truth on Issues from Tobacco Smoke to Global Warming*. New York: Bloomsbury Press, 2010.

Palmer, Parker J. *Let Your Life Speak: Listening for the Voice of Vocation*. Hoboken, NJ: John Wiley & Sons, 1999.

Penniman, Leah. "All That Breathes Gives Praise: A Conversation with Ibrahim Abdul-Matin and Chris Bolden-Newsome." In *Black Earth Wisdom: Soulful Conversations with Black Environmentalists*, 20–34. New York: HarperCollins, 2023.

Pierre-Louis, Kendra. "Wakanda Doesn't Have Suburbs." In *All We Can Save*, edited by Ayana Elizabeth Johnson and Katharine K. Wilkinson, 138–144. New York: One World, 2020.

Pihkala, Panu. "Anxiety and the Ecological Crisis: An Analysis of Eco-Anxiety and Climate Anxiety." *Sustainability* 12, no. 19 (2020): 7836.

———. "Toward a Taxonomy of Climate Emotions." *Frontiers in Climate* 3 (2022): 738154.

Prakash, Varshini. "People Power and Political Power." In *Winning the Green New Deal: Why We Must, How We Can*, edited by Varshini Prakash and Guido Girgenti, 137–163. New York: Simon & Schuster, 2020.

Price, Jennifer. *Stop Saving the Planet!: An Environmentalist Manifesto*. New York: W. W. Norton, 2021.

Ray, Sarah Jaquette. *The Ecological Other*. Tucson: University of Arizona Press, 2013.

Reznicek, Jessica, and Ruby Montoya. "Why We Acted." *Via Pacis* 41, no. 3 (2017): 1, 3.

Rich, Nathaniel. *Losing Earth: A Recent History*. New York: MCD Books, 2019.

Riley, Shamara Shantu. "Ecology Is a Sistah's Issue Too: The Politics of Emergent Afrocentric Ecowomanism." In *Ecofeminism and the Sacred*, edited by Carol J. Adams, 191–204. New York: Continuum, 1993.

Rios, Jill. "Faith and Flight: Immigration, the Church and the Climate." In *Sacred Acts: How Churches Are Working to Protect Earth's Climate*, edited by Mallory McDuff, 167–181. Gabriola Island, BC: New Society Publishers, 2012.

Rolen, Emily. "Gubernatorial Candidate Scott Wagner Called This 18-Year-Old 'Young and Naive' When She Asked Him about Climate Change." *Philly Voice*, 2018.

Ross, Alexander Reid, and Emmi Bevensee. "Confronting the Rise of Eco-Fascism Means Grappling with Complex Systems." *CARR Research Insight* 3 (2020): 27. London: Centre for the Analysis of the Radical Right.

Rowe, Terra Schwerin. *Of Modern Extraction: Experiments in Critical Petro-Theology*. London: Bloomsbury, 2022.

Rude, Ron. *(Re)considering Christianity: An Expedition of Faith Joining Science, Ancient Wisdom, and Sustainability*. St. Paul, MN: Beavers Pond Press, 2012.

The School of Life. *The School of Life: An Emotional Education*. London: School of Life, 2019.

Schumacher, E. F. *Small Is Beautiful: Economics as If People Mattered*. New York: Harper & Row, 1973.

Scranton, Roy. *We're Doomed. Now What?: Essays on War and Climate Change*. New York: Soho Press, 2018.

Seymour, Nicole. *Bad Environmentalism: Irony and Irreverence in the Ecological Age*. Minneapolis: University of Minnesota Press, 2018.

Shakespeare, Tom. *Disability: The Basics*. New York: Routledge, 2017.

Shearer, Christine. *Kivalina: A Climate Change Story*. Chicago: Haymarket Books, 2011.

Sherrell, Daniel. *Warmth: Coming of Age at the End of Our World*. New York: Penguin, 2021.

Shipley, Julia. "'You Strike a Match': Why Two Women Sacrificed Everything to Stop the Dakota Access Pipeline." *Grist Magazine*, May 26, 2021.

Si, Yutong, Dipa Desai, Diana Bozhilova, Sheila Puffer, and Jennie C. Stephens. "Fossil Fuel Companies' Climate Communication Strategies: Industry Messaging on Renewables and Natural Gas." *Energy Research and Social Science* 98 (2023): 103028.

Solnit, Rebecca. *Call Them by Their True Names: American Crises (and Essays)*. London: Granta, 2018.

Southgate, Christopher. *The Groaning of Creation: God, Evolution, and the Problem of Evil*. Louisville, KY: Westminster John Knox Press, 2008.

Spotts, Christopher. "The Possibilities of the Hebrew Sabbath for Black Theology." *Journal of the Society of Christian Ethics* 33, no. 2 (2013): 41–56.

Stanley, Samantha K., Teaghan L. Hogg, Zoe Leviston, and Iain Walker. "From Anger to Action: Differential Impacts of Eco-Anxiety, Eco-Depression, and Eco-Anger on Climate Action and Wellbeing." *Journal of Climate Change and Health* 1 (2021): 100003.

Stanton Anleu, Billie. "Protestors Turn to Humor in Plea for Drake Closure." *Gazette*, 2015.

Stop Fossil Fuels. "Ruby Montoya & Jessica Reznicek: DAPL Ecosaboteurs." Accessed October 11, 2023. https://stopfossilfuels.org/ecosabotage/ruby-montoya-jessica-reznicek-dapl-ecosaboteurs/.

Stringfellow, William. *An Ethic for Christians and Other Aliens in a Strange Land*. Eugene, OR: Wipf and Stock Publishers, 2004.

Sultana, Farhana. "Decolonizing Climate Coloniality." In *Not Too Late: Changing the Climate Story from Despair to Possibility*, edited by Rebecca Solnit and Thelma Young-Lutunatabua, 58–65. Chicago: Haymarket Books, 2023.

Supran, Geoffrey, and Naomi Oreskes. "Addendum to 'Assessing ExxonMobil's Climate Change Communications (1977–2014).'" *Environmental Research Letters* 15 (2020): 119401.

———. "Assessing ExxonMobil's Climate Change Communications (1977–2014)." *Environmental Research Letters* 12 (2017): 084019.

Szeman, Imre, and Dominic Boyer. *Energy Humanities: An Anthology*. Baltimore: Johns Hopkins University Press, 2017.

Taylor, Bron Raymond. *Dark Green Religion: Nature Spirituality and the Planetary Future*. Berkeley: University of California Press, 2010.

Thomas, Leah. *The Intersectional Environmentalist: How to Dismantle Systems of Oppression to Protect People + Planet*. New York: Voracious, 2022.

Thunberg, Greta. *No One Is Too Small to Make a Difference*. New York: Penguin, 2019.

———. "Our House Is Still on Fire and You're Fueling the Flames." January 21, 2020. https://www.weforum.org/agenda/2020/01/greta-speech-our-house-is-still-on-fire-davos-2020/.

———. "Six Months on a Planet in Crisis: Greta Thunberg's Diary From the U.S. to Davos." *Time Magazine*, July 10, 2020.

Thunberg, Greta, Isabelle Axelsson, Sophia Axelsson, Iqbal Badruddin, Danielle Ferrieira de Assis, Holly Gillibrand, Julia Haddad et al. "At Davos We Will Tell World Leaders to Abandon the Fossil Fuel Economy." *Guardian*, January 10, 2020.

Thunberg, Greta, Svante Thunberg, Beata Ernman, and Malena Ernman. *Our House Is on Fire*. New York: Penguin Books, 2020.

Tippett, Krista. "Interview with Christiana Figueres." 2023. https://onbeing.org/programs/christiana-figueres-ecological-hope-and-spiritual-evolution/#transcript.

United Nations Framework Convention on Climate Change. "First Global Stocktake: Draft Decision as of 13 December 2023." 2023. https://unfccc.int/sites/default/files/resource/cma2023_L17_adv.pdf.

United Nations High Commission on Refugees. *Focus Area Strategic Plan for Climate Action: 2024–2030*. Geneva: United Nations High Commission on Refugees, 2023.

United States District Court for the Northern District of California Oakland. "C 08-1138 SBA." *Native Village of Kivalina v. ExxonMobil Corporation et al.* https://climatecasechart.com/wp-content/uploads/case-documents/2009/20090930_docket-408-cv-01138-SBA_order.pdf.

US Energy Information Administration. "Coal and Coke Reserves." 2021. https://www.eia.gov/international/data/world/coal-and-coke/coal-reserves.

"U.S. Environmental Footprint Factsheet." 2023. https://css.umich.edu/publications/factsheets/sustainability-indicators/us-environmental-footprint-factsheet.

Veldman, Robin Globus. *The Gospel of Climate Skepticism*. Oakland: University of California Press, 2019.

Warrior, Robert Allen. "Canaanites, Cowboys, and Indians." *Christianity and Crisis*. September 11 (1989): 21–26.

Weiss, Daniel J. "Anatomy of a Senate Climate Bill Death." 2010. https://www.americanprogress.org/article/anatomy-of-a-senate-climate-bill-death/.

Welsby, D., J. Price, S. Pye, and P. Ekins. "Unextractable Fossil Fuels in a 1.5 °C World." *Nature* 597, no. 7875 (2021): 230–234.

"What We Do." Accessed September 28, 2023. https://cornwallalliance.org/about/what-we-do/.

White, Gregory. "'Climate Refugees'—A Useful Concept." *Global Environmental Politics* 19, no. 4 (2019): 133–138.

Whyte, Kyle Powys. "The Dakota Access Pipeline, Environmental Injustice, and U.S. Colonialism." *Red Ink* 19, no. 1 (2017): 154–169.

———. "Indigeneity in Geoengineering Discourses: Some Considerations." *Ethics, Policy and Environment* 21, no. 3 (2018): 289–307.

———. "Indigenous Climate Change Studies: Indigenizing Futures, Decolonizing the Anthropocene." *English Language Notes* 55, no. 1–2 (2017): 153–162.

———. "Is It Colonial Déjà Vu? Indigenous Peoples and Climate Injustice." In *Humanities for the Environment: Integrating Knowledges, Fording New Constellations of Practice*, edited by Joni Adamson, Michael Davis, and Hsinya Huang, 88–104. New York: Earthscan Publications, 2016.

Williams, Delores S. "Black Women's Surrogacy Experience and the Christian Notion of Redemption." In *After Patriarchy: Feminist Transformations of the World Religions*, edited by Paula M. Cooey, William R. Eakin, and Jay B. McDaniel, 1–14. Maryknoll, NY: Orbis, 1991.

———. "Sin, Nature, and Black Women's Bodies." In *Ecofeminism and the Sacred*, edited by Carol J. Adams, 24–29. New York: Continuum, 1993.

Wink, Walter. *Engaging the Powers: Discernment and Resistance in a World of Domination*. Minneapolis: Fortress Press, 1992.

———. *Jesus and Nonviolence: A Third Way*. Minneapolis: Fortress Press, 2003.

———. *My Struggle to Become Human*. Minneapolis: Fortress Press, 2017.

———. *Naming the Powers: The Language of Power in the New Testament*. Minneapolis: Augsburg Fortress, 1984.

———. *The Powers That Be: Theology for a New Millennium*. New York: Doubleday, 1998.

———. *Unmasking the Powers: The Invisible Forces That Determine Human Existence*. Minneapolis: Augsburg Fortress, 1986.

———. *When the Powers Fall: Reconciliation in the Healing of Nations*. Minneapolis: Augsburg Fortress, 1998.

Wynes, Seth. *SOS: What You Can Do to Reduce Climate Change—Simple Actions That Make a Difference*. Washington, DC: National Geographic Books, 2019.

York, Richard, and Shannon Elizabeth Bell. "Energy Transitions or Additions?" *Energy Research and Social Science* 51 (2019): 40–43.

Zakaras, Alex. *The Roots of American Individualism: Political Myth in the Age of Jackson*. Princeton, NJ: Princeton University Press, 2022.

INDEX